Coder to Developer:
Tools and Strategies for Delivering Your Software

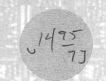

Coder to Developer:
Tools and Strategies for Delivering Your Software

Mike Gunderloy

SYBEX

San Francisco · London

Associate Publisher: Joel Fugazzotto
Acquisitions and Developmental Editor: Tom Cirtin
Production Editor: Leslie E.H. Light
Technical Editor: John Paul Mueller
Copyeditor: Liz Welch
Compositor: Happenstance Type-O-Rama
Graphic Illustrator: Happenstance Type-O-Rama
Proofreader: Laurie O'Connell, Nancy Riddiough
Indexer: Lynnzee Elze
Cover Designer: Ingalls+Associates
Cover Illustrator: Rob Atkins, The Image Bank

Library of Congress Card Number: 2003116217

ISBN: 0-7821-4327-X

SYBEX and the SYBEX logo are either registered trademarks or trademarks of SYBEX Inc. in the United States and/or other countries.

Screen reproductions produced with PaintShop Pro. PaintShop Pro is a trademark of Jasc Software Inc.

Internet screen shot(s) using Microsoft Internet Explorer reprinted by permission from Microsoft Corporation.

TRADEMARKS: SYBEX has attempted throughout this book to distinguish proprietary trademarks from descriptive terms by following the capitalization style used by the manufacturer.

The author and publisher have made their best efforts to prepare this book, and the content is based upon final release software whenever possible. Portions of the manuscript may be based upon pre-release versions supplied by software manufacturer(s). The author and the publisher make no representation or warranties of any kind with regard to the completeness or accuracy of the contents herein and accept no liability of any kind including but not limited to performance, merchantability, fitness for any particular purpose, or any losses or damages of any kind caused or alleged to be caused directly or indirectly from this book.

Manufactured in the United States of America

10 9 8 7 6 5 4 3 2 1

For Dana, once again—and always.

Foreword

You know what drives me crazy?

"Everything?" you ask. Well, OK, some of you know me a bit too well by now.

But seriously, folks, what drives me crazy is that most software developers don't realize just how little they know about software development.

Take, for example, me.

When I was a teenager, as soon as I finished reading Peter Norton's famous guide to programming the IBM-PC in Assembler, I was *convinced* that I knew everything there was to know about software development in general. Heck, I was ready to start a software company to make a word processor, you see, and it was going to be *really good*. My imaginary software company was going to have coffee breaks with free donuts every hour. A lot of my daydreams in those days involved donuts.

When I got out of the army, I headed off to college and got a degree in Computer Science. Now I *really* knew everything. I knew *more* than everything, because I had learned a bunch of computer-scientific junk about linear algebra and NP completeness and frigging *lambda calculus* which was *obviously* useless, so I thought they must have run out of *useful* things to teach us and were scraping the bottom of the barrel.

Nope. At my first job I noticed how many things there are that many Computer Science departments are too snooty to actually teach you. Things like software teamwork. Practical advice about user interface design. Professional tools like source code control, bug tracking databases, debuggers, and profilers. Business things. Computer Science departments in the most prestigious institutions just won't teach you this stuff because they consider it "vocational," not academic; the kind of thing that high school dropouts learn at the local technical institute so they can have a career as an auto mechanic, or an air-conditioner repairman, or a (holding nose between thumb and forefinger) "software developer."

I can sort of understand that attitude. After all, many prestigious undergraduate institutions see their goal as preparing you for life, not teaching you a career, least of all a career in a field that changes so rapidly that any technologies you learn now will be obsolete in a decade.

Over the next decade I proceeded to learn an incredible amount about software development and all the things it takes to produce software. I worked at Microsoft on the Excel team, at Viacom on the web team, and at Juno on their e-mail client. And, you know what? At every point in the learning cycle, I was completely convinced that I knew everything there was to know about software development.

"Maybe you're just an arrogant sod?" you ask, possibly using an even spicier word than "sod." I beg your pardon: this is my foreword; if you want to be rude, write your own damn foreword, tear mine out of the book, and put yours in instead.

There's something weird about software development, some mystical quality, that makes all kinds of people think they know how to do it. I've worked at dotcom-type companies full of liberal arts majors with no software experience or training who nevertheless were convinced that they knew how to manage software teams and design user interfaces. This is weird, because nobody thinks they know how to remove a burst appendix, or rebuild a car engine, unless they *actually know how to do it*, but for some reason there are all these people floating around who think they know everything there is to know about software development.

Anyway, the responsibility is going to fall on your shoulders. You're probably going to have to learn how to do software development on your own. If you're really lucky, you've had some experience working directly with top notch software developers who can teach you this stuff, but most people don't have that opportunity. So I'm glad to see that Mike Gunderloy has taken it upon himself to write the book you hold in your hands. Here you will find a well-written and enjoyable introduction to many of the most important things that you're going to need to know as you move from being a person who can *write code* to being a person who can *develop software*. Do those sound like the same thing? They're not. That's roughly the equivalent of going from being a six year old who can crayon some simple words, backwards N's and all, to being a successful novelist who writes books that receive rave reviews and sell millions of copies. Being a software developer means you can take a concept, build a team, set up state of the art development processes, design a software product, the *right* software product, and produce it. Not just any software product: a high-quality software product that solves a problem and delights your users. With documentation. A web page. A setup program. Test cases. Norwegian versions. Bokmål *and* Nynorsk. Appetizers, dessert, and twenty seven eight-by-ten color glossy photographs with circles and arrows and a paragraph on the back of each one explaining what each one was.*

And then, one day, finally, perhaps when it's too late, you'll wake up and say, "Hmm. Maybe I really *don't* know what it really takes to develop software." And on that day only, and not one minute before, but on that day and from that day forward, you will have earned the right to call yourself a software developer. In the meantime, all is not lost: you still have my blessing if you want to eat donuts every hour.

—Joel Spolsky
Founder, Fog Creek Software

*Apologizes to Arlo Guthrie.

Acknowledgments

Once again, it's been a long road from original idea to finished book. And I could never have navigated that road without the help of all the folks on the editorial team: Joel Fugazzotto, Tom Cirtin, Liz Welch, Leslie Light, and John Mueller. Thanks also to the production team at Happenstance Type-O-Rama, who performed the magic of turning my Word documents and Visio sketches into a finished product.

Thanks to Joel Spolsky for contributing the foreword and allowing me to quote some of his work (and borrow liberally from a few of his ideas). Roy Osherove provided valuable suggestions on various chapter drafts, and Dan Frumin inspired some of my thoughts about team management. Eric Sink from SourceGear kindly donated a copy of his company's Vault source code control software for the book's website.

I feel a great debt to all the authors of computer books whose work I've tried to build on. There are too many to list here (and inevitably I'd forget some), but certainly everyone in the field owes something to Frederick P. Brooks Jr. Without his pioneering example, who would have thought of thinking about the process of development?

Many of the ideas in this book came out of work I did on the *Developer Central* newsletter, at first for Di Schaffhauser at *MCP Magazine* and then for Mike Bucken at *ADT Magazine*. I'm happy that both of them have let me get into as much trouble as I like by spreading my opinions around the Internet. The readers of *Developer Central*, too, have helped hone my ideas by pointing out my errors and omissions.

Of course, none of these people are responsible for the remaining errors and omissions. I blame gremlins for those. That's my story and I'm sticking to it.

Finally, thanks go out to my family for putting up with the long hours I spent pounding away at this book instead of reading stories, dispensing cookies, or indulging in adult conversation. Adam and Kayla provide the leavening of childish energy that I need to remind me that there's a world outside of books. Dana Jones keeps me on an even keel, and helps out with the million and one chores of growing a family (not to mention doing all the work of growing #3). I couldn't write without them.

Contents at a Glance

Contents

Introduction

This book won't teach you how to write code. In fact, I'm going to assume that you already know how to write code. Oh, you might pick up a tip here and there, but by and large, my focus isn't on helping you write better C# applications. You've finished a university course on the subject, or spent long winter nights huddled up to the .NET Framework SDK figuring it out on your own. Now if someone asks you for a doubly linked list or a class to represent customers, you're all set.

But when you take your coding skills out to the real world (or what passes for the real world in software circles), you'll discover that there's more to the job than that. I like to draw a distinction between *coders*, who know the syntax and semantics of a computer language, and *developers*, who can apply that knowledge to turning out a working application with all the necessary supporting details. This book is dedicated to helping you make the transition from coder to developer.

Because of my own background, most of the advice here is aimed at developers working alone or in small groups. If you're a corporate developer stuck in a regimented cubicle farm, you may find less here that applies to you (though I certainly encourage you to look!). If you've got an idea for a product, or have been given an assignment to build an internal application and don't know quite how to go from concept to execution, then this book is for you.

Tools of the Trade

I've used C# and Visual Studio .NET 2003 throughout this book as the core of my development process. Of course, much of the advice I have to offer isn't specific to this particular language or development environment, but by focusing in one direction I can cover the topics more coherently. You'll see as you go along that there are dozens of other tools, large and small, that I find helpful in development. It's hard to overemphasize the importance of good tools in this business. Every repetitive or difficult task in development, save one, is subject to being automated and made trivial by the proper tool.

That one task, of course, is the actual writing of the code. Although design tools can help you come up with an initial code structure, and refactoring tools can help make that structure more sensible (you'll learn about both of those topics in this book), ultimately it's up to you to create your application out of pure thought. By removing busywork tasks from your to-do list, however, good tools can give you the time and energy you need to indulge your creativity.

Keep in mind, though, that you don't need every tool that I mention to turn out good software. You'll have to be hardheaded and sensible when evaluating trial versions and deciding which ones are worth their purchase price.

With the large number of tools in the text, you'll find an equally large number of URLs. To save you the bother of typing these in by hand, you can visit the book's website (`www.CoderToDeveloper.com`) for links directly to the tools. You'll also find the code for the sample application on both `www.CoderToDeveloper.com` and `www.Sybex.com`; see the inside back cover for more details.

Also, of course, there are new tools every day that would fit right in with this book. I keep a daily weblog of such finds at my other website, `www.larkware.com`. Feel free to drop by for updates.

How This Book Is Organized

This books contains 15 chapters, covering a set of skills that I think are essential for any serious developer. I've tried to organize them into a sensible order that follows roughly the tasks that you'll need to complete to ship a successful software product. Feel free to jump around or to dip in if you need a quick course on a particular topic; each chapter can stand alone for the most part.

The first two chapters are about some essential planning tasks that any project should start with. Chapter 1, "Planning Your Project," covers managing requirements, choosing a methodology, and using project-tracking tools. Chapter 2, "Organizing Your Project," concentrates on overall architecture and delivery schedules.

The next three chapters cover some necessary coding skills that you might have missed along the way. Chapter 3, "Using Source Code Control Effectively," shows you how and why to use this most necessary of development tools. Chapter 4, "Coding Defensively," tackles assertions, exceptions, and how to write useful comments. Chapter 5, "Preventing Bugs with Unit Testing," is an introduction to unit testing, test-driven development, and refactoring—all key skills when you're trying to turn out high-quality code quickly.

Tools occupy the next three chapters. Chapter 6, "Pumping Up the IDE," focuses on the numerous tools available to help you make Visual Studio .NET a productive development environment. This chapter also gives you a crash course in customizing the IDE to be more useful to you. Chapter 7, "Digging Into Source Code," turns the focus in the other direction, showing you how to use a variety of tools to investigate other code, and discusses sources for high-quality reusable code. Chapter 8, "Generating Code," is a first look at code generation, a current hot topic in development circles.

Chapters 9 and 10 discuss the tasks that go along with sending the first few test releases out into the world. Chapter 9, "Tracking and Squashing Bugs," discusses effective bug management, quality assurance, and the importance of a good bug-tracking tool. Chapter 10, "Logging

Application Activity," brings in a variety of tools and techniques for recording useful information as end users bang on your code.

Chapter 11 is titled "Working with Small Teams," but it features a twist. Rather than focus on people-management skills (which are well covered elsewhere), I've tried to give you specific advice on techniques and tools that work for small software development teams. In particular, I discuss what you can do to make a team work even when it's distributed around the world.

The final four chapters cover some of the tasks that surround any good software but that are often neglected. Chapter 12, "Creating Documentation," talks about writing useful help files and manuals. Chapter 13, "Mastering the Build Process," will help you turn the complex dance of creating software into a unified process. Chapter 14, "Protecting Your Intellectual Property," shows you how licensing and obfuscation can help you keep your source code safe. And finally, Chapter 15, "Delivering the Application," looks at the process of creating a setup program for your application.

About the Sample Application

To help tie the various parts of this book together, I've created a sample application named Download Tracker. The goal of Download Tracker is simple: to help me (and anyone else who finds it useful) keep track of the code and documents downloaded from the Internet. Right now I have more than 8GB of code samples tucked away on one of my hard drives, and I have no idea what some of them are. With Download Tracker, I can enter basic information to catalog a download as I make it, and so build up a searchable database to help me find things again in the future.

The book will give you glimpses of the Download Tracker application being built, but you won't get a step-by-step guide to creating it. Remember, the point of the book is the process and the tools, not the actual code. But if the application looks useful to you, you can get the code from the book's website. In fact, you can get the code in every state from beginning to end. That's because I've installed a SourceGear Vault server at the website, which lets you obtain your own copy of the source code from the development database. You'll learn more about source code control in Chapter 3, "Using Source Code Control Effectively."

I've tried to write production-quality code in Download Tracker, but I'm sure there are oversights. I welcome your comments and suggestions for making it a better application for the next edition of the book.

NOTE   You can download all the code for this book, including the complete Download Tracker, from the book's websites at www.sybex.com (search for the book's ISBN, 4327) and www.CoderToDeveloper.com.

Keeping Up to Date

This book was written in late 2003 and early 2004 using the then-current versions of the software it discusses, starting with Visual Studio .NET 2003. As new versions are released, I'll note them on www.CoderToDeveloper.com. When in doubt, you can always check there for updates. And if you find any problems with the sample code, or have any questions or suggestions, I'll be happy to hear from you via e-mail. You can reach me at MikeG1@larkfarm.com. Of course, I can't guarantee an answer to every question, but I'll do my best.

CHAPTER 1

Planning Your Project

How does one design an electric motor? Would you attach a bathtub to it, simply because one was available? Would a bouquet of flowers help? A heap of rocks?

—Professor Bernardo de la Paz, quoted in *The Moon Is a Harsh Mistress*, by Robert A. Heinlein

So there you are with your shiny new IDE and your coding skills and a vague idea of what it is that you want to produce. The temptation can be almost overwhelming to dive right in and start typing.

Don't do it. Even the smallest of projects benefits from at least a little bit of planning up front, and yours is no different. In this chapter, I'll discuss some of the basic planning steps, including requirements management and choosing a methodology, that you should consider before you write a single line of code.

Nailing Down a Feature Set

Before you write a single line of code, there's a simple yet difficult question that you must answer: What are you writing? You need to have more than a vague idea of the end product before you can finish building an application. If you don't know what you're trying to produce, then you're not really writing an application; you're just noodling around with code. There's nothing wrong with that as a learning activity, but as a developer, you need to be more focused.

"What" is not the only question you should be asking about your application at this point. In fact, you should think about the same set of questions that a good newspaper reporter asks:

- What are you writing?
- When do you want to finish writing it?
- Where do you expect it will be used?
- Why are you writing this software?
- How will you write the software?

I've found it useful to start the process of software development with some brainstorming activities. The goal of brainstorming is not to come up with all the answers, but to develop a set of ideas that you can reasonably expect will include the answers. In the context of focusing your software development, that means that you want to have a pretty good idea of the features of the finished product before you start building it. It's possible, even likely, that this list of features will change as you actually build the application. That's OK; for right now, you just want to have a clear direction, even if the ultimate destination changes later.

If you read the Introduction, you know that my sample application for this book is named Download Tracker, and that it has something to do with downloading software from the Internet. So far, Download Tracker is just a vague idea: I want to keep track of things I download from the Internet. To come up with an initial feature set, I'll develop an *elevator pitch* and a *mind map*.

The Elevator Pitch

The elevator pitch is an idea that was popularized during the peak of the dot-com era, when it seemed as if there were buckets of money out there to be had—and a lot of competition for having them. The scenario goes like this: You're on your way to a meeting with the venture capitalists on the 87th floor of the skyscraper. You've got your laptop loaded with PowerPoint slides, and collateral to hand out. Your 15-minute presentation is honed to a glittering edge.

Then, just as you step into the elevator in the building lobby, the senior partner from the VC firm steps in with you. "So, Bill," he says, "what have you got for us today?" Forget the 15-minute presentation. You've got a 30-second elevator ride to impress this guy and convince him to add zeroes to your bank balance. What do you say?

You're probably not going to get an eight-figure investment from someone who thinks your idea is fabulous, but coming up with an elevator pitch is still a very useful exercise. The important thing is not to create your elevator pitch quickly, but to be able to explain your software quickly. You might also think of this as coming up with "100 words or less" to explain your software.

> **RULE** Write a short statement describing what your software will do, and why, to help keep you on track.

If you're unsure whether a potential new feature should be added, ask yourself whether it fits in with the elevator pitch. If not, either the pitch needs to be modified or the feature should be discarded. When in doubt, discard the feature. Feature creep—the continuing addition of new functionality while you're still writing the code—is one of the biggest enemies that keep you from actually finishing a project.

Here are some things to think about when you're coming up with your elevator pitch:

- Short is better than long. A long and rambling elevator pitch probably means you haven't really decided what you're building yet.

- Functionality trumps technology. Potential customers care about what your software will do. They usually don't care how your software does it.

- Solve a problem. If you can't explain what problem your application will solve, customers won't know why they should buy it.

- Pitch the benefits, not yourself. Customers won't be buying you, your superior knowledge, or your development team (if you're lucky enough to be working with a team). They'll be buying the software.

- Figure out what's important to your audience, and make sure you address that. Are the people buying your product most interested in cost, innovation, features, compatibility, or something else entirely?

With those points in mind, here's an elevator pitch for Download Tracker:

Download Tracker builds a personal catalog of all the software that you download from the Internet. You can add descriptions and keywords to identify each software package. Later on you can edit this information and add your own ratings. With Download Tracker, you'll never forget where you saved a program again, or lose track of the name of the file that installs your favorite freeware application. If you run a website, you can even use Download Tracker to automatically generate a list of your favorite downloads, complete with hyperlinks.

The Mind Map

The elevator pitch is a great tool for gaining focus on your application. You can print it out and nail it to the wall over your monitor to keep you motivated when you're chasing bugs at 3 A.M. and that last slice of pizza puts you into the heartburn zone. But after you've achieved that focus, you need to expand your view. This is the point where I'll typically start brainstorming a more detailed list of the things that the software will do.

There are a lot of ways to do this brainstorming, and choosing between them is largely a matter of personal preference. Some people like to use a text editor or a word processor and just type ideas, perhaps organizing them into an outline. Many developers are happy with a whiteboard for this purpose, although that leaves you with the problem of saving the whiteboard contents for later reference. If you have this problem, take a look at PolyVision's Whiteboard Photo (`www.websterboards.com/products/wbp.html`), though at $249 it may be too pricey if you're not a frequent whiteboard user.

NOTE   The software prices I quote in this book are current in early 2004. Prices do change, though, so check at the relevant websites before making up your budget. I'm including prices so you know which tools are free, which are inexpensive, and which are potential budget-busters.

My own personal choice for freeform brainstorming is the mind map. Tony Buzan, who invented this form of diagram, describes a mind map as "a powerful graphic technique which provides a universal key to unlock the potential of the brain. It harnesses the full range of cortical skills—word, image, number, logic, rhythm, color, and spatial awareness—in a single, uniquely powerful manner." You can think of a mind map as a sort of two-dimensional outline; rather than organizing ideas into a linear list, you spread them around the page and connect them. Mind maps can also use icons, graphics, fonts, colors, hyperlinks, and other techniques to include information that's hard to put into words.

NOTE   For general information on mind mapping, visit Tony Buzan's website at `www.mind-map.com/`.

There are several software packages out there to create mind maps, which is a good thing, because most developers don't have the graphic skills to create a nice one by hand. Table 1.1 lists some of the mind-mapping software available for Windows.

TABLE 1.1 Mind-Mapping Software for Windows

Product	URL	Description
ConceptDraw MINDMAP	`www.conceptdraw.com/en/products/ mindmap/main.php`	Cross-platform Mac/PC product that strives for a "hand drawn" creative look.
FreeMind	`http://freemind.sourceforge.net/`	A free version written in Java. It's quite a mature product, but concentrates on text rather than embellishments.
MindManager	`www.mindjet.com/`	High-end dedicated mind-mapping software with Microsoft Office integration and many features.
SmartDraw	`www.smartdraw.com/index2.htm`	General-purpose diagramming package with mind maps as one of its possible outputs.
Visual Mind	`www.visual-mind.com/`	Inexpensive commercial program concentrating on text output with a browser plug-in.

Figure 1.1 shows a mind map of features, ideas, and notes for Download Tracker. This mind map was created with MindManager X5 Pro. As you can see, I've got a fair number of things in mind for this product.

One of the best features of software-generated mind maps is that they're dynamic. It's easy to move branches around, add or delete text or images, and otherwise update mind maps. If you're using a mind map for brainstorming, consider updating it as your project proceeds to give you a continuously current snapshot of your ideas. If you do this, I suggest you archive a copy of the original version first. When the project is released, it's fun to look back and see how your ideas about it have changed and evolved.

FIGURE 1.1
Mind map for Download Tracker

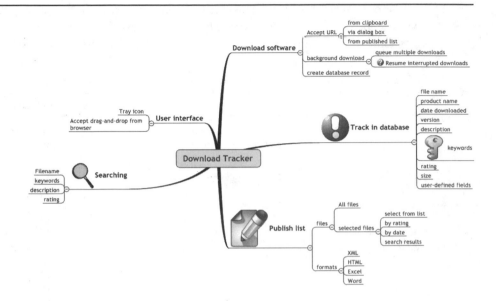

Handling Requirements

Depending on the project, coming up with your initial feature set can ease into a formal process for handling requirements. One thing needs to be clear right up front, though: Not every software project needs a formal requirements process. In general, I've found that requirements management is more important when the requirements come from someone other than the software developer. If you're building software to implement your own vision, you can probably get by without anything more than a mind map or feature list to cover your product's requirements. But if you're building an application to handle data entry for an insurance office, you're probably not an expert in the *problem domain* (that is, in the details of the business of selling insurance). In that case, paying more formal attention to requirements can save you lots of grief down the road.

> **TIP**   As a middle path, you might like to track your product's requirements with a bug-tracking tool. I'll talk more about this in Chapter 9, "Tracking and Squashing Bugs."

Defining Requirements

Broadly speaking, the requirements for a piece of software define what the software should do. But it helps to have a framework for classifying requirements. One useful framework comes from Karl Wiegers' book *Software Requirements* (Microsoft Press, 2003). Wiegers distinguishes four types of requirements in his taxonomy:

Business requirements   High-level objectives of the organization or customer who requests the system.

User requirements   User goals or tasks that the users must be able to perform with the product.

Functional requirements   Software functionality that the developers must build into the product to enable users to accomplish their tasks, thereby satisfying the business requirements.

System requirements   Top-level requirements for a product containing multiple subsystems. Note that not all of the subsystems will be software!

TECHNOLOGY TRAP

This Year's Model

Developers tend to be a bit like magpies. When we see something new and bright, our instinctive reaction is to cart it back to our nests. "Ooooh, shiny!" could be the slogan on our coat of arms.

One place this is evident is in the way that fads sweep the development universe. For example, take peer-to-peer. For a while, it seemed as if everyone was building their software to be peer-to-peer enabled. "Our product will be the best peer-to-peer enabled fish scaler on the market" isn't a real elevator pitch, but it surely could have been. There are plenty of other technology fads that I'd put in this category, for example:

- Distributed computing

- Banner-ad supported

- Web services

Now, certainly all of these are useful technologies *for some things*. But they clearly don't belong in every single product on the market. Particularly when you're a small shop, it's important to concentrate on adding real value, rather than simply buzzword compliance. Restraining yourself will also prevent you from wasting time learning a new technology, only to find that it's a dead end (anyone remember Data Reports from Visual Basic 6?).

Here's a tip: When you read an article about some hot new technology, resist the temptation to immediately add it to your code. Instead, write it down on a sticky note and stick it to your monitor. If your application *really* needs a distributed reflection-based plug-in API, it will still need it in the morning. If not, it's a lot easier to rip off the sticky note than to roll back the code changes.

Wiegers divides the process of working with these requirements into *requirements development* and *requirements management.* Requirements development further divides into a complex set of elicitation, analysis, specification, and validation activities, with feedback loops between them. After requirements development has teased out the requirements for a product, requirements management entails the process of coming to an agreement with the customer as to what the requirements are, and tracking the progress of the product to meet those requirements.

WARNING   Requirements are rarely static. If you're building software for an external customer, make sure you and the customer agree on how the requirements can be amended, and decide up front who bears the burden of any additional costs.

Eliciting Requirements Checklist

If you're working with an external customer, this checklist will help you elicit the requirements for the software:

- Talk to the actual end users of the software. Ask them what they expect the software to do.

- Watch how the end users perform their job now. Make sure you understand how the software will change things.

- Write a vision and scope document, explaining what's a part of the project and (equally important) what is not. Make sure the customer agrees with you.

- Hold an informal group discussion with the users over lunch or a night out. People will speak up in a group of their peers even when they won't tell you things one on one.

- Document the requirements you determine in plain English, and then check with the users to see if they make sense.

- If you're replacing existing software, find out what's wrong with the current system. Your requirements will often boil down to fixing the problems.

- Arrange the requirements in priority order and make sure the customer agrees on the priority.

At the end of the requirements elicitation process, you should know what the software will do. Just as important, the customer should have confidence that you understand their requirements.

Eliciting and Documenting Requirements

If you're writing software for yourself, eliciting requirements (often called *needs assessment*) is simply a matter of writing down what you think the software should do. If you're dealing with an external customer, the process can be much more complex. There's no alternative to getting the customer to tell you what the requirements are, but you have many ways to go about this. You might observe them at work, exchange frequent e-mails, or even convene a formal requirements workshop. For this book, I'm going to assume that you are your own customer, and hence, a formal requirements elicitation process is unnecessary. If you're working for an external customer, the sidebar "Eliciting Requirements Checklist" will help you get started, but you should also read *Software Requirements* or another book on the subject.

The issue of documenting requirements still remains. One useful tool for a formal requirements document is the *use case*. A use case describes one or more interactions between an external actor (which might be a person or another application) and your application. Here's a partial list of use cases for Document Tracker:

- Download Software
- Annotate Software
- Rate Software
- Publish Software List
- Search for Software

Two or three words isn't much in the way of documentation, of course. To seriously employ use cases for requirements, you'll need a more formal document for each use case. Typical contents of a use case document include:

1. A unique identifier for the use case
2. The use case name
3. A short text description
4. A list of preconditions that must be satisfied before the use case can start
5. A list of postconditions that must be satisfied when the use case ends
6. A numbered list of steps that are carried out in the use case

See the sidebar "A Download Tracker Use Case" for one simple use case document.

A Download Tracker Use Case

Use Case ID: UC-1

Use Case Name: Download Software

Description: The user initiates a software download by notifying Download Tracker of the desired file. Download Tracker prompts for a download location and identifying information. When the download is completed, Download Tracker displays a success message.

Preconditions:

1. Download Tracker is already running.

Postconditions:

1. Software is stored on hard drive.

2. Database contains a record for the software.

Normal Course:

1. User drags a URL from Internet Explorer and drops it on the Download Tracker tray icon (see Alternative Courses 1.1 and 1.2).

2. Download Tracker prompts for a download location, starting from its default directory.

3. User confirms download location.

4. Download Tracker initiates download.

5. Download Tracker prompts for identifying information such as program name, description, and keywords.

6. User enters desired information and clicks OK.

7. Download Tracker creates and saves database record.

8. Download Tracker notifies user when download is complete.

Alternative Courses:

1.1 (alternative to step 1): User pastes a URL to the Clipboard, then right-clicks on Download Tracker icon and selects Download From Clipboard. Continue with step 2 of Normal Course.

1.2 (alternative to step 1): User right-clicks on Download Tracker icon, selects Download URL, and enters a URL. Continue with step 2 of Normal Course.

Exceptions:

E1. URL is not valid

1. Download Tracker displays a message if it cannot download from the specified URL.

NOTE   As you can probably guess, people have written software specifically for requirements management. Most of these packages are directed at large organizations and require a fairly serious commitment of time and resources to install and master. You'll find a comprehensive list on the Requirements Management website at `www.jiludwig.com/Requirements_Management_Tools.html`. For small projects, you'll probably do just as well to write your use cases in Word or Excel.

Project-Tracking Tools

You may be content to just write code until the program is done, whenever that happens. But often there are constraints that prevent such a "we'll ship it when it's done" mentality from working. For instance, you might need to get a product on the market so as to be able to sell some copies so that you can afford to buy something other than ramen noodles, rice, and beans for dinner. Or you might want to be first to the market to gain a strong competitive advantage. In such cases, you're going to want to track the progress of your project.

Painless Software Scheduling

Scheduling software is a difficult problem. In fact, it's a *very* difficult problem. It's so difficult that almost no one does it well, despite the fact that as an industry we have over 60 years' experience in trying to predict how long it will take to write applications. Still, if you're trying to allocate resources and finish a product, you've got to come up with a schedule.

Most of what you'll find written about scheduling software projects is aimed at people building very large applications that involve thousands of requirements and large teams of developers (the classic work here is Fred Brooks' excellent *The Mythical Man-Month*, 2nd edition, Addison-Wesley, 1995). That's not us. If you're developing software in the small, the place to start thinking about scheduling is with Joel Spolsky's essay "Painless Software Schedules" (`www.joelonsoftware.com/articles/fog0000000245.html`). In this essay Joel comes up with a set of rules that I'll quote here with permission:

1. Use Microsoft Excel.

2. Keep it simple.

3. Each feature should consist of several tasks.

4. Only the programmer who is going to write the code can schedule it.

5. Pick very fine-grained tasks.

6. Keep track of the original and current estimate.

7. Update the elapsed column every day.

8. Put in line items for vacations, holidays, etc.

9. Put debugging time into the schedule.

10. Put integration time into the schedule.

11. Build a buffer into the schedule.

12. Never, ever let managers tell programmers to reduce an estimate.

13. A schedule is like wood blocks: If you have a bunch of wood blocks, and you can't fit them into a box, you have two choices: get a bigger box, or remove some blocks.

Some of these rules require a bit more amplification; I urge you to go read Joel's original essay for the details. But I do want to talk about fine-grained tasks for a moment. There's an art to picking the right tasks to include on a schedule. Inexperienced developers and managers often try to just schedule the major milestones: "user interface," "downloading code," and so on. Experienced developers seem to universally agree that *this doesn't work*. No matter how much experience you have, any number that you pull out of thin air for developing the user interface will be wrong. In fact, no matter how hard you try, you won't allow enough time for such major milestones.

TIP   If you're absolutely forced to estimate a schedule based only on milestones (say, because the customer is sitting across the desk from you and wants a number right away), come up with the absolute best, most realistic numbers you can, and then multiply them by three. You can always deliver early, but you can't slip the schedule without making someone unhappy. A far better plan is to simply say, "I'll let you know as soon as I can work up a detailed schedule."

Instead of milestones, when you're scheduling a software project you should think in terms of inch-pebbles. What's an inch-pebble? It's a teeny-tiny task, a small part of a milestone. Instead of scheduling the entire user interface as a single task, schedule individual dialog boxes and forms. You probably have a much better idea of how long it takes to build an individual dialog box than of how long it takes to build an entire user interface for a vaguely defined product. There's also a great side effect here: By the time you create a schedule at the inch-pebble level, your product will be much less vaguely defined.

I know of two products that implement the Painless Software Scheduling method. One is Positive-g's Task Tracker (`www.positive-g.com/tasktracker/index.html`), a stand-alone application that's available as shareware with a $25 registration fee. The other is Safari Software's MasterList-XL, a free Microsoft Excel application (`www.safarisoftware.com/intro.htm`).

Figure 1.2 shows a first cut at a schedule for the DownloadTracker application.

FIGURE 1.2
Scheduling a new
project using Task
Tracker

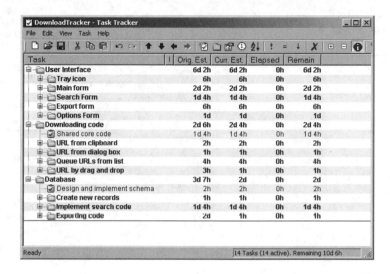

Time and Billing Tools

There's a second aspect of project tracking that some developers need to worry about: time and billing tracking. If you're getting paid by the hour by an external customer, they probably want you to provide an accurate accounting of your time, and to generate reasonably professional-looking invoices. While you can use a general-purpose accounting package for this, my recommendation is that you evaluate time and billing software aimed specifically at software developers. Two such packages are AllNetic's Working Time Tracker (`www.allnetic.com/`) and Atozed Software's A to Z Project Billing (`www.atozedsoftware.com/project/`).

These packages are designed to make it easy for you to allocate billable time to projects by recording the time as you work. Either one lets you easily start a timer when you begin a task, and then assign the time to a particular task when you finish. They can then produce reports showing the total time that was assigned to each task. In addition, the Atozed product includes a complete billing system, with clients, employees, and accounts receivable. Both packages have trial versions that you can download and try. If you're billing by the hour, either one will definitely beat trying to track hours on a scrap of paper or in a spreadsheet. Figure 1.3 shows just one of the reports that you can get from A to Z Project Billing.

FIGURE 1.3
Tracking hours with A
to Z Project Billing

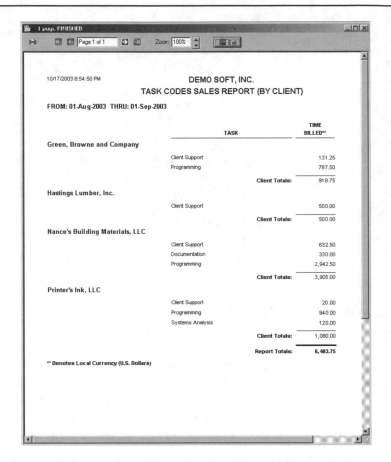

Some developers don't want to have anything to do with bookkeeping. Unfortunately, unless you're big enough to hire someone to do nothing but keep track of billing, you're going to have to pay some attention to that side of the business. It makes sense to spend a little money on a package to make this as painless as possible.

Choosing a Methodology

A methodology is a framework for constructing software. I almost decided not to mention methodologies at all in this book. That's because they've been a source of much debate over the years. This debate has often generated more heat than light; people seem to feel compelled to defend their own preferred methodology, if not to the death, at least to the point of extreme discomfort.

Using Microsoft Project

Developers sometimes get seduced into trying to use Microsoft Project for software project management. After all, it's a dedicated project-management tool, and it comes as part of your MSDN subscription, so why not?

Because it's overkill, that's why not. Microsoft Project is made for managing huge projects—say, building a new dam or office park. Project (and other high-end project-management software) is at its best when a project involves a complex web of interdependencies and pools of interchangeable workers. Neither of those tends to be true for software projects. The dependencies in a program are usually pretty obvious, and software construction seldom proceeds along more than two or three main paths at once. And developers are certainly not interchangeable; Mary won't be able to debug Bill's code efficiently, and adding a database developer to an overdue Internet integration project is unlikely to speed up its delivery.

For very large projects, you may find something like Project necessary. But in that case, you have gone beyond the scale that I'm concerned with in this book. For small applications, take a look at the other programs I mentioned earlier, and stay away from Project.

Nevertheless, there's a lot of good stuff in the various methodologies that have been proposed over the years. As a developer, you can't afford to turn your back on the wisdom of your peers. But you probably don't want to spend years learning about methodologies either. So in this section, I'm going to present a very personal and biased view of methodologies by mentioning three schools of thought that you should be aware of.

For a more thorough review of software methodologies, see Steve McConnell's *Rapid Development* (Microsoft Press, 1996).

The Waterfall Approach

Much of the early work on methodologies came from organizations such as NASA's Software Engineering Laboratory (SEL) and Carnegie-Mellon's Software Engineering Institute (SEI). The focus here was on rigorous methods for developing large applications in an age of relatively primitive software tools.

The methodologies to come out of this era were relatively bureaucratic, emphasizing lots of planning and documentation. At a time when assembling a working program out of small routines was a heroic task, that made sense. And with the proving ground for much of the work being the manned space program, where errors in software are measured in human lives, a heavy process was affordable.

These early methodologies were characterized by a "waterfall approach," in which activities flow smoothly into one another. At the top of the waterfall, you start with requirements analysis.

From there, the project flows downhill through preliminary design, detailed design, implementation, and system testing, coming to rest in an acceptance testing phase. At that point, the software is finished, and the development team goes on to something else.

If you're interested in this set of methodologies, NASA's SEL has a large selection of documents online at http://sel.gsfc.nasa.gov/website/documents/online-doc.htm. *Manager's Handbook for Software Development* and *Recommended Approach to Software Development* in particular will make for interesting reading for those with a sense of history.

Iterative Approaches

As time went on, waterfall methodologies were found to be a poor fit for the way that software development was actually carried on in real organizations. Part of this mismatch was the effect of better tools. Moving from mainframe work, with decks of cards submitted to run overnight, to compilers and editors that actually ran on the desktop made it possible to speed up the software development process immensely. The compile-run-debug cycle decreased in length from days to hours and then minutes. As it became easier to try out ideas before designing them in detail, more exploratory coding went on. The different phases of design, implementation, and testing all started to muddle together.

In response to these changes, some iterative methodologies came to the fore in the software industry (or at least in that part of it concerned with software for personal computers). Two of these are the Rational Unified Process, or RUP (developed by Rational Software, which is now owned by IBM) and the Microsoft Solutions Framework (MSF). You can find their respective home pages at http://www-3.ibm.com/software/awdtools/rup/ and www.microsoft.com/technet/itsolutions/tandp/innsol/default.asp.

Iterative methodologies are characterized by an explicit representation that project phases such as development, testing, or planning may be repeated many times in the course of a project. Figure 1.4, for example, is a schematic diagram of the current version (3.1) of MSF. Although it includes many of the activities you'll find in classic waterfall models of software development, the key feature here is that the process loops back on itself. When one iteration of deployment is finished, another iteration of envisioning is just beginning. A large project might move through this cycle half a dozen times before release.

Agile Approaches

In the mid- to late 1990s, a new group of methodologies started garnering increasing attention. Generically referred to as agile methodologies, this group includes such processes as Extreme Programming (XP), Scrum, and Crystal. In some quarters these developments have been greeted with relief; in others they've been condemned as a complete abandonment of any sort of reasonable process control. One reasonably fair overview is Martin Fowler's essay "The New Methodology" (www.martinfowler.com/articles/newMethodology.html#N4001F4).

FIGURE 1.4
Schematic diagram of
the Microsoft Solu-
tions Framework

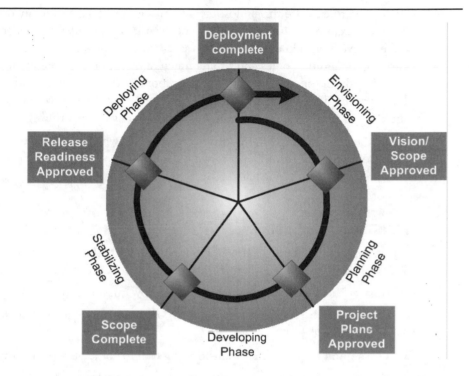

The agile methodologies look at the transition from waterfall to iterative methods and continue the trend. If faster cycles are useful, why not reduce the cycles to weeks or even days? If bureaucracy can be cut down, why not cut it out entirely? These are attractive notions, especially to developers who like rapid development and dislike bureaucracy.

The best known of the agile methodologies is XP. XP is a collection of practices, some of which (such as pair programming, which involves having two developers work together to write code) are quite controversial. Nevertheless, it's also the site of much of the most interesting research in software development being done today. You should at least read Kent Beck's slim book *Extreme Programming Explained* (Addison-Wesley, 2000) to get an idea of the issues here. On the Web, check out the Agile Alliance (`www.agilealliance.org/home`).

Settling on a Methodology

So which methodology should you choose for your software development work? Frankly, I don't think that you really need to choose. Instead, I recommend what might be called a meta-methodology:

RULE   Take what works for you and leave the rest.

I've tried to exercise this philosophy in writing this book, and in my own software development. For example, estimating the costs of an entire project up front is a practice from waterfall and iterative methodologies, where it's assumed that you know where you're going when you start. Agile methodologies don't think much of this approach, preferring instead to deliver small chunks of functionality until time or money runs out. On the other hand, test-driven development (which you'll meet in Chapter 5, "Preventing Bugs with Unit Testing") is straight out of XP; I find it a useful practice even without any of the other XP methods.

Inevitably, as you write more software you'll learn which tools and techniques work for you. Over time, this will result in your own personal methodology. If it lets you deliver working software, don't let anyone tell you that you're doing it wrong.

Planning Checklist

If you don't plan your software, you'll never know whether you're building the right thing. Think about these points when you're planning your software and development process:

- Answer the what, when, where, why, and how questions about your software.
- Come up with a succinct "elevator pitch" that you can refer to when deciding what belongs in the project.
- Use a mind map or other brainstorming tool to come up with a feature set.
- Define and document the requirements for your software.
- Use a scheduling program to keep yourself on track.
- Choose a methodology that works for you.

Are you ready to write code now? Not quite! In the next chapter I'll talk about software architecture for small projects. Architecture provides the scaffolding that your code will hang on, and is an essential part of your project.

CHAPTER 2

Organizing Your Project

"Begin at the beginning," the King said gravely, *"and go on till you come to the end: then stop."*

—Lewis Carroll, *Alice's Adventures in Wonderland,*
Chapter 12

I s it time for code now? Well, not quite yet. At this point, you may know where you want your application to end up, but not how to get there. Before you write any code, it's helpful to think a bit about how that code will be organized. In this chapter, I'll look at several different ways to organize your project: the architectural perspective, the new project perspective, and the staged delivery perspective:

- The architectural perspective addresses the overall shape of the application.
- The project perspective addresses the construction of the application.
- The staged delivery perspective addresses the release of the application.

Thinking about Architecture

Architecture is one of the trendy terms in software development these days. Many people who used to present themselves as developers now have business cards that read "Software Architect," and you'll find institutes, certifications, and websites galore for architects. But don't let yourself get turned off by the trendiness. There is a valuable discipline of software architecture, and for even small projects it remains a good starting point.

What Is Software Architecture?

Darned good question, that. Although most authorities agree that there is a need for architecture in the software field, there's no generally accepted definition. Martin Fowler offers a definition in his book *Patterns of Enterprise Application Architecture* (Addison-Wesley, 2003) that I rather like:

> *There are two common elements: One is the highest-level breakdown of a system into its parts; the other, decisions that are hard to change.*

The goal of creating an architecture for your software is to have a general idea of what you're going to build, before you start building it. Commonly, you'll use pictures, sketches, and diagrams to communicate this information.

Architecture vs. Design

It's easy to get misled by analogies between software and other fields. The fact that we reuse words from other fields makes it even easier. *Architecture* is one of those words. In the real world of buildings and bridges, architects are responsible for design at all levels of detail: Everything from the outside view of the skyscraper to the location of each sink in the janitorial closets will be on the architectural plans somewhere. In computer software, though, most people distinguish between architecture and design.

Generally, when developers speak of architecture, they mean very broad decisions: what database the application will use, whether Extensible Markup Language (XML) should be used as a file storage format, how many tiers the overall solution will use for its structure. Once the architecture is in place, you can proceed to detailed design: what objects the data access code will use, which variables will hold global state, and so on. One way to make the distinction is that you shouldn't be writing any code in the architecture phase, but once you get into design, you might well dictate such implementation details. Of course, it's a fuzzy line: Does choosing a collection type to hold a set of objects fall under architecture or design? It's the sort of decision that's hard to change, but it's also an implementation detail. But since one of the themes of this book is that you need to be prepared to move back and forth between different tasks as you develop an application, there's no need to find a hard boundary between architecture and design.

Software construction is often divided into three stages:

- In the architecture stage, you nail down the most important decisions about the application.

- In the design stage, you make more detailed plans for writing the application.

- In the implementation stage, you actually write the code.

Although this breakdown provides a convenient framework for large projects, a small project might only require two stages (architecture/design—design/implementation). You might characterize these as "thinking about the code" and "writing the code." Of course, you'll probably shift back and forth between these two activities several times in the course of developing an application.

Architecture in Small Projects

For small projects (those that will require a single developer or perhaps several developers working closely together), my own feeling is that you don't need to go overboard on your architecture. A simple sketch, perhaps on the whiteboard in your office, is often enough. If you want something electronic, I recommend a drawing package such as Microsoft Visio. Figure 2.1 shows my initial architectural diagram for Download Tracker.

This diagram captures some of the decisions I've already made about how Download Tracker will be structured:

- Data will be stored in a Microsoft Access database. I doubt that I'll outgrow that, but for flexibility I'll use a separate data access layer to present a structured, object-oriented view of the database.

- Most of the code should be contained in a logic layer. I don't quite know what that will look like yet, but I intend to separate it from the user interface (UI).

- Downloading will be handled by a separate downloading engine. I see this as an object that can go off and handle downloads on its own thread and notify the main logic when it's done.

- I plan to use a pluggable architecture for output formats. That way, it's easy to include additional formats in the future—or to delete some if I run into a scheduling problem.

FIGURE 2.1
Architectural diagram
for Download Tracker

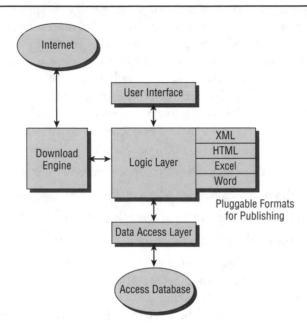

What about UML?

It's impossible to read much about software architecture these days without running into the Unified Modeling Language (UML). UML is the closest thing we've got to a standard for architectural diagrams, and it's implemented by quite a few products. These range from the $95 Enterprise Architect (www.sparxsystems.com.au/) to the $3000 IBM Rational XDE (http://www-3.ibm.com/software/rational/). The more expensive products such as XDE can actually go beyond architectural modeling to generating code to implement the model.

TIP   A good starting point in finding a UML tool is Bruce Eckel's collection of reader feedback at http://mindview.net/WebLog/log-0041. Bruce has collected information on a wide array of tools from his readers.

UML is a powerful tool, but I find that it's mainly useful for straightforward line-of-business applications. If you're going to be working out an invoicing system for your employer, you might well find UML models to be a good place to start. For small tools and utilities, though, I don't find that the exercise of going through formal UML diagrams helps much.

TECHNOLOGY TRAP

The Map Is Not the Territory

"The map is not the territory" is one of the maxims set forth by Alfred Korzybski, founder of General Semantics. It seems obvious when you think about it: There's a difference between a thing and our written representations of the thing. But despite this, people regularly confuse maps and territories. For example, the word *surgeon* calls forth your mental map of the concepts surrounding surgeons; for many people, it's then jarring to be told "This surgeon is a woman." Somehow their mental map includes the concept "All surgeons are male," despite good real-world evidence to the contrary.

Why this digression into semantics? Because I've seen developers get into trouble when they start to confuse the architecture with the actual code. The architecture represents an ideal view of your application, but you need to be prepared to change the architecture if the application demands it.

One place this turns up is in database design. Most developers know that the ideal database is in third normal form, which means that it complies with a set of rules for avoiding redundant data. Nevertheless, sometimes trying to work with a third normal form database can be a problem, particularly when you need fast access to derived data. In some cases, the best answer is to selectively denormalize the data for increased performance. If your developers are confusing the architecture with the application, you can expect strong opposition to this move, no matter how sensible it is.

The bottom line is that the architecture documents should provide guidance for design and coding, but you shouldn't be afraid to revisit the architecture if you're running into a problem.

If you're interested in learning more about UML, many excellent books are available on the market. I like Sinan Si Alhir's *Learning UML* (O'Reilly, 2003) and Jason T. Roff's *UML: A Beginner's Guide* (McGraw-Hill Osborne, 2002). For Rational XDE in particular, try Wendy Boggs's and Michael Boggs's *Mastering Rational XDE* (Sybex, 2003).

Introducing Patterns

Here's one thing to keep in mind when you're thinking about architecture: You are not the first person to be designing this sort of application. Oh, sure, the sum total of all your work will likely be something new and wonderful. However, the individual problems and subsystems will no doubt resemble those of other applications. There are only so many ways to set up an event with multiple listeners, for example.

In the computer world, these similarities are called patterns. The term is borrowed from Christopher Alexander's seminal work in architecture *A Pattern Language: Towns, Buildings, Construction* (Oxford University Press, 1977), though truthfully, there's not all that much similarity between architecture patterns and software patterns. Patterns are a specific type of best practices. In fact, it might have been simpler to call them architectural best practices. Still, the term is common now and we're stuck with it. While a small project may not need to make use of the knowledge stored in patterns, you should have at least a general overview of the field.

RULE   In software it's often more important to know where to go to find things than it is to memorize them.

The Gang of Four

In the software world, patterns start with the Gang of Four. That's the common nickname for Erich Gamma, Richard Helm, Ralph Johnson, and John Vlissides, who in 1995 published *Design Patterns: Elements of Reusable Object-Oriented Software* (Addison-Wesley, 1995). The Gang of Four (sometimes you'll see this abbreviated as GOF), brought Alexander's concept to computing, identifying 23 patterns that applied to many object-oriented software systems.

The GOF patterns are things like "Chain of Responsibility." The description of the pattern starts with its intent (in this case, to avoid coupling the sender of a request to its receiver by giving multiple objects a chance to handle the request). The authors then go on to give some motivation for the pattern (context-sensitive help is a good example when you want to fall back on increasingly general objects if specific ones do not have help of their own). The next step is a section on the applicability of the pattern to various problems, followed by a diagram of its structure, a list of the classes that participate in it, and the consequences of implementing this pattern. Each pattern also includes implementation issues and sample code, plus examples from situations where it's known to be used.

The original patterns book spawned something of an industry in computer science. Hundreds of books are now available on software patterns; I even have several on my shelf that deal with Visual Basic .NET and C# design patterns.

TIP   A good place to start learning more about patterns (although fraught with dead links) is the Patterns Home Page at `http://hillside.net/patterns/`.

Why Patterns?

Patterns are complex and hard to describe. Some of the design patterns in the GOF book stretch over many pages of discussion and sample implementations (in C+ and Smalltalk). Just understanding the details of a pattern such as Observer can take quite a bit of study. So why take the time to make the study? Because if you're working in systems architecture, the vocabulary of patterns can help you solve design problems quickly and with known-good solutions.

For example, consider the Observer pattern identified by the GOF. The Observer pattern shows you how to define a one-to-many dependency between an object and its dependents. When the object changes state, all of its dependents are notified and updated.

Now suppose your application deals with medical imaging data in a multiwindows UI. You might find yourself showing a rotating image in one window while simultaneously tracking the point of view numerically in another and updating a graph of transparency values in a third. A team without pattern experience might spend a long time working out a combination of objects, events, and algorithms to make everything work smoothly together. Or, if they were all familiar with the patterns in the original GOF book, it's likely that someone would suggest the Observer pattern as an appropriate answer, and the discussion could move immediately to solving details like the unexpected update problem.

Design patterns make such discussions possible by giving the participants a shared vocabulary at a high level of abstraction. And by encapsulating the wisdom of members of the object-oriented design community who share decades of experience, design patterns help you benefit from that experience as well. You don't need to reinvent the wheel if you have a design pattern that points out how well circular objects roll.

Patterns at Microsoft

A few years ago, I could have just left this section out of the book entirely. While Microsoft has been making excellent developer tools for a long time, its traditional attitude toward developers has been something like, "You're smart people, you'll figure this stuff out." The release of a new version of Visual Basic or Visual C++ was an occasion for the Microsofties to go back to work on the next version while the rest of us figured out how to effectively use the current one.

That has largely changed since the release of the .NET Framework. Whether it's feeling growing pressure from the Java camp, or whether it has just matured as an organization, Microsoft now offers substantial help to developers on the effective use of its products. In particular, you can gain a lot of knowledge with a visit to the Microsoft Patterns & Practices website (`www.microsoft.com/resources/practices/`).

The Patterns & Practices site provides an amazing amount of information. This ranges from entire books on topics like enterprise application patterns using Microsoft products (and you can download the books or order paper copies) to articles on best practices with Exchange Server and Active Directory. The patterns and practices here cut across both development and systems administration, just as Microsoft's products do.

TIP   The Patterns and Practices Group posts some material for public review before it's officially published. You can keep up with the latest by visiting TheServerSide.NET at `www.theserverside.net`.

As a .NET developer, you should know in particular about the application blocks. The application blocks are fully developed chunks of reusable source code designed to solve particular problems. As I write this, the available application blocks include:

- Aggregation application block, for aggregating and transforming information from multiple sources

- Asynchronous Invocation application block, for agent-based asynchronous processing

- Caching application block, for caching information in distributed applications (note that for pure ASP.NET applications you should probably use the ASP.NET cache instead)

- Configuration Management application block, for securely reading and writing configuration information from a variety of sources

- Data Access application block, to simplify ADO.NET data access

- Exception Management application block, which provides an extensible framework for handling exceptions

- Logging application block, to enable distributed and asynchronous logging across an entire application

- Updater application block, which provides a "pull model" for updating desktop applications over a network

- User Interface Process application block, a model for writing UI and workflow processes as a distinct layer

You can find further information on these application blocks (and keep track of new application blocks) in the Patterns & Practices library at `www.microsoft.com/resources/practices/completelist.asp`.

NOTE　I'll discuss the application blocks in more detail in Chapter 7, "Digging Into Source Code."

Starting a New Project

If you've come this far, you've got an idea for a new application. You've brainstormed a list of requirements and come up with an architecture at a level of detail that suits you. Now you're ready to set pen to paper (or, much more likely, fingers to keyboard) and start writing code. But where to start? There are three basic ways to get going on a new and reasonably large coding method:

- Breadth-first

- Depth-first

- Mixed

Breadth-First Coding

In a breadth-first strategy, the object is to rough in the entire application at once, and then go back and fill in the details later. When working this way, you'll probably concentrate first on the interfaces between the various components. For example, defining how the core logic of Download Tracker will call the download engine would tell me something about both components; I could write the skeleton of the method in the engine, and the code to call it, without actually implementing anything.

A breadth-first approach brings some advantages with it:

- You can quickly scope out whether you left anything out of your architecture.
- It's possible to demonstrate the overall flow of an application early in the coding cycle.

But breadth-first coding has disadvantages as well:

- If you're working for customers, they may mistake the shell of the application for a nearly complete version, resulting in unrealistic schedule expectations.
- It can be hard to manage a team of developers on a breadth-first project, because splitting off parts of separate developers to work on is challenging.

Depth-First Coding

With a depth-first strategy, you concentrate on one piece of the application at a time. For example, using a depth-first approach to the Download Tracker application, I might start by writing the entire download engine before any other part of the application. Only when that part was written and debugged would I turn to the next task, perhaps setting up the database and data access layer.

Of course, depth-first coding offers advantages:

- By concentrating on a single task, you can research and remember the code issues associated with that task to the exclusion of all else.
- If you have a team of developers, they can work on separate components without bumping into each other's code.

To balance these, you have to consider the disadvantages of the depth-first approach:

- You won't have a sanity check on your architecture until late in the game.
- While you can demonstrate individual components, there's no way to get a sense of overall application flow until you're nearly done coding.

Mixed Models

So which approach do I advocate? For a small project, I like to take a mixed approach to development. Most of the work I do involves some UI, with functionality behind it. Download Tracker is a good example: there are UI bits, but there are also plenty of non-UI bits to work on. (Class libraries, by contrast, are all code with no UI.)

In such cases, I usually start by at least roughing in the UI. This gives me a chance to check that the application will behave in a sensible way and to think in more depth about the way that a user will interact with it. So this part of the process is breadth-first; the UI is a façade with nothing behind it, at least to begin with.

After I'm satisfied that the UI is close to what I want, I'll switch to depth-first development, tackling one component at a time. This lets me focus my skills and knowledge on a single problem, without worrying about the entire application at once. In Download Tracker, for example, it makes sense to write the download engine and the data access layer as two separate tasks, since there's not likely to be much code that can be shared between the two.

Scheduling Deliveries

Software projects are never on time. OK, maybe there are exceptions to that rule, but it's a good starting point for thinking about delivery schedules. Most developers are very aware of the three-cornered trade-off shown in Figure 2.2.

One way or another, this triangle has to stay in balance. If you have to add more features to the product corner, then either the time or cost (or both) have to be increased. If time and cost are fixed, then the amount of product you can deliver is also fixed. (If you have a boss that dictates product functionality, time, and cost, beware; he or she may have an impossible combination in mind.)

FIGURE 2.2
Trade-offs in software
development

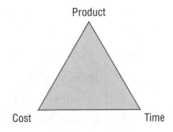

The realities of business are such that cost and time are usually pretty well fixed, and your only flexibility is in how much product you can deliver on time and within budget. Given this equation, it's not smart to plan on an all-or-nothing strategy that leaves you with no software at all if the cost and time factors prove to be wrong. By delivering your software in multiple stages, you can be sure to produce something even if your initial estimate of what you can accomplish is wrong.

RULE   Plan on multiple deliveries of any project of reasonable size.

The Beta Testing Approach

One way to handle this is to deliver your entire application in a very crude form at first, and then to refine it into successively better-working builds. Typically, the builds will have names like this:

- Alpha
- Beta 1
- Beta 2
- Release Candidate
- Release

This is the approach that Microsoft takes with its large applications like Office or Visual Studio. The alpha builds go to a few selected people to look at; the beta builds to a somewhat wider audience; and the release candidate builds are widely distributed to catch obscure problems that affect only a few people.

How does this approach handle the trade-offs? Usually, Microsoft fixes the time and cost points by planning a schedule that runs from alpha to final release. The trade-offs are then within product functionality. It's not unusual, with this approach, for a feature that's in an alpha or beta build to mysteriously disappear before the product's final release. This could be because feedback from testers indicated that the feature was unwanted, or it could simply be that the developers ran out of time and money to implement it.

The XP Approach

Note that the beta testing approach amounts to delivering broken software repeatedly, with the hopes that each build will be less broken than the one before. If you're sure you have the resources to get to a final release version, that's fine, but what if you run out of time and money at the Beta 1 stage? Software that's almost totally broken is worse than no software at all.

This problem has led advocates of Extreme Programming (XP) to a different philosophy about releasing software. They advocate a series of small releases. The idea is to put a simple version of the program in operation as quickly as possible, with a high quality bar. Then you prioritize the requirements, and add them in one at a time on successive releases. Releases are spaced close to one another (perhaps two to three weeks apart), and each represents a minimum increment of functionality above the previous release.

The XP approach handles resource constraints almost the same way as the beta testing approach, by adjusting product functionality. But there's a difference between the two if the constraints get unexpectedly tight. Suppose your development budget were chopped off halfway through the project. With a beta testing approach, your final release might have implemented 100% of the planned functionality, but with lots of bugs in every function. With the XP approach, your final release might only have implemented 50% of the planned functionality, but that 50% will be close to bug-free.

Choosing a Scheduling Approach

Choosing between a typical beta testing approach and an XP "small releases" approach is usually a matter of understanding your resources and audience. If you're working in a business setting with uncertain requirements and a potentially shaky contract, I urge you to go for a more XP-like schedule. You can maximize your chance of a happy customer by making sure that they have a working system at all times, even if it doesn't (yet) do everything that they're hoping for.

On the other hand, if you're creating a utility for sale on the Internet, you might find a beta testing approach more to your liking. Even if you're not facing external constraints on your time, the feedback from beta testers has a value all by itself. By pushing out an early version with a rough cut of your planned functionality, you can get an idea as to whether the market is really interested in this software.

> **TIP** Before releasing a beta test version, you should think about licensing issues. I'll talk more about this in Chapter 14, "Protecting Your Intellectual Property."

Whatever you do, don't make the mistake of thinking of the Product corner of the triangle (Figure 2.2) as "product quality" instead of "product functionality." It can be tempting at the end of a long development cycle to shove a product out the door even if you know that it's full of bugs. Resist the temptation. There's no better way to lose customers permanently than to sell them software that doesn't work.

Organization Checklist

You could start writing code without organizing your project—but that lowers your chance of actually finishing a project. Before you charge into the coding phase, make sure you know where you're going:

- Plan an overall architecture for the project.
- Be flexible but cautious about changing the architecture.
- Decide between a depth-first, breadth-first, or mixed approach to coding.
- Choose an XP scheduling approach if you're working with uncertain requirements.
- Choose a beta testing scheduling approach if external feedback is important.

There's one more decision to make before writing your code: where you're going to store the code. In the next chapter, I'll discuss source code control, and explain why every application should make use of this critical facility.

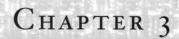

CHAPTER 3

Using Source Code Control Effectively

Those who cannot remember the past are condemned to repeat it.

—George Santayana

If Santayana were writing computer books, he might have put that a little differently: Those who cannot remember the source code are compelled to re-create it. We live in a world where things go wrong. Hard drives crash, taking precious files with them. Libraries change their interfaces. The brilliant idea you had at 3A.M. looks a lot stupider after some sleep, and you're faced with ripping out all that code you wrote last night. For these reasons, and many others, any serious software project must use source code control.

The Three Levels of Source Code Control Enlightenment

Most developers start out writing code without any sort of source code control, except perhaps for making occasional backups of an entire directory of stuff. But gradually, most of us realize that having a tool help keep track of code changes and prevent code loss is a good idea. We tend to go through three levels of enlightenment in this process, starting as beginning users and gradually developing expertise. In this section, I'll review the three levels so that you can judge where you are in the process—and how much of the journey might remain.

TIP	I'll be describing general source code control concepts and commands in this section, without reference to actual products. Not every product will implement all of these commands, and the actual operations may differ. For example, Concurrent Versions System (CVS) has no concept of checking out a file, while Visual SourceSafe (VSS) insists on it.

Level 1: Opening Your Eyes

The first level of enlightenment is simple: You start using source code control. For developers who are familiar with Microsoft tools, this normally takes the form of installing VSS, setting up a server, and putting a project into the VSS database. From there, you can get by with only six commands: Create Project, Add, Get, Check Out, Undo Check Out, and Check In:

- The Create Project command creates a new area in the source code control database (sometimes called a repository) to hold files. Projects can generally be nested.

- The Add command adds a file to the source code control database. When you use the Add command, you're stating that it's important to keep track of this file.

- The Get command is the reverse of the Add command; it gets the current version of a file from the source code control database and places it on your hard drive. If you already have a copy of the file, Get checks to see if there are any changes in the database, and if so, overwrites your local copy.

- The Check Out command says that you're going to actively work on a particular file. Depending on your source code control system, this may prevent others from making changes to the file. Check Out normally performs an implicit Get to make sure you start with a current copy of the file.

- The Undo Check Out command says that you've decided you didn't want to make any changes after all. It throws away any changes you've made and unlocks the file. This is the easiest way to get rid of changes that didn't turn out to be a good idea after all.

- The Check In command says that you're done making changes, and puts your current version of the file back into the source code control database. It also unlocks the file so that others may make changes.

Going from no source code control at all to this first level has two main benefits: code protection and code history.

When you have only a single copy of your source code, you're risking everything to the vagaries of your hardware. What happens if your hard drive crashes and you haven't backed up the code? Using a source code control server can help protect against this sort of catastrophic failure. Ideally, the source code control server is a separate computer from the client machine where you're writing the code. But even if it's on the same machine, you can store the source code control database on a separate hard drive. Doing so gives you automatic protection against single hardware failures (though it still won't protect you against site-wide catastrophes like a fire; for important code, you should do periodic off-site backups as well).

Why is code history important? Imagine you've been working on an application for a while, and versions 1.0, 1.1, 1.2, 1.3, and 1.4 have all shipped to clients. Now a customer reports a bug in version 1.3. Is that same bug in earlier versions? Is it in later versions? If your computer only has the latest version of the source code for your application, you'll never know the answer to those questions. A good source code control system will let you look at your application's code as it existed at any point in time, so you can tell when a particular bug snuck into the code stream.

Source code control history can also help you keep track of the work that's been done on any particular file. Most source code control systems let you add a comment whenever you add or check in a file. The summary of these comments can provide a pretty good look at who did what and when they did it, as shown in Figure 3.1.

FIGURE 3.1
Viewing a file's history using SourceGear Vault

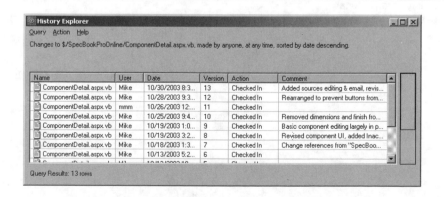

Level 2: The SCC Journeyman

The next step in your path to source code enlightenment is to be able to effectively manage your source code tree. Storing code in the source code control system is a good first step, but you'll need to learn a few more tricks if you want to be able to use it effectively. In particular, you should know about the Label, Share, Branch, and Merge commands:

- The Label command assigns a friendly name to a specific version of a file or set of files so that you can find them again by name in the future.

- The Share command allows a single file to appear in more than one project, while maintaining only one copy in the source code control database.

- The Branch command lets development diverge, making copies of a file in two separate branches and letting them change independently.

- The Merge command takes changes from one branch and applies them to another branch.

NOTE   One typical use for the Label command is to apply a new label to the build tree every night so that you can easily recover the state of the project on any specified day. For more information, see Chapter 13, "Mastering the Build Process."

When you master these commands, you'll be prepared to manage fairly complex release scenarios. Sharing and labeling are fairly obvious, but you might not immediately see a use for branching and merging. One typical situation where these commands are useful is in preparing to release a product while simultaneously working on the next version. You don't want bits of the version 2 feature set creeping into version 1, but you still need to fix bugs in version 1. In that case, you'd choose to create a Version1Release branch, as shown schematically in Figure 3.2. This lets one group of developers tidy up the last few bugs in version 1, while another group works on version 2 features.

FIGURE 3.2
Creating a branch for a release

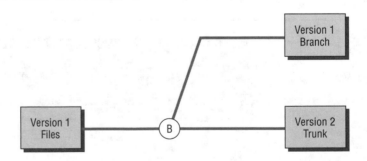

In this diagram, development proceeds in a single group of version 1 files until the branch, marked with a B. After that, there are two separate sets of the same files, with differing contents. Most source code control systems identify one branch as the trunk; here I've assigned that designation to the version 2 files.

But what happens after the version 1 release? It's quite possible that some of the bug fixes on the version 1 branch should also be made to the version 2 branch. Rather than retype those fixes yourself, you can use your source code control system's Merge command. Merge takes changes from one branch and applies them to another branch, as shown schematically in Figure 3.3.

FIGURE 3.3
Merging changes
from a branch back
to the trunk

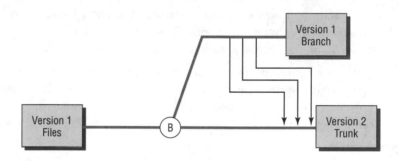

You might also find yourself creating a branch but never merging it back. For example, if you're unsure whether a major refactoring of your code will leave things in a better state, start a branch to test it out. If the refactoring works, you can merge the changes back into the main line of development. If not, simply abandon the branch.

Level 3: Experts Only

Many users will be able to do all of their source code control work with just the 10 commands that I've discussed so far. But depending on your source code control system, lots of other commands may be available. Some of these are useful in specialized situations; others sometimes appear to exist just so a package can boast of more choices than the competition. Table 3.1 lists some of the commands that you might find in a source code control system.

TABLE 3.1 Advanced Source Code Control Features

Command	Description
Cloak	Hides a project in the repository so that it doesn't appear when you're working with files. There's normally an Uncloak to reverse this.
Delete	Removes a file from the repository. Depending on the product, this may actually destroy all trace of the file, or simply hide it.

TABLE 3.1 CONTINUED Advanced Source Code Control Features

Command	Description
Move	Relocates a file or subproject to a new parent project.
Pin	Freezes a shared file at a particular version in a particular project. There's normally an Unpin to reverse this.
Rename	Renames a file or project.
Rollback	Reverts a file to an earlier version, destroying all changes made after that version.

In addition, most source code control systems have some way to manage security. This may take the form of integration with Windows security, or there may be an entirely separate list of users and passwords that someone has to manage.

Whatever product you're using, it's worth spending a few hours to read the manual, so you know what advanced capabilities it has. Don't try to use all of the commands immediately, however; start with the basic set. Then when you run into an unusual situation, you can consider whether there's some product-specific way to handle the problem.

NOTE   Whatever your level of source code control expertise, you should recognize that in some cases source code control is overkill. For example, small bits of code for articles or training, or utility code that you'll run only once and then throw away, probably don't need to be in your source code control system.

Source Code Control Alternatives

There are many choices in the source code control marketplace. I've listed a few in Table 3.2, but this is certainly not an exhaustive list. When you're ready to start shopping seriously, spend a few minutes with Google or talk to developers you know to get other recommendations.

TABLE 3.2 Some Representative Source Code Control Software

Package	URL
AccuRev	www.accurev.com/
BitKeeper	www.bitkeeper.com/
ClearCase	www.rational.com/products/clearcase/
CVS	www.cvshome.org/
Perforce	www.perforce.com/

TABLE 3.2 CONTINUED Some Representative Source Code Control Software

Package	URL
StarTeam	www.borland.com/starteam/
Subversion	http://subversion.tigris.org/
Vault	www.sourcegear.com/vault/index.asp
Visual SourceSafe	http://msdn.microsoft.com/ssafe/

The following list explains these in some detail:

AccuRev   AccuRev is a high-end source code control system that uses a client-server architecture. It uses a lightweight TCP/IP protocol, so it's well suited for distributed teams working over the Internet. It emphasizes atomicity of all operations and immutability of everything in the repository. It also features a set of graphical management tools that provide one of the easiest-to-use IDEs of any of the products I've looked at. It's very well suited for projects that have many versions or complex branching. AccuRev is available for both Windows and UNIX systems.

BitKeeper   BitKeeper is a cross-platform solution, supported on Windows, Linux, Unix, and MacOS/X. BitKeeper is free for open source projects, but commercial use requires purchasing or leasing a license for each developer. It uses a distributed repository design so that it is very scalable and easy to use for developers who are only occasionally connected to the main repository. BitKeeper is the source code control system that's currently used by the Linux kernel developers. This is an excellent indication of its ability to handle large projects involving many developers distributed around the globe.

ClearCase   IBM Rational ClearCase is one of several systems available for medium and large enterprises. IBM calls ClearCase a Software Asset Management system, indicating that it does more than just source code control. For example, ClearCase can handle build management for you, as well as disconnected and replicated work scenarios. There's also a built-in change management process to structure your team's activities. Cross-platform support includes Windows, Unix, Linux, and some mainframes. You're probably not going to use ClearCase or one of its direct competitors for a small team, but you might run into it if you're consulting for a large organization.

CVS   CVS is the most widespread open-source source code control system out there. It's used by thousands of projects, many of which are available over the Internet at sites like SourceForge (http://sourceforge.net/). It uses a client-server model, with files being stored in a central repository, and is specifically oriented toward the edit/merge/commit style of working. Although it lacks advanced features found in some other systems, it's a well-tested piece of software that will be all that many teams will ever need. There are CVS clients and add-ons for almost any purpose you can name. One intriguing add-on is TortoiseCVS (www.tortoisecvs.org/), which lets you work with CVS directly from Windows Explorer.

Perforce   Perforce is a client-server system that boasts of being optimized for speed, so that developers are never bogged down by their source code control. It offers strong support for complex branching, and emphasizes atomic change sets—checking in multiple files as a single unit of work. Perforce probably supports a wider variety of operating systems than any of its competitors, making it ideal for cross-platform development. Microsoft is rumored to be using a custom version of Perforce for at least some of its internal projects.

StarTeam   StarTeam is Borland's entry in the high end of this market, and may be overkill for the small development team. StarTeam offers extensive customization through Java, COM, and .NET APIs, so you can integrate it with just about any process you like. StarTeam includes serious security capabilities, as well as integration with requirements, change management, and workflow systems. Like ClearCase, StarTeam will show you some of the possibilities that exist if your projects ever outgrow simple source code control.

Subversion   Subversion is an open-source attempt to build a "better CVS." Among the differences between Subversion and CVS are support for arbitrary properties attached to files, the use of the Apache Web server as a network server, increased protocol efficiency, and efficient handling of binary files. The jury is still out on how well they've succeeded, but if you're cash-poor it's worth a look.

Vault   SourceGear got its start by providing a means for VSS users to work more efficiently over the Internet. Now SourceGear has launched its own source code control system using a modern architecture; Vault uses Microsoft SQL Server for its repository and web services for much of its communications. It supports both edit/merge/commit and check-out/edit/ check-in styles of working (I'll explain these two styles in detail later in this chapter), includes relatively fine-grained security features, and integrates well with Visual Studio .NET.

Visual SourceSafe   VSS, of course, is the source code control system that Microsoft ships to customers (though not the one that most Microsoft projects use internally). It supports only check-out/edit/check-in, and is horridly inefficient over the Internet. For relatively small projects, VSS may be adequate, but it's not state of the art.

Choosing Your Source Code Control System

Although most developers I know have started with VSS for source code control, by and large they don't remain with it. VSS may have been a state-of-the-art system a decade ago when it was first designed, but it hasn't been seriously revised in the intervening years. Some versions got a well-deserved reputation for corrupting files, which is simply a disaster in the application you're depending on to keep your code safe. Current versions seem to have fixed that problem, but they still depend on an obsolete file-locking scheme, lack the flexibility of some other products, and have an overall bad reputation.

The main advantage to VSS is that it's "free"—more precisely, if you own Visual Studio .NET or another Microsoft development tool, you probably own a bundled copy of VSS. If you're just getting started with source code control, particularly if you're on a limited budget, you might want to use that copy. But I recommend you look around at the source code control landscape to see what else is out there. In this section, I'll suggest some factors you can use to evaluate which product to use in your own development.

TECHNOLOGY TRAP

Penny-wise, Pound Foolish? Or, a Fool and His Money Are Soon Parted?

Deciding how much to spend on software tools is a tough question, especially if you're an independent developer or a small business. Good tools protect you from disasters or make it easy to write good code fast. However, they also come with a price tag, and that price tag can be significant.

For any given tool, the decision may be easy. That $500 expense for a source code control system seems like cheap insurance. The $100 add-in to handle unit testing will save you much more than that in time that would otherwise be spent fixing bugs. But add up enough of these easy decisions, and suddenly you've spent $10,000 on tools with no income to show for it.

The key, especially when you're starting out, is not to make these decisions on a tool-by-tool basis. Instead, come up with a tools budget and stick to it. After you figure out what you can spend, start making lists of all the tools that you want to buy. Go wild at this stage; put on everything that you'd like to have on your desk to help you write better code.

Now figure out what it will all cost. If it's more than your budget (and it will be, if you're even half trying), prioritize the list and start looking for alternatives. Do you need unit testing or automatic documentation more? Can you get by with fewer features in your performance-testing tools? Eventually, you'll either get the list down to something you can afford, or you'll have an ordered list of tools that you're not willing to compromise further.

Buy what you can from the top of the list and go to work. If you want more tools, keep the list handy to review after your next big sale. That's a good time to plow some money back into getting a solid toolset in place for future productivity. Repeat until you've bought everything you want.

Price

Prices for these products vary widely. At one end, you have the free open-source products (CVS is the best-known of these). At the other, some of the commercial applications will cost you hundreds of dollars per user, and may have a minimum number of users that you can buy licenses for at one time.

Although cost is certainly a factor, especially for a small shop, I urge you not to let it be the only factor. Source code control is something like insurance in this regard—not buying it will save you money, but in the long run you're risking much larger costs. Think about what it would cost you to re-create your entire code base if there were a hard drive crash and you didn't have the code saved safely elsewhere.

Concurrent Development Style

I cheated a bit when I described the basic source code control commands. There are actually two distinct ways to handle concurrent development, and I described only one of them. So here's the bigger picture.

VSS uses the check-out/edit/check-in style. In this style, a typical editing session works like this:

1. Developer A decides to work on Module 1, so he checks it out of the repository.

2. While he's editing the module, no one else can check it out.

3. When he's done with changes, Developer A checks in the module. At this point, Developer B can check it out and repeat the cycle.

By contrast, CVS and some other systems implement the edit/merge/commit style. Here's how a session might go under this style:

1. Developer A decides to work on Module 1, so he just starts editing it.

2. Meanwhile, Developer B also decides to work on Module 1. CVS doesn't lock anything, so she just starts editing.

3. Developer A finishes his changes, so he commits them to the repository and goes on to something else.

4. Developer B finishes her changes and attempts to commit them. But the system notices that someone else changed the module in the repository after the last time that Developer B got a copy.

5. Rather than throw away her work, Developer B merges her changes into the copy in the repository. Now she can commit the merged copy, and everyone is happy.

Whether one style or the other of handling concurrent development is superior is one of those hotly fought battles in software development that never seems to come to a resolution. Proponents of check-out/edit/check-in worry about the chaos of having two developers make conflicting changes in the same source code file. Proponents of edit/merge/commit complain about the inefficiency of waiting for files to be checked in so that they can make unrelated changes.

In practice, I haven't found either one of these issues to be a real problem, at least on small teams. It's rare to have two developers decide to work on the same part of the same file at the same time. But it's also rare to have a developer who has absolutely nothing to do but wait for someone else to unlock a file.

If you (or your team) are used to one style or the other, make sure that your product of choice supports that style. Otherwise, you might like to experiment a bit to see which style makes more sense to you.

The Repository

Every source code control system stores the code somewhere. Repository-related issues that you should consider when choosing a system include the following:

- How open is the repository? Can you get the data out easily if you ever switch systems?
- How stable is the repository? Does it use disk files, database records, or some other means to store the code you place in it?
- How secure is the repository? Does it protect source code from people who should not have access?
- How easy to manage is the repository? Does the source code control system offer good administrative tools?

You should also consider the network overhead that the repository adds. Does it require you to set up a separate server? Do you need to buy separate database-client licenses? Choosing the wrong product might involve substantial hidden costs.

Internet Friendliness

If your development team is distributed, you also need to find out how well your source code control system will work over the Internet. Some products, such as VSS, have network performance that is frankly unacceptable. If it takes 5 minutes to check out a file, developers simply won't bother, and your source code control system will fail at its tasks of tracking and protecting code.

Other products were designed for the Internet from the start, using Transmission Control Protocol/Internet Protocol (TCP/IP) as their communications protocol and passing information in small chunks. Even if you're not using the Internet to distribute work now, you might want this flexibility in the future.

IDE Integration

Modern integrated development environments (IDEs), such as Visual Studio .NET, support source code control operations directly from within the IDE. Figure 3.4 shows the Solution Explorer window in Visual Studio .NET 2003.

As you can see, Visual Studio .NET lets you get the latest version of a file, check out a file (and later check it in), or compare two versions of a file without leaving the IDE. In this case, I'm using VSS as a source code control system, but the same capabilities are available with many other products. That's because Microsoft has published the API that it uses for source code control, and this has become a de facto standard across many products and IDEs.

> **TIP**   If you have multiple source code control clients installed on your computer, you can use only the default client from within Visual Studio .NET. If you're in this situation, grab a copy of Source Control Provider Selector from `www.kilic.net/weblog/archives/000183.html`. This free utility gives you a taskbar icon that lets you switch quickly between providers.

Although IDE integration can be convenient, I've stopped using it in my own projects. Only a small subset of source code control commands are available in the IDE, so you need to switch to a dedicated source code control client application from time to time anyhow. Given this requirement, I find it more convenient to do all of my source code control work in one place. You might feel otherwise, of course.

FIGURE 3.4
Source code control in the Visual Studio .NET IDE

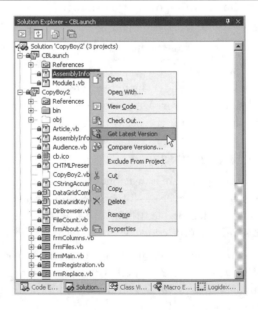

If you do decide to work within the Visual Studio .NET IDE, Microsoft has issued guidelines on how to most effectively use source code control in this environment. You can download a copy of "Structuring Solutions and Projects" from `http://msdn.microsoft.com/library/default.asp?url=/library/en-us/dnbda/html/tdlg_ch3.asp`.

Advanced Commands

As I mentioned earlier, different systems support different advanced commands. If you absolutely must have Cloak, or Pin, or Move, this will narrow down the list of products that you'll find acceptable.

Cross-Platform Support

A final consideration is whether your development is completely tied to Windows, or whether you might need to do cross-platform development at some time in the future. Some source code control systems, such as VSS, are tightly tied to Windows. Others, like CVS, are available for a wide variety of operating systems. If you need to share files across operating systems, life will be easier if you settle on a cross-platform-capable system in the first place.

Best Practices in Source Code Control

Deciding on and installing a source code control system is only half the battle. You also need to learn how to use it effectively. While I can't offer detailed instructions on every product out there, I can pass on quite a few tips about using source code control effectively. Some of these might not be applicable to your particular project or platform, but in general, I think you'll find this a useful list of best practices.

What Belongs in the System?

What belongs in your source code control system? Not just source code! You should use the repository as a central place to store and manage any artifact that is not built from other artifacts.

"Artifact" is used here as a general term for anything having to do with your software product. Here are a few things you might consider storing in your source code control system:

- Source code
- Windows Installer databases
- Database build scripts
- Icons, bitmaps, and other graphics
- License files

- Readme files
- Informal development notes
- Documentation
- Help files
- Build scripts
- Test scripts

The goal is simple: if someone comes to you a year from now and wants you to rebuild version 1.0.5 of your product, you should be able to pull everything that you need out of the source code control system.

Note that this doesn't mean that you need to store everything in the system. Consider documentation, for example. If you're using a product such as RoboHelp to build help files and other documentation, there's no need to store the final help files and documentation in the source code control system. Instead, store the RoboHelp files, and you can always re-create the documentation if you need to by running the source files through RoboHelp again.

NOTE	I make one exception to the rule of not storing generated artifacts: I store log files from my build and test tools. It's useful to be able to look back and see whether a particular build was successful, and if not, what went wrong, without getting all of the source files and running the entire build again.

The goal is simple: If you pull the files for a particular release out of your source code control system, you should have everything you need to re-create the build exactly as it was that day. If your build process includes manual steps, your source code control system should contain documentation on those steps, and you need to keep that documentation up-to-date as things change.

As a corollary, once you store something in the system, you *must* manage it through the system—and this rule needs to be enforced across your entire organization. Don't let developers (or anyone else) copy things off to a private sandbox with the intent of checking them in later. Once a file escapes from source code control, you lose the ability to easily re-create the state of your project at a point in time.

Source Code Control Etiquette

The cardinal rule of effective use of source code control is to work with as few files as possible at one time. If you're working in a check-in/edit/check-out system, this means checking out only enough files to complete one task, and then checking them back in. If you're working in an edit/merge/commit system, this means remembering to commit your changes at the end of each task.

This is important for several reasons. First, if you are working with a system that locks files, you can avoid locking other people out for longer than necessary. Second, by keeping your commits small, you vastly lower the chance of needing to merge two incompatible versions of code. Finally, by working in small chunks, you can keep the comments in the source code control system targeted and informative.

Whenever you check in a new file or make a change, be sure to put a comment into the system along with the code. Occasionally, developers think that the comments in the code should be sufficient; if anyone wants to know what happened, they can compare two versions and see what's changed. This turns out to be a very inconvenient attitude when you want to view the entire history of a file and see how it evolved. (Developers with this attitude often don't want to write comments at all; I'll talk about that in Chapter 4, "Coding Defensively.")

The Proper Use of Labels

Labels (called tags in some systems) offer a way to mark a file version or, more usefully, a versioned set of files with some friendly name. This is useful because human beings are much better at remembering "Beta 1" than "Version 254" or "3 April 2004 10:12 AM" when they're trying to find a set of files. But when should you apply a label to your files?

The answer is that you should label significant points in time. Certainly a public release counts as such a point in time, but there may be other events worthy of a label as well. Consider again the task of making a major change to your code. You might want to label the start of this change (assuming that you don't do it in a branch) to make it easy to back up to before the change if you need to do so.

Depending on your system, you may find that it's easier to retrieve files by label than by date. If that's the case with your system, you might find it worthwhile to label every daily build.

Branching Discipline

When should you create a branch in a project under source code control? The answer is simple: You should create a branch whenever different developers in the same project are following different rules. In the example I used earlier (starting work on version 2.0 while finishing up version 1.0), one group of developers is checking in small, careful changes, while the other is roughing out the broad outlines of new features. That's a good example of the need for a branch.

Branching is useful for exploration as well. If your main line of code is using a known, stable technique but you want to explore a faster and potentially unstable way of accomplishing the same objectives, you should create a branch to explore the consequences. If the branch works out well, merge its changes back to the main line. If not, just stop working in the branch.

Don't create a branch just because you know you're going to need it at some point in the future. If nobody is working on version 2.0 yet, then it's too soon to create separate 1.0 and 2.0 branches. To do so only results in extra merging work as you try to keep the two branches in sync before they're really needed.

Make sure that you handle branching by actually creating branches. Sometimes a developer will copy a project and check the copy into the source code control system as the basis for a new version. Don't let this happen. If you do, then the files in the new version will not have any connection to the files in the original, making it impossible to trace their history back to their starting points.

If you know you're going to merge code from a branch back to the main line of development, do the merge sooner rather than later. The longer you wait to perform a merge, the more likely you are to have to resolve incompatible changes in the other line of code. And the longer you wait, the more likely you are to forget exactly which changes you wanted to merge, and why.

Miscellaneous Rules

Some bug-tracking systems offer an interface to some source code control systems. If your two products of choice work together this way, use the integration! When you check in a file in response to a bug report, be sure to note the bug number that it fixes. This will allow you to view the applicable changes directly from the bug-tracking system. For more on bug tracking, see Chapter 9, "Tracking and Squashing Bugs."

If you're working in an organization with several developers, you'll likely end up creating your own "best practices" document, describing how your team handles builds and source code control. Consider checking that document into the source code control system too. In fact, you might create a special project in your system to hold nothing but documentation of company standards. That way, developers can always refer to the most recent version of the standards documentation, no matter where they're working (at least, as long as they can connect to the source code control system).

Source Code Control for Download Tracker

At last, we're ready to create some code! Figure 3.5 shows the source code control repository for the Download Tracker project. I'm using SourceGear Vault as my source code control system.

FIGURE 3.5
Source code control tree for Download Tracker

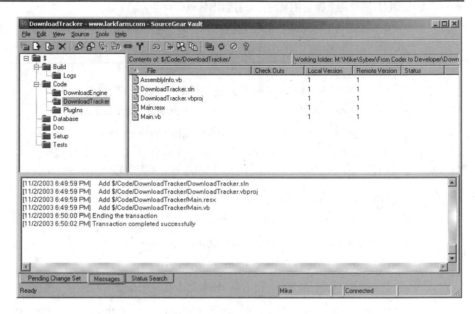

I've set up a number of folders in the repository to hold the artifacts that I anticipate this project will generate:

- /Build will hold the build scripts, as well as any documentation of the build process.

- /Build/Logs will hold the results of each build that I do.

- /Code is the overall starting point in the tree for source code.

- /Code/DownloadEngine will hold the code for the download engine project.

- /Code/DownloadTracker will hold the main Download Tracker code.

- /Code/Plugins will hold the code for publishing plug-ins.

- /Database will hold the SQL statements to rebuild the database.

- /Doc will hold source files for end-user documentation.

- /Setup will hold a Windows Installer project to set up Download Tracker on an end user's computer.

- /Tests will hold code and instructions for automated testing.

As you can see, I've checked the first project into the /Code/DownloadTracker folder. There's a lot left to do on this project, but at least it's started now.

Source Code Control Checklist

After you've been working with it for a while, source code control should be as natural as breathing. Review these basic points to check the effectiveness of your own source code control process:

- Use a source code control system to protect your code and keep track of its history.
- Learn how to effectively use commands such as Label, Share, Branch, and Merge.
- Evaluate several source code control alternatives and choose the one that fits best with your budget and style of work.
- Place all development artifacts under source code control.
- Check out files only when you need them.
- Comment changes at check-in time.
- Label your code at significant points in time.
- Create a branch whenever the rules change.
- Use source code control together with bug tracking.

Although this isn't a book primarily about coding style, some coding topics are too important to overlook. In the next chapter you'll learn about assertions and comments, and what they can do to improve the quality of your code.

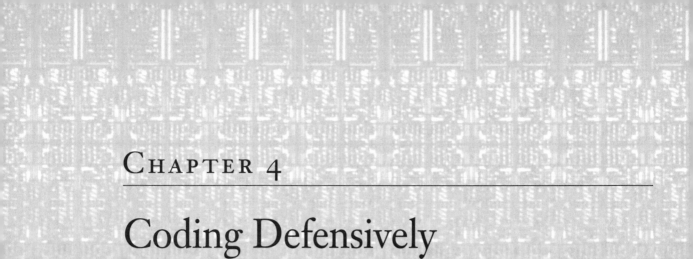

CHAPTER 4

Coding Defensively

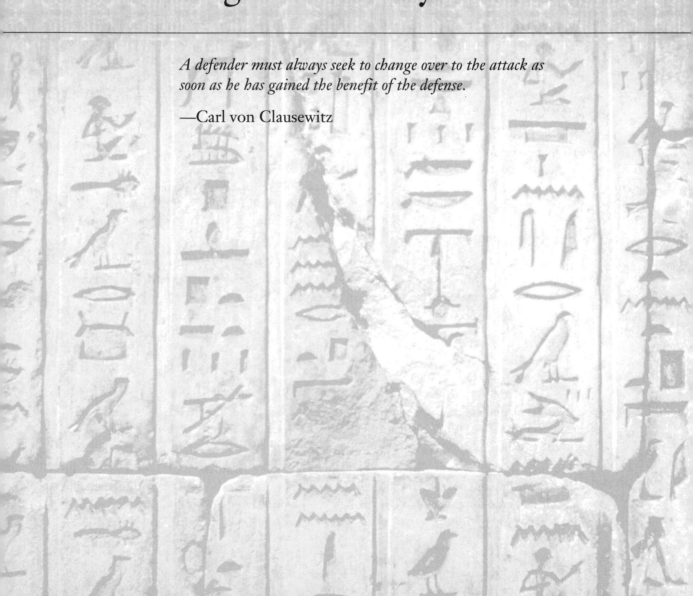

A defender must always seek to change over to the attack as soon as he has gained the benefit of the defense.

—Carl von Clausewitz

This is a book about going beyond coding, but there are still parts of coding that I want to talk about. In particular, when you start writing code that you intend to develop and maintain for the long run, you need to pay attention to defensive coding. When you get into a defensive coding mindset, you recognize that despite your best efforts, your code is going to have some problems and will need to be modified. The goal of defensive coding is to write code that makes it easy to find problems and make any necessary modifications.

Assertions and Exceptions

Assertions and exceptions have similar purposes; they both notify you that something is not right in your application. In general, you'll want to reserve assertions for design-time debugging issues and use exceptions for runtime issues that might have an impact on users. Nevertheless, you should know how to use both tools to catch problems early.

Assertions

When you use an assertion, you *assert* that a particular Boolean condition is true in your code and that you want the Microsoft .NET runtime to tell you if you're wrong about that. For example, in the DownloadEngine component of Download Tracker, it doesn't make sense to try to download a file from an empty URL. Ideally, I'll never write code that attempts this; there should be validation of user input to prevent this situation. But if it does happen, through some mistake on my own part (or as a result of some undue sneakiness on the part of the user), I'd rather know immediately.

To use assertions in .NET, you need to set a reference to the System.Diagnostics namespace. Then you can use the Debug.Assert or the Trace.Assert method. For example, here's a snippet of code to verify the presence of some data in the SourceUrl property:

```
// This method should never be called without
// a Source URL
Debug.Assert((((d.SourceUrl != string.Empty) &&
    (d.SourceUrl != null)),
    "Empty SourceUrl",
    "Can't download a file unless a Source URL is supplied");
```

The first argument to the Assert method is a Boolean expression that the Common Language Runtime (CLR) will evaluate at runtime. If it evaluates to true, then nothing happens, and the code keeps running with the next line in the application.

However, if the Boolean expression evaluates to false, the CLR halts execution and uses the other two arguments to construct a message to the developer. I can test this with the aid of a quick little harness application. Figure 4.1 shows the result of calling into this method with an empty SourceUrl property.

FIGURE 4.1
Assertion at runtime

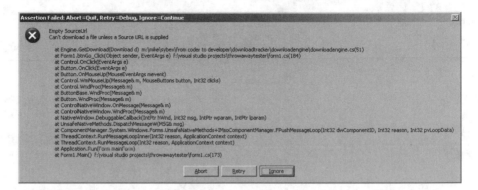

Notice the truly horrid caption of the message box that displays the assertion, which tells you that the buttons do something other than what their captions might lead you to believe. Apparently Microsoft decided to overload the existing system message box API rather than design some custom user interface for assertions. Don't do this in your own code!

> **NOTE**   In Chapter 5, "Preventing Bugs with Unit Testing," you'll learn about a superior alternative to quick and dirty testing applications.

Mechanics of .NET Assertions

As I mentioned earlier, you can use either the `Trace.Assert` or the `Debug.Assert` method in your code. These classes are identical, except that the `Debug` class is active only if you define the DEBUG symbol in your project, and the `Trace` class is active only if you define the TRACE symbol in your project. These constants are commonly defined in the Build section of the project properties (available by right-clicking on the project node in Solution Explorer and selecting Properties), as shown in Figure 4.2.

By default, the Debug configuration defines both the TRACE and DEBUG constants, and the Release configuration defines the TRACE constant. Thus, `Trace.Assert` is active in both default configurations, whereas `Debug.Assert` is active only in the Debug configuration. I tend to use `Debug.Assert` because I usually reserve assertions for design-time debugging rather than end-user error logging. Because assertions are an aid for the developer rather than the end user, I don't believe they have a place in release code. Instead, code you release to other users should implement an error-handling and logging strategy that precludes the necessity for any assertions.

> **NOTE**   I'll talk more about error-logging strategies in Chapter 10, "Logging Application Activity."

FIGURE 4.2
Defining build
constants

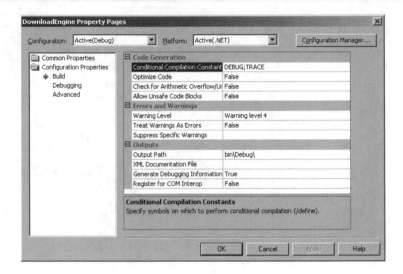

The Trace and Debug classes can send their output to more than one place. There are special classes within the System.Diagnostics namespace called Listener classes. These classes are responsible for forwarding, recording, or displaying the messages generated by the Trace and Debug classes. The Trace and Debug classes have a Listeners property, which is a collection capable of holding objects of any type derived from the TraceListener class. The TraceListener class is an abstract class that belongs to the System.Diagnostics namespace, and it has three implementations:

DefaultTraceListener   An object of this class is automatically added to the Listeners collection of the Trace and Debug classes. Its behavior is to write messages to the Output window or to message boxes, as you saw in Figure 4.1.

TextWriterTraceListener   An object of this class writes messages to any class that derives from the Stream class. You can use a TextWriterTraceListener object to write messages to the console or to a file.

EventLogTraceListener   An object of this class writes messages to the Windows event log.

You can also create your own class that inherits from the TraceListener class if you want custom behavior. You could, for example, export all assertion results to an XML file. When doing so, you must at least implement the Write and WriteLine methods.

Assertions in Other Languages

Most modern computer languages have some built-in assertion facility similar to the Trace and Debug support in .NET. Even if your language of choice doesn't support assertions, it's easy enough to add them by writing a small bit of code. In general, you'd use a structure something like this:

```
Public Sub Assert (Assertion As Boolean, Message As String)
    If Not Assertion Then
        MsgBox Message, "Assertion Failed"
        Stop
    End If
End Sub
```

That is, if the asserted condition is false, you want to display the message and halt the program. Otherwise, the procedure will return to the calling code.

Guidelines for Good Assertions

Generally, you don't want end users to see the results of assertions. Ideally, you'll fix any problems that lead to assertions firing before you ship the code, but even if you don't manage to do that, you should develop a friendlier strategy for end users than just dumping stack traces on their screen. That's why I suggest using Debug.Assert rather than Trace.Assert in most cases. Assuming that you're shipping the release configuration to your users (and you should), debug assertions will simply vanish when you compile the code.

That leads to another guideline for the good use of assertions: Make sure assertions don't have side effects. Assertions should check that something is true, not execute any other code. For example, here's a bad use of an assertion:

```
// Make sure path is OK
Debug.Assert(
    (newPath = Path.Combine(foldername, filename)) != string.Empty,
    "Bad path to download");
```

See the problem? If you take out the assertion, then newPath will never get initialized. Putting executable statements into assertions is a good way to introduce such mysterious errors when you switch from debug to release builds.

Another mistake is to use assertions to verify that your compiler and language are working properly:

```
int[] intSizes = new int[3];
Debug.Assert(intSizes.GetUpperBound(0) == 2,
    "Failed to initialize array");
```

If you can't trust your compiler to allocate three array members when you tell it to declare an array with three members, you might as well just give up now. No amount of assertions will make your applications any more reliable.

So what *should* you use assertions for? One excellent use for assertions is to verify that input data is reasonable. If you refer back to the first code snippet in this chapter, you'll see that is what I'm doing with the SourceUrl argument. Note that I'm checking in the method that uses the value, not in the method that sets the value. By placing the assertion here, I can make sure that any code that calls this method is using reasonable values.

Another good use for assertions is to check your assumptions after a particularly involved or tricky piece of code executes. For example, you might make some calculations that are designed to yield a percentage based on a complex set of inputs. When the calculations have finished, you could use an assertion to verify that the final result is between zero and one.

RULE   Avoid writing involved or tricky code. There are no points for being exceptionally clever in the real world—only for writing code that works the way it should.

Exceptions

Exceptions represent another way to handle problems with your code. As the name implies, exceptions are for exceptional situations—primarily errors that cannot be avoided at runtime.

For example, consider the DownloadEngine component within Download Tracker. I'm developing this as a general-purpose library that any application can use. In particular, the application can pass in a URL to be downloaded. But there's no way for the DownloadEngine component to prevent the calling application from passing in "Mary had a little lamb" instead of a valid URL. So what should the component do when that happens? That's where exceptions come into play. An exception signals an exceptional problem in your code that will be handled in another part of your code. As an example, the DownloadEngine component uses this code structure to handle problems with the actual downloading process:

```
public void GetDownload(Download d)
{
    string filename = string.Empty;
    string foldername = string.Empty;
    WebClient wc = new WebClient();

    try
    {
        // Code to perform the actual download goes here
    }
    catch (Exception e)
    {
```

```
            // Bubble any exception up to caller, with custom info
            throw new DownloadException("Unable to download" ,d, e);
    }
    finally
    {
        wc.Dispose();
    }

}
```

In the case of Download Tracker, of course, I'm in control of the input layer as well as the
library. That means that I can prevent this exception from happening in many cases by
checking the input. For example, I can use a .NET regular expression to make sure that the
URL typed by the user is actually a URL. Generally, it's good programming practice to catch
errors as soon as possible. But it doesn't hurt to have a backup plan, as in this case.

Exception Mechanics

You should already be familiar with the coding mechanics of exceptions in C#, but here's a
quick review just in case. The following four statements together make up the exception-handling mechanism:

- The try statement indicates the start of an exception-handling block. If any code within the
  block raises an exception, that exception is handled by the associated catch statement.

- The catch statement indicates the start of the actual exception handling. The CLR trans-
  fers execution here if an exception is raised in the associated exception-handling block.

- The finally statement indicates the start of code that will always run, whether or not an
  exception occurs. Typically, the finally block is used for cleanup.

- The throw statement is used to generate an exception. If you throw an exception in a catch
  block, it will be handled by the parent routine's exception-handling block (if any).

So, the DownloadEngine component takes a relatively straightforward approach to exception handling. It catches any exception in its own operations, wraps this exception in a new custom exception (more on that in a moment), and throws it to the parent code. This is a typical
pattern for library code, which doesn't have a user interface to present errors directly to the end
user. Ideally, every user interface component will validate the input so that such errors never
happen. But as a library writer, you can never be quite sure that's going to happen (unless the
library is purely for internal use, and you have control over every single application that calls
the library).

Custom Exceptions

You'll want to create custom exception classes in two situations:

1. There is no existing exception class that correctly represents the exceptional condition.

2. You want to pass additional information to the parent code with the exception.

In the case of the DownloadEngine component, I want to pass the actual failing Download object back to the caller so that it can determine which download failed. Thus, I've created a custom DownloadException class in my code.

TIP   To quickly review the built-in exception classes in the .NET Framework, use the Object Browser or a tool such as Lutz Roeder's Reflector (www.aisto.com/roeder/dotnet/) to search for classes containing the word "Exception" in their names.

Here are some guidelines that you should follow when creating a custom exception class:

- Derive your exception classes from the System.ApplicationException class.

- End the name of custom exception class with the word *Exception*.

- Implement three constructors with the signatures shown in the following code:

```
public class MyOwnException : System.Exception
{
    public MyOwnException() : base()
    {
    }

    public MyOwnException(string message) : base(message)
    {
    }

    public MyOwnException(string message, System.Exception e) :
    base(message, e)
    {
    }
}
```

Here's the code for the DownloadException class. In addition to implementing the required constructors, it supplies two other constructors that accept a Download object.

```
/// <summary>
///      Custom exception class to handle download errors
/// </summary>
/// <remarks>
///      Additional fields:
///          d: The failing download to pass with the exception
/// </remarks>
```

```csharp
public class DownloadException : System.Exception
{

    // Define the additional fields
    private Download _d;

    // Define read-only properties for the additional fields

    /// <summary>
    ///      The associated Download object
    /// </summary>
    public Download d
    {
        get
        {
            return _d;
        }
    }

    /// <summary>
    ///      Parameterless (default) constructor
    /// </summary>
    public DownloadException() : base()
    {
    }

    /// <summary>
    ///      Constructor for an exception with text message
    /// </summary>
    public DownloadException(string message) : base(message)
    {
    }

    /// <summary>
    ///      Constructor for an exception with text
    ///      message and inner exception
    /// </summary>
    public DownloadException(string message,
        System.Exception e) : base(message, e)
    {
    }

    /// <summary>
    ///      Constructor for an exception with text
    ///      message and Download object
    /// </summary>
    public DownloadException (
```

```
        string message, Download d) : this(message)
{
    _d = d;
}

/// <summary>
///     Constructor for an exception with text
///     message, inner exception and Download object
/// </summary>
public DownloadException(
    string message, Download d, System.Exception e) :
    this(message, e)
{
    _d = d;
}

}
```

NOTE   The comment lines starting with /// are C# XML comments for the benefit of documentation generators. Other languages might offer their own syntax for such comments. I'll discuss this further in Chapter 12, "Creating Documentation."

Guidelines for Good Exceptions

In addition to the rules for creating exception classes, other guidelines you should keep in mind
when using exceptions in your code include the following:

Exceptions are for exceptional situations.   Don't use exceptions as an alternative to
other control-of-flow statements. As with other software tools, many developers have a tendency to overuse exceptions when they're first exposed to the concept. Don't, for example,
use an exception to signal to the calling code that a download was completed successfully.
That's what the return value from your method is for. Alternatively, your method could raise
an event for the calling code to handle.

**In general, you should use the exception constructors that include a string value for
additional information.**   This approach lets the calling application display the string to the
end user if it can't figure out what else to do with the exception.

**If you're throwing an exception to pass error information from lower-level code to
higher-level code, use one of the constructors that accepts an** Exception **object.**   This
lets you wrap the exception that you received. The calling code can drill into that exception, if
necessary, by using the InnerException property of your exception class.

Don't create custom exceptions when the built-in ones will do.   For example, you should use the build-in `InvalidOperationException` if calling code attempts to set a property before your class is completely initialized, or `ArgumentException` if inputs are out of the allowed range.

Comments or Self-Documenting Code?

The issue of whether to write comments in your code, and what kind of comments to write, has a tendency to make developers argue with one another. On the one side, you have people who feel that the code should be its own documentation and that comments are superfluous. On the other side are people who think that well-written comments make code easier to read. I personally tend to side with the latter group, with one caveat: Writing good comments is not an excuse to write bad code.

Noise Comments

There are a couple of commenting styles that I don't care for in source code. I tend to think of these as "noise comments"—comments that make the code longer without really bringing any value to it. The first type of noise comment is the comment that simply repeats the code:

```
// DefaultDownloadFolder property
public string DefaultDownloadFolder
{
    // Public getter
    get
    {
        // Return the internal variable's value
        return _DefaultDownloadFolder;
    }
    // Public setter
    set
    {
        // Store the supplied value
        // in the internal variable
        _DefaultDownloadFolder = value;
    }
}
```

The comments in this code block don't add anything to the code. Indeed, they're just a restatement of the code into some sort of stilted English. If someone was absolutely unfamiliar with C#, such comments might help that person to understand what the code is doing. However, it's safe to assume that most people who will read your source code have a pretty good grasp of the language already and are trying to figure out what your program is doing, not what individual statements are saying.

The other form of noise comment is the formal procedure header:

```
// Procedure: GetDownload
// Module: DownloadEngine.cs
// Author: Mike Gunderloy
// Creation Date: 5 November 2003
//
// Inputs:
//    d: A Download variable with information
//       on the file to be downloaded
//
// Outputs:
//    NONE
//
// Revision History:
//    5 Nov 2003: Initial creation
//    8 Nov 2003: Downloading code implemented
//    9 Nov 2003: Added custom exception
//
public void GetDownload(Download d)
{
    // Method body goes here
}
```

I admit it—I've written plenty of formal procedure headers in the past, particularly when I was working as a contract programmer. They're a great way to make yourself look busy under the guise of adding value to the source code when you can't figure out how to solve the actual problem. But everything in this comment is purely redundant information:

- The module name is on the tab at the top of the IDE or in the title bar of your text editor.

- The procedure name, inputs, and outputs are right there in the source code for anyone to read.

- The author, creation date, and revision history are all in your source code control system, where they can be easily retrieved when you need them, and where they won't get in the way when you don't need them.

If you're getting paid by the hour and no one is checking your work carefully, write all the noise comments that you want. Of course, such behavior is not the hallmark of a real professional! If the goal is to get your own product to market without wasting time, and to do so with maintainable code, don't bother.

RULE   Use comments to convey information, not just to repeat information that is stored elsewhere.

Placeholder Comments

Some comments are merely placeholders or notes to your future self:

```
// HACK: Brute-force search, can replace if this becomes a perf issue
// TODO: Add code to make sure user has access to folder
// POSTPONE: This is where we'll want to create custom properties
```

Visual Studio .NET offers good support for placeholder comments by letting you tie them to the Task List. Select Options from the Tools menu, and then navigate to the Task List section of the Environment options, as shown in Figure 4.3. You can use this section of the Options dialog box to define comment tokens that indicate a task.

The Task List window, shown in Figure 4.4, will automatically keep itself up-to-date as you add and remove the indicated comments. You can double-click on any task comment to go directly to that comment in your code. This is a handy way to remind yourself to fix things. As a general rule, you shouldn't be shipping code that still contains UNDONE or TODO tasks.

FIGURE 4.3
Defining comment tokens

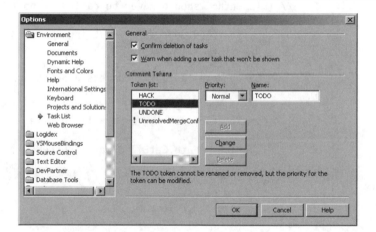

FIGURE 4.4
The Visual Studio .NET
Task List

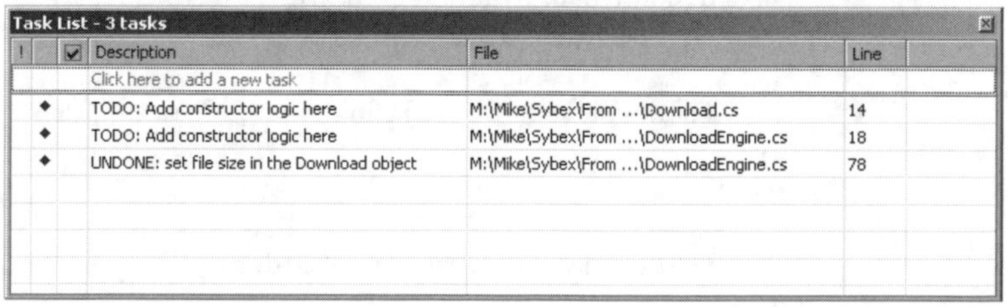

Summary and Intent Comments

Like assertions and exceptions, comments should have a reason to exist. The noise comments I mentioned earlier fail this simple test, while placeholder comments pass it. Two other types of comments are also useful.

Summary comments are superficially similar to comments that just repeat the code in that they tell you things you could learn by reading the code carefully. For example, here's a block of the DownloadEngine component with summary comments inserted:

```
public void GetDownload(Download d)
{
    string filename = string.Empty;
    string foldername = string.Empty;
    WebClient wc = new WebClient();

    try
    {
        // This method should never be called without
        // a Source URL
        Debug.Assert(((d.SourceUrl != string.Empty) &&
            (d.SourceUrl != null)),
            "Empty SourceUrl",
            "Can't download a file unless a Source URL is supplied");

        // If no filename specified, derive from SourceUrl
        if((d.FileName == string.Empty) || (d.FileName == null))
        {
            filename = Path.GetFileName(d.SourceUrl);
        }
        else
        {
            filename = d.FileName;
        }

        // If no download folder specified, use default
        if((d.DownloadFolder == string.Empty) ||
            (d.DownloadFolder == null))
        {
            foldername = DefaultDownloadFolder;
        }
        else
        {
            foldername = d.DownloadFolder;
        }
        // Ensure that we got a folder name somehow
        Debug.Assert(foldername != string.Empty,
```

```
            "Empty foldername",
            "Download folder not set and no default supplied");

        // Use WebClient to do the download
        wc.DownloadFile(d.SourceUrl, Path.Combine(foldername, filename));

        // UNDONE: set file size in the Download object

    }
    catch (Exception e)
    {
        // Bubble any exception up to caller, with custom info
        throw new DownloadException("Unable to download" ,d, e);
    }
    finally
    {
        wc.Dispose();
    }
}
```

In this case, the comments don't add anything that a good programmer couldn't figure out by reading the code. But they're still useful, simply because the comments are shorter than the code. With the default color-coding in Visual Studio .NET, you can skim for green text to easily read just the comments. Such summary comments give you a faster way to grasp what a procedure is doing without having to read every single line of code.

Some programmer's editors offer a "collapse to comments" feature that can hide all of the source code in a procedure and show you just the comments. Alas, Visual Studio .NET doesn't have this capability.

Even better than summary comments are intent comments. *Intent* comments are the hardest type to write, but they're often the most useful. With intent comments, instead of explaining how the code works, you explain why it's there in the first place. An intent comment for the GetDownload method might look like this:

```
// GetDownload uses the information in a Download object
// to get the specified file from the Internet to a local
// hard drive. Any download errors are wrapped in a
// custom exception and returned to the caller, along with
// the failing Download object.
```

Intent comments are great when you need to maintain code, especially code that you've been away from for a long time (defined as any more than a few days). By skimming the intent comments, you can quickly locate the section of the code that you need to work on.

TECHNOLOGY TRAP

When Good Comments Go Bad

There's one major problem with writing good comments: They're not tightly coupled to the code that you're commenting on. What this means is that comments and code can (and do) drift out of synchronization. If you dive into the code for a quick fix to respond to a problem that just turned up in the debugger, you may forget to review the comments and fix them as well.

People who focus on this problem tend to be in the "self-documenting code" category. If the comments are going to drift away from the code, and the code itself is definitive, why bother with comments in the first place? Just write understandable code and be done with it.

I'm sympathetic to this point of view, but I don't agree with it. The basic mistake here, I think, is to view comments as just a restatement of the code. For noise comments, that's true. But if you're writing good summary or intent comments, there's more to the comments than just restating the code in English. Comments offer a more efficient way to get to the part of the code you want, just as an index helps you find the page in a book that you want to read. A "self-documenting book" wouldn't need an index; you just read the book to find the page you want. But most of us would agree that the index adds efficiency in some situations.

The real cure for the comment synchronization problem is to exercise some discipline. When you change code, make sure the comments are still sensible, and change the comments if they need to be resynchronized with the code. You'll also find that this is less of a problem if you concentrate on writing a few good intent comments. Most bug fixes change the implementation of code, but not its intent.

Another approach to keeping code and comments synchronized is to use literate programming, in which special tools let you write documentation and code together, separating them out for printing and compiling. In this approach, a program is considered a work of literature rather than source code to be commented on separately. You can find more information at the Literate Programming website (`www.literateprogramming.com/`). I'm not aware of any literate programming tools specifically targeted at C#, but the LEO text editor (`http://personalpages.tds.net/~edream/front.html`) lets you experiment with literate approaches in any source code language.

Defensive Coding Checklist

Defensive coding can be the difference between an application that never quite works and one that you can easily maintain and improve. When you're writing code, you should try to adhere to good defensive coding habits:

- Use assertions to catch design-time errors.
- Use exceptions to handle runtime errors.
- Use exceptions only for exceptional situations.
- Avoid peppering your code with noise comments.
- Use comments as placeholders for future work.
- Use comments to summarize and document the intent of your code.
- When you change code, make sure you keep the comments up-to-date.

Of course, you need to perform other activities at the same time you're writing code. One of the most important of these is testing your code. In the next chapter, I'll introduce unit testing and test-driven development, and show how you can use these tools to help you write better code.

CHAPTER 5

Preventing Bugs with Unit Testing

Never stop testing, and your advertising will never stop improving.

—David Ogilvy, *Confessions of an Advertising Man*

Ogilvy made quite an impact on the advertising world (if you're old enough, you may remember the Maxwell House percolator in time with the music, or the guy with the eye patch wearing Hathaway shirts), but if you change "advertising" to "software" his dictum applies equally well to development. Developers are recognizing that testing is not something to be left to other people, or to be done only at the end of a project. By integrating testing directly into your development process, you can produce more robust and error-free code. In this chapter, I'll show you how to do that with unit testing. I'll also introduce you to the basics of two related subjects: test-driven development and refactoring.

The Testing Landscape

If you're employed by a large organization, you may have the luxury of working with a well-staffed and trained quality assurance (QA) department who will test your code. If you're in a small shop, you might well do most of your own testing. Either way, you should have some feel for the major types of testing that most software is subjected to, and you should appreciate that part of your job as a developer is to perform your own testing.

Types of Testing

Every developer knows that software requires testing, but that simple word "testing" encompasses quite a few activities. Here are half a dozen types of testing that you might consider for any given application:

Unit testing   Testing very small pieces of code is called *unit testing*. These are the units that make up an entire application. These tests focus on very small sections of the code to ensure that those small sections are doing what they are supposed to do.

Integration testing   When different developers are working on different parts of the code, it doesn't always fit together as it should. The goal of *integration testing* is to ensure that your code doesn't break someone else's code, and vice versa. Integration testing might consist of simply running all the various unit tests to make sure the various bits of code continue to perform as designed.

System testing   When you have a separate QA group, they often focus on system testing: exercising the entire application to see if they can make it fail. *System testing* often consists of a mix of automated tests and ad hoc "banging on" the application to see if it can be made to fail. System testing can uncover interactions between components and bugs that the developers never even considered.

NOTE   Testing is a laborious task, and very few good tools are available to help you. You might want to take a look at *Developing an Automated Software Testing Tool*, by Kanglin Li and Mengqi Wu (Sybex, 2004), which teaches testing procedures and takes the reader through the steps for developing a powerful automated testing tool. All of the code for the tool is provided with the book.

Stress testing   The goal of *stress testing* is to push the limits of an application until it fails. This might mean using a large number of simulated users, or huge database records, or running the application on a computer with limited RAM.

Beta testing   *Beta testing* involves giving copies of the unfinished code to testers outside of your organization so that they can exercise the code and report on their findings. Beta testing can also be used as a marketing tool to expose large numbers of prospective customers to a new product before it is shipped.

Acceptance testing   Depending on the process you're using, you might formally verify that an application meets each of the requirements precisely. Such formal *acceptance testing* can verify that software will do its job, but it tends to miss bugs caused by unexpected usage.

Testing for Developers

As a developer, you might engage in any or all of the forms of testing I've discussed. But unit testing and integration testing are typically the most important of these activities for developers. One typical pattern of work for developers in a team looks like this:

1. Check out the module that you'll be working on.

2. Write the code for the next feature you're implementing.

3. Write the unit tests to test the feature.

4. Make sure the code passes the unit tests.

5. Get the latest code for the entire application from your source code control system.

6. Make sure the whole project passes the integration tests.

7. Check in your code and unit tests.

RULE   When there are multiple developers on a project, it's important to run the integration tests *before* you check in your changes.

Running the integration tests before checking in the code is the easiest way to make sure that your code doesn't inadvertently break some other part of the application or interact poorly with another change that was checked in while you were working on your own changes.

> **WARNING**   Although developers sometimes do their own system testing, it's definitely a better prac-
> tice to have someone else do this. It is very, very difficult to give code a thorough systems
> test when you're the one who wrote the code. If you had a blind spot about a potential prob-
> lem when you were writing the code, you probably won't think to test that problem later on.

Unit Testing in Action

When I got started writing software, unit testing was a purely ad hoc (and often manual) process. After writing each small chunk of code, I'd run the application and test it by hand to see
whether it worked properly. Sometimes I'd have an automated testing tool that could simulate
key presses and mouse clicks to make this easier. Sometimes I'd write custom code in a separate
module in the program to exercise the code I was planning to ship. But all in all, my unit testing
was a chaotic process.

In recent years, unit testing has become a much more structured process for many developers.
The major cause for this change was the release of JUnit, a unit-testing framework for Java code
written by Erich Gamma and Kent Beck (if you're doing Java development, you can download
JUnit from `www.junit.org/index.htm`). JUnit lets you construct unit tests in a separate Java module. It runs the tests for you and keeps track of which tests your code passes at any given point.

JUnit has been ported to many other development environments. By now there are dozens
of tools, both free and commercial, that owe their basic design to the JUnit project. These are
the tools that many of us now automatically think of when you mention unit testing, and
they're the ones that I'll be using in this chapter.

> **NOTE**   For a quick tutorial on using JUnit with Java, see *Java Programming 10-Minute Solutions*, by
> Mark Watson (Sybex, 2004).

Unit Testing Tools for .NET

As I mentioned, the basic unit-testing framework has been ported to many different languages
and development environments. In fact, there are at least five unit-testing tools for Microsoft
.NET developers:

NUnit   A free, open-source unit-testing framework. This is probably the best known of the
.NET unit-testing tools, and there are several other projects that build on NUnit to offer
additional functionality. These include NUnitAddin (`http://sourceforge.net/projects/`
`nunitaddin/`) and TestRunner for NUnit (`www.mailframe.net/Products/TestRunner.htm`),
each of which integrates NUnit with Visual Studio .NET, and NUnitAsp (`http://`
`nunitasp.sourceforge.net/`), which extends NUnit to support testing ASP.NET pages.
(`http://nunit.org`)

csUnit   Another free, open-source implementation. It offers a slightly different set of features from NUnit, including built-in integration with Visual Studio .NET. It also includes project wizards to build new testing projects easily, as well as a user interface that shows more information than NUnit's interface does. (`www.csunit.org/`)

HarnessIt   A commercial product with a price of $199 per user. It uses a pluggable test engine architecture to extend its reach. This allows for easy testing of web applications and remote applications using the same tools that you use for local Windows applications. HarnessIt also offers a way to explore exceptions in detail and good reporting tools. (`www.unittesting.com/default.aspx`)

X-Unity   A commercial product with pricing starting at $129 per user. It features Visual Studio .NET integration, a separate development kit for unit tests, and integration with X-Unity's continuous integration product (see Chapter 13, "Mastering the Build Process," for more on continuous integration). (`http://x-unity.miik.com.ua/`)

.TEST   A commercial product that costs $900. Its claim to fame is that it will actually write many unit tests for you. It uses a rules-based engine to do this, and helps you ensure that your code conforms to various design guidelines as well as letting you write your own custom tests. (`www.parasoft.com/jsp/products/home.jsp?product=TestNet`)

All of these products offer versions that you can download and evaluate. When you're ready to start unit testing, you should look at the products within your price range to determine which one works best for you. In this chapter, I'll use NUnit to demonstrate the principles of unit testing and test-driven development.

TIP	XProgramming.com maintains an excellent and comprehensive list of unit-testing and related tools for many languages and development environments at `www.xprogramming.com/software.htm`. Check there from time to time to find new and updated testing tools.

Using NUnit for Unit Testing

In this section, I'll work through the mechanics of using NUnit for unit testing. I'll use the DownloadEngine component as my example component for testing.

First Steps with NUnit

NUnit recognizes classes decorated with the `TestFixture` attribute as containing unit tests. Although you can put these classes directly into the code that you're testing, I prefer to create a separate class library project to hold the tests. This makes it easy for me to be sure that I don't accidentally ship testing code with the final product. So to begin, I've created a new C# class library project named DownloadEngineTests.

To use NUnit, you need to set a reference within the test project to the nunit.framework assembly. When you install NUnit, it automatically places this assembly into the Global Assembly Cache and makes it available in the Add Reference dialog box.

You can have any number of test methods within a single test class. Test methods are methods where both of these things are true:

- The method type is public void.

- The method is decorated with the Test attribute.

The following code listing shows the new test class with a single test method:

```
using DownloadTracker.DownloadEngine;
using NUnit.Framework;
using System;

namespace DownloadEngineTests
{
    /// <summary>
    /// Tests for the DownloadEngine class
    /// </summary>
    [TestFixture]
    public class DownloadEngineTests
    {
        public DownloadEngineTests()
        {
            //
            // TODO: Add constructor logic here
            //
        }

        /// <summary>
        ///     Make sure we can set and retrieve
        ///     the default download path
        /// </summary>
        [Test]
        public void TestDownloadPath()
        {
            Engine eng = new Engine();
            eng.DefaultDownloadFolder = @"c:\Tcmp";
            Assert.AreEqual(eng.DefaultDownloadFolder, @"e:\Temp");
        }

    }
}
```

The test here is the `TestDownloadPath` method. This test first creates an instance of the `Engine` object exposed by the DownloadEngine project. It then sets the `DefaultDownloadFolder` property of that object to a fixed string. Finally, it uses the `AreEqual` method of the NUnit `Assert` object to assert that the retrieved property will be that same string. If the string has the expected value, NUnit will consider the test to be a success. If the string has any other value, the test will fail.

At this point, you're ready to run the first test. Compile the test assembly to make sure that you didn't make any syntax errors.

Nunit lets you run tests from either a console application or a GUI application. For now, I'm going to use the GUI application. By default, it installs to Program Files ➢ NUnit v2.1 ➢ Nunit-Gui. Launch the application and select Open from the File menu. Open the `Download-EngineTests.dll` assembly. This will display the DLL name, the namespace name, the class name, and the test name in a tree view. Click the Run button. NUnit will run the tests and display the results, as shown in Figure 5.1. All of the bullets in the tree view will turn green, indicating successful tests.

FIGURE 5.1
First test run
with NUnit

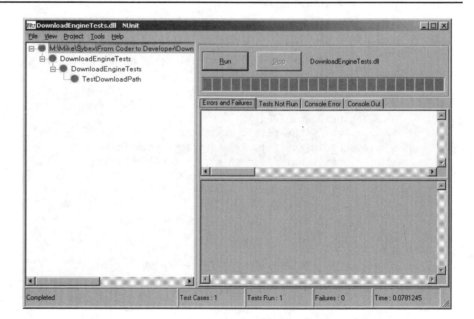

Testing the Download Engine

The next step is to write unit tests for the actual downloading functionality. Here are two new tests: one that downloads a file to the engine's default folder, and one that downloads a file to a specified folder.

```
/// <summary>
///     Download a file to the default folder
///     for the download engine
/// </summary>
[Test]
public void TestDownloadToDefaultFolder()
{
    Engine eng = new Engine();
    eng.DefaultDownloadFolder = @"e:\Temp";
    Download dl = new Download();
    dl.SourceUrl = @"http://localhost/DownloadEngine/DLTest.txt";
    // delete any existing file
    try
    {
        File.Delete(@"e:\Temp\DLTest.txt");
    }
    catch (Exception e)
    {
        // no existing file to delete
        // not a problem
    }
    // perform the download
    eng.GetDownload(dl);
    // verify the file's existence
    Assert.IsTrue(File.Exists(@"e:\Temp\DLTest.txt"),
        "File not found in expected folder");
}

/// <summary>
///     Download a file to a specified folder
/// </summary>
[Test]
public void TestDownloadToSpecifiedFolder()
{
    Engine eng = new Engine();
    eng.DefaultDownloadFolder = @"e:\Temp";
    Download dl = new Download();
    dl.SourceUrl = @"http://localhost/DownloadEngine/DLTest.txt";
    dl.DownloadFolder = @"e:\Temp\Test";
```

```
          // delete any existing file
          try
          {
              File.Delete(@"e:\TempTest\DLTest.txt");
          }
          catch (Exception e)
          {
              // no existing file to delete
              // not a problem
          }
          // perform the download
          eng.GetDownload(dl);
          // verify the file's existence
          Assert.IsTrue(File.Exists(@"e:\Temp\Test\DLTest.txt"),
              "File not found in expected folder");
      }
```

These tests are pretty straightforward: Each one starts by setting up the required objects. It then deletes any existing file from the target location, downloads the file, and checks that it ended up in the expected place. NUnit's `Assert.True` method lets me use any method that returns a Boolean value; in this case, the `File.Exists` method (from the `System.IO` namespace) provides an easy way to see whether a file exists after the download finishes.

NOTE   Remember the rule to check everything you need into your source code control system? At this point, I added the `DLTest.txt` file, and a command file to build the necessary folders, to my Vault database.

When you recompile a class containing NUnit tests, NUnit automatically adds the new tests to the tree view (assuming that you're using the GUI tester). So all you need to do is switch back to the tester and click the Run button. Figure 5.2 shows the results in this case.

One of the new tests passed, but the TestDownloadToSpecifiedFolder test failed. The main bar in the NUnit window is now an angry red. This means that at least one of the tests failed.

RULE   When a unit test fails, it's time to stop adding new tests and fix the problem.

FIGURE 5.2
Test run with a failing
test

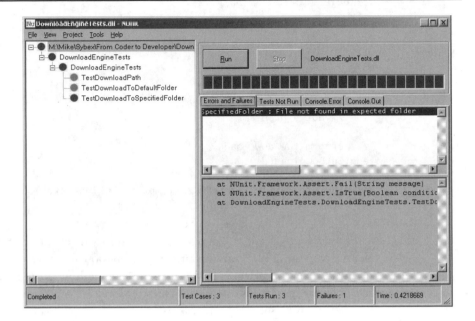

Debugging NUnit Tests

Looking at the NUnit interface, you'll see that the file didn't end up in the right place on the hard drive. Why is that happening? The obvious approach to this problem is to set a breakpoint inside the test code and find out. But if you try this, you'll discover that your breakpoint is never hit. That's because NUnit launches its tests on a separate thread. You can debug the code that NUnit is testing, but it takes a bit of extra work. Follow these steps to debug a unit test in action:

1. Set a breakpoint in the test code where you want to drop into the debugger.

2. Launch NUnit.

3. Select Debug ≻ Processes in Visual Studio .NET. This will open the Processes dialog box, shown in Figure 5.3.

4. Scroll down the Available Processes list to find the nunit-gui.exe process, and then click Attach. This will open the Attach To Process dialog box.

5. Select the CLR debugger and click OK. nunit-gui.exe will now show up in the Debugged Processes list.

6. Select the option to detach from the process when debugging is stopped and click Close.

Now when you run the tests in the NUnit GUI, Visual Studio .NET will stop on the breakpoint and let you debug using all the normal Visual Studio .NET tools.

FIGURE 5.3
Attaching to a process
to debug

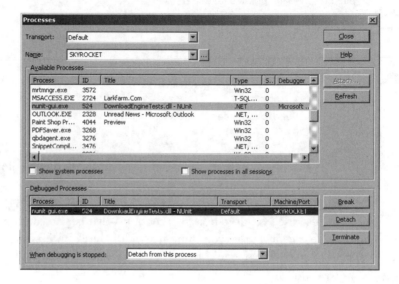

For a less-cumbersome debugging experience, you might like to experiment with the TestRunner or NUnit Addin projects that I mentioned earlier in the chapter.

Oh, the error? Just a bit of late-night coding stupidity on my part. Here's the code that I originally saved to handle the `DownloadFolder` property of the `Download` class:

```
/// <summary>
/// The folder where the file will be saved
/// </summary>
public string DownloadFolder
{
    get
    {
        return _DownloadFolder;
    }
    set
    {
        _DownloadFolder = DownloadFolder;
    }
}
```

Of course, with the test failing, it's easy to see that this code should be changed:

```
/// <summary>
/// The folder where the file will be saved
/// </summary>
```

```
public string DownloadFolder
{
    get
    {
        return _DownloadFolder;
    }
    set
    {
        _DownloadFolder = value;
    }
}
```

With this change, all three of the unit tests pass with flying colors.

Testing an Exception

You can also use NUnit to test an exception—that is, you can test whether a piece of code throws the exception that you think it should. Here's an NUnit test for the exception that I expect DownloadEngine to throw when it's given an invalid URL:

```
/// <summary>
///     Make sure an invalid URL throws the proper
///     exception
/// </summary>
[Test]
[ExpectedException(typeof(Engine.DownloadException))]
public void TestInvalidURL()
{
    Engine eng = new Engine();
    eng.DefaultDownloadFolder = @"e:\Temp";
    Download dl = new Download();
    dl.SourceUrl = @"http://localhost/DownloadEngine/BadFile.txt";
    // perform the download
    eng.GetDownload(dl);
}
```

When you want NUnit to check that your code throws a particular exception, you need to add the ExpectedException attribute to the test in question. This attribute has a property that indicates the type of exception that you're expecting. If the test throws the specified exception, it's considered as passing.

Testing with Mock Objects

One problem you may face from time to time is how to test parts of a project before other parts are finished. For instance, here's a little preliminary code from the logic layer of the Download Tracker application:

```
public bool SaveDownload(string SourceUrl,
```

```
        string DownloadFolder, string FileName)
    {
        // Set up the download engine and a download
        DownloadEngine.Engine eng = new DownloadEngine.Engine();
        eng.DefaultDownloadFolder = GetDefaultDownloadFolder();
        DownloadEngine.Download d = new DownloadEngine.Download();
        d.SourceUrl = SourceUrl;
        d.DownloadFolder = DownloadFolder;
        d.FileName = FileName;
        // Perform the download
        eng.GetDownload(d);
        // Save to the database and return the result
        return _DB.SaveDownload(d);
    }

    public DownloadEngine.Download GetDownload(string ProductName)
    {
        // Pass the request to the database layer and
        // return the result
        return _DB.GetDownload(ProductName);
    }
```

This code handles moving downloads to the database and back, using an object, _DB, supplied by the database layer code. Although the code is simple, it's a good practice to write unit tests for everything. After all, you can't be sure that things will stay simple. But without having yet written the database layer, how can you test this code?

One answer to that question is to use mock objects. A *mock object* has the same interface as the real object that it's imitating but contains only test code. To use mock objects for testing, you declare and use interfaces rather than classes in your main code. Then that code can use either the real object or the mock object without changes. In this case, I can begin by declaring an interface that the data access layer will ultimately implement:

```
namespace DownloadTracker
{
    public interface IDBAccess
    {
        bool SaveDownload(DownloadEngine.Download d);
        DownloadEngine.Download GetDownload(string ProductName);
    }
}
```

Of course, it's likely that I'll add more methods to this interface later. But if you're serious about unit testing (and you should be), writing just enough code to test is always a good idea. That way, you're more likely to write the tests, instead of postponing them until later.

To use this strategy, ensure that the database layer object is passed into the logic layer rather than declared inside it. It's convenient to provide a constructor to handle this. Note that the constructor is declared with the interface. This allows me to pass in any object that implements that interface:

```
public class DTLogic
{
    IDBAccess _DB;

    public DTLogic()
    {
        //
        // This constructor should not be used
        //
    }

    /// <summary>
    ///     Constructor including data access
    /// </summary>
    public DTLogic(IDBAccess DB)
    {
        _DB = DB;
    }
```

When the code is in actual production use, I'll pass in a real database layer object here. For testing, though, I want to use a mock object. So this means building NUnit test code for the SaveDownload and GetDownload methods that use a mock object. Here's the code:

```
using DownloadTracker;
using DownloadTracker.DownloadEngine;
using NUnit.Framework;
using System;

namespace DownloadTrackerTests
{
    /// <summary>
    /// Tests for the main Download Tracker logic
    /// </summary>
    [TestFixture]
    public class DownloadTrackerTests
    {
        public DownloadTrackerTests()
        {
        }

        /// <summary>
        ///     Exercise the DTLogic.SaveDownload method
```

```
        /// </summary>
        [Test]
        public void TestSaveDownload()
        {
            DTLogic DT = new DTLogic(new MockDBAccess());
            bool retval = DT.SaveDownload(
                @"http://localhost/DownloadEngine/DLTest.txt",
                @"e:\Temp", "");
            Assert.IsTrue(retval);
        }


        /// <summary>
        ///     Exercise the DTLogic.GetDownload method
        /// </summary>
        [Test]
        public void TestGetDownload()
        {
            DTLogic DT = new DTLogic(new MockDBAccess());
            Download D = DT.GetDownload("MyProduct");
            Assert.AreEqual("MyProduct", D.ProductName);
        }

    }

    public class MockDBAccess: IDBAccess
    {
        public MockDBAccess()
        {
            //
            // TODO: Add constructor logic here
            //
        }
        #region IDBAccess Members

        public bool SaveDownload(DownloadTracker.DownloadEngine.Download d)
        {
            // always mock a successful save
            return true;
        }

        public DownloadTracker.DownloadEngine.Download GetDownload(string
ProductName)
        {
            // return a synthetic object
            Download d = new Download();
            d.ProductName = ProductName;
            d.Description = "Download containing " +
```

```
            ProductName;
        return d;
    }

  }

}
```

Running these tests exercises the `SaveDownload` and `GetDownload` methods without requiring a real implementation of the database layer (and, in fact, the tests both pass). There's an additional benefit here as well: Because the tests don't make any actual database changes, I don't need to worry about cleaning up the database in between test runs.

Mock objects come in handy in many situations:

- The real object doesn't exist yet.
- The real object takes a long time to do its work.
- The real object is hard to set up or clean up after.
- The real object depends on unreliable resources (such as network connectivity).
- The real object returns nondeterministic results. For example, if you're retrieving stock prices, you can't determine in advance what the correct number will be. This makes it impossible to test the results.
- The real object requires user input (and so can't be used in automated tests).

But there are also drawbacks to testing with mock objects. In particular, the need to factor out interfaces can make your code more complex. Also, you need to be careful that the mock object behaves exactly like the real object. Otherwise, your test is worthless.

In some situations, you may want to generate mock objects to replace quite complex real objects. In that case, you should investigate some of the products that exist to automatically create mock objects from real objects. I know of three for .NET:

NMock   An open-source mock object library. (http://nmock.truemesh.com/)

.NET Mock Objects   Another open-source mock object library, which includes prebuilt implementations of some Framework mock objects. (http://sourceforge.net/projects/dotnetmock/)

POCMock   A commercial implementation that lets you create mock objects or add validation code to existing objects. It costs $49.95 to register. (www.prettyobjects.com/english/Products/POCMock.asp)

As of this writing, neither of the open-source projects appears to be actively maintained.

Test-Driven Development

Unit testing has been around for a long, long time. It was recognized as an essential part of developing software decades ago. However, in the last few years a new testing technique, test-driven development (TDD), has gained increasing prominence. TDD is one of the practices recommended by advocates of Extreme Programming (usually abbreviated as XP). One excellent introduction to TDD is Kent Beck's *Test-Driven Development: By Example* (Addison-Wesley, 2003). Beck boils down TDD to two simple rules:

- Write a failing automated test before you write any code.

- Remove duplication.

That's right—in TDD, you write the test *before* you write the code. Here's the general plan of action in a bit more depth:

1. Quickly add a test.

2. Run all tests and see the new one fail.

3. Make a little change.

4. Run all tests and see them all succeed.

5. Refactor to remove duplication.

TDD in Action

An example will make the TDD process more clear. Right now, there's a bit of undone code in the middle of the Engine object:

```
public void GetDownload(Download d)
{
    string filename = string.Empty;
    string foldername = string.Empty;
    WebClient wc = new WebClient();

    try
    {
        // ... some code omitted ...

        // Use WebClient to do the download
        wc.DownloadFile(d.SourceUrl, Path.Combine(foldername, filename));

        // UNDONE: set file size in the Download object

    }
    catch (Exception e)
    {
```

```
        // Bubble any exception up to caller, with custom info
        throw new DownloadException("Unable to download" ,d, e);
    }
    finally
    {
        wc.Dispose();
    }

}
```

The intent is clear: When the engine downloads a file, it should fill in the property of the Download object that records the size of that file. To get this working using TDD, I start by writing a new test in the DownloadEngineTests project:

```
/// <summary>
///     Make sure the engine properly sets
///     the size of the downloaded file
/// </summary>
[Test]
public void TestDownloadSize()
{
    Engine eng = new Engine();
    eng.DefaultDownloadFolder = @"e:\Temp";
    Download dl = new Download();
    dl.SourceUrl = @"http://localhost/DownloadEngine/DLTest.txt";
    // delete any existing file
    try
    {
        File.Delete(@"e:\Temp\DLTest.txt");
    }
    catch (Exception e)
    {
        // no existing file to delete
        // not a problem
    }
    // perform the download
    eng.GetDownload(dl);
    // verify the file's size in the Download structure
    Assert.AreEqual(57, dl.Size);
}
```

Not surprisingly, the test fails, as shown in Figure 5.4. Note that NUnit assumes that the first argument to the AreEqual method is the expected value and the second is the actual value.

RULE   When using TDD, keep code changes as small as possible.

FIGURE 5.4

A failing test for new functionality

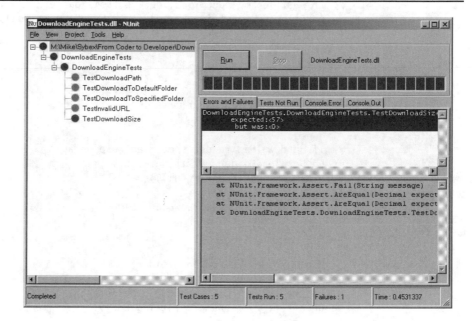

The next step is to make a small change—in fact, the smallest change that will make the test work. It's important to not get ahead of yourself by writing a bunch of code at once. The goal of TDD is to make certain that all of your code gets tested by writing the tests before the code. The revised GetDownload method with code to fill in the file size:

```
// GetDownload uses the information in a Download object
// to get the specified file from the Internet to a local
// hard drive. Any download errors are wrapped in a
// custom exception and returned to the caller, along with
// the failing Download object.
public void GetDownload(Download d)
{
    string filename = string.Empty;
    string foldername = string.Empty;
    WebClient wc = new WebClient();

    try
    {
        // This method should never be called without
        // a Source URL
        Debug.Assert(((d.SourceUrl != string.Empty) &&
            (d.SourceUrl != null)),
            "Empty SourceUrl",
            "Can't download a file unless a Source URL is supplied");
```

```
            // If no filename specified, derive from SourceUrl
            if((d.FileName == string.Empty) || (d.FileName == null))
            {
                filename = Path.GetFileName(d.SourceUrl);
            }
            else
            {
                filename = d.FileName;
            }

            // If no download folder specified, use default
            if((d.DownloadFolder == string.Empty) ||
                (d.DownloadFolder == null))
            {
                foldername = DefaultDownloadFolder;
            }
            else
            {
                foldername = d.DownloadFolder;
            }
            // Ensure that we got a folder name somehow
            Debug.Assert(foldername != string.Empty,
                "Empty foldername",
                "Download folder not set and no default supplied");

            // Use WebClient to do the download
            wc.DownloadFile(d.SourceUrl, Path.Combine(foldername, filename));

            // Set file size in the Download object
            FileInfo fi = new FileInfo(Path.Combine(foldername, filename));
            d.Size = fi.Length;

        }
        catch (Exception e)
        {
            // Bubble any exception up to caller, with custom info
            throw new DownloadException("Unable to download" ,d, e);
        }
        finally
        {
            wc.Dispose();
        }

    }
```

After making this change, I compile everything, run the tests again—and they all pass. That shows me that not only did I implement the file size code correctly but that I didn't break anything else in the process. Now I can move on to other tasks.

Effects of TDD

It's pretty typical to start writing more code when you commit to TDD. I find that my test harnesses run up to twice as large as the code that they're testing. Of course, much of the test code is pretty routine; it consists of creating objects, invoking methods, and checking the return values. When I'm heavily into the TDD mindset, I might write a dozen tests for a new method. When I can't think of anything else to test, then the method is done, and it's time to go on to something else.

The key that makes TDD work (at least for me) is the discipline of writing the test before writing the code. That's the only way that I know of to make sure that I really write the tests. Otherwise, they tend to be left until, well, later—and later seldom (if ever) arrives. Writing the tests first means the tests get written. It also means that I think about what I'm building and how it might fail. The delay of writing the tests gives me a little more time to plan and results in better code.

Writing better code is a major benefit of TDD, but it's not the only one. I find that the most important plus to test-driven development is the sense of confidence that it gives me in my code. It's difficult to describe this feeling unless you've experienced it. By writing many fine-grained tests, and knowing that the code passes those tests, I'm sure that it meets the requirements as embodied in the tests. This is especially critical when new requirements come up that I didn't think of when I was starting out. Surely you've been in the situation where adding a new property required tinkering with code all over the place. Scary, wasn't it? Well, with TDD, you can banish that fear forever.

The major problem in tinkering with your code is that you might break something unexpectedly. But if you've been doing TDD, you will have tiny tests that cover every bit of code you've written. In that case, you can make your changes and run your tests. Either they'll all pass (great!), a few will fail and you'll figure out how to fix them, or things will be horribly broken—in which case you can toss out your changes and start over (another reason to use source code control!). What you can avoid is the horrible uncertainty of not knowing whether things are broken. That confidence translates into a direct productivity boost.

Refactoring

You might have noticed that I didn't carry out the final step of the TDD plan: refactoring to remove duplication. Refactoring is another concept that deserves a section of its own. This concept was also publicized by XP advocates, with Martin Fowler's *Refactoring: Improving the Design of Existing Code* (Addison-Wesley, 1999) remaining the best work on the subject. Fowler defines refactoring as "the process of changing a software system in such a way that it does not alter the external behavior of the code yet improves its internal structure."

Refactoring *GetDownload*

As an example, there are several bits of duplication in the code that you just saw for the GetDownload method. Now that I have unit tests that cover the expected behavior of the code, I can refactor the code to remove this duplication. Here's the revised code:

```
// GetDownload uses the information in a Download object
// to get the specified file from the Internet to a local
// hard drive. Any download errors are wrapped in a
// custom exception and returned to the caller, along with
// the failing Download object.
public void GetDownload(Download d)
{
    string filename = string.Empty;
    string foldername = string.Empty;
    WebClient wc = new WebClient();

    try
    {
        // This method should never be called without
        // a Source URL
        Debug.Assert(((d.SourceUrl != string.Empty) &&
            (d.SourceUrl != null)),
            "Empty SourceUrl",
            "Can't download a file unless a Source URL is supplied");

        // If no filename specified, derive from SourceUrl
        filename = ReplaceNull(d.FileName,
            Path.GetFileName(d.SourceUrl));

        // If no download folder specified, use default
        foldername = ReplaceNull(d.DownloadFolder,
            DefaultDownloadFolder);
        // Ensure that we got a folder name somehow
        Debug.Assert(foldername != string.Empty,
            "Empty foldername",
            "Download folder not set and no default supplied");

        string TargetFile = Path.Combine(foldername, filename);

        // Use WebClient to do the download
        wc.DownloadFile(d.SourceUrl, TargetFile);

        // Set file size in the Download object
        FileInfo fi = new FileInfo(TargetFile);
        d.Size = fi.Length;
```

```
        }
        catch (Exception e)
        {
            // Bubble any exception up to caller, with custom info
            throw new DownloadException("Unable to download" ,d, e);
        }
        finally
        {
            wc.Dispose();
        }
    }


    // Replace a possibly-null string with another string
    // Returns the original string if it's not null or
    // empty, otherwise returns the replacement string
    private string ReplaceNull(string MaybeNull, string Replacement)
    {
        if((MaybeNull == string.Empty) ||
            (MaybeNull == null))
        {
            return Replacement;
        }
        else
        {
            return MaybeNull;
        }
    }
```

The new code isn't shorter than the original, but most developers would agree that it's a bit "cleaner" or "more beautiful." These are terms that are difficult to define, but for the most part, developers know cleaner code when they see it.

More important, the code still passes the unit tests after these changes. Without the unit tests, it's difficult or impossible to have the confidence that your refactorings won't break something.

Refactoring Tools

Some refactoring patterns occur frequently (Fowler's book is largely a catalog of such patterns). For instance, you might pull out repeated code to its own procedure, as I did in refactoring GetDownload. Or you might turn fields into properties, or vice versa, or create a superclass based on two similar classes. Making such changes is routine work—and routine work is a good source of automated tools.

TECHNOLOGY TRAP

Code Thrashing

You should always have a purpose in mind when you refactor your code. Perhaps it's time to remove duplicated code caused by cut-and-paste programming. Perhaps you've realized that a class isn't general enough and needs a new superclass. But beware of refactoring just because you can. When your next coding task looks difficult or boring, it's easy to decide that it's time to clean up the existing code. A session of converting fields into properties can be just the ticket when you're trying to avoid real work.

There's a second problem that sometimes turns up in refactoring when a team of developers is involved. If different developers have different ideas about what makes for beautiful code, they can waste a lot of time second-guessing each other. A tip-off to this behavior is a set of source code check-in comments like this:

- 4-7-04 MG Converted fields to properties

- 4-8-04 SJ Converted properties to fields

- 4-10-04 MG Converted fields to properties

- 4-11-04 SJ Converted properties to fields

If you find such a list of comments in your own source code control system, it's time to get the team together over a pot of coffee or a pizza and discuss the problem. Shared vision and coding standards can help you avoid the issue in the first place, but be ready to listen to everyone concerned. It's possible that one of the developers involved has spotted a problem with the code that the rest of the team doesn't yet understand.

Automated refactoring is an area where several other development environments (notably Smalltalk and Java) are well ahead of .NET. However, some tools are available for .NET:

dotEasy   A free Visual Studio .NET add-in that evaluates code based on various metrics and that plans to support automatic refactoring of problematic code. (www.doteasy.com.uy/)

The C# Refactoring Tool   Supports a number of standard refactorings, including smart renaming, encapsulating fields, extracting methods, moving members, and more. Costs $110 per user. (http://dotnetrefactoring.com/)

C# Refactory   A full-featured refactoring tool that integrates with Visual Studio .NET. At $99, it offers a solid set of refactorings in a well-designed interface. (www.xtreme-simplicity .net/CSharpRefactory.html)

Flywheel   A $449 tool for designing and refactoring .NET code. It supports refactoring by drag and drop in the Flywheel interface. (www.velocitis.com/)

If you find that TDD works well for you, or you're faced with a complex pile of existing object-oriented code that needs to be cleaned up and rearranged, it's worth evaluating these tools to see whether they can help.

Unit Testing Checklist

If you don't test your code, you can never know for sure that it's working. Beyond just catching bugs, a thorough suite of unit tests can give you the confidence you need to fine-tune your code. Think about these points when evaluating your own unit-testing practices:

- Write unit tests for all code.

- Write the tests as you go along. Don't leave them for a "later" that may never come.

- Make sure code passes unit tests and integration tests before you check it into the source code control system.

- Use an automated tool such as NUnit to make the unit-testing process easy and repeatable.

- Check the tests and any necessary setup files into your source code control system.

- Consider using TDD to ensure 100% testing coverage.

- Refactor code only when you have a thorough set of tests for the code.

Now that the code is starting to pile up, I want to turn our attention to the development environment itself. Visual Studio .NET is a fine IDE, but as you'll see in the next chapter, many tools are available that can make it even better.

CHAPTER 6

Pumping Up the IDE

"I am Hans and he is Franz. And we want to pump you up!"

—Dana Carvey as Hans, *Saturday Night Live*

It may not be a 98-pound weakling, but Visual Studio .NET (VS .NET) can still use a bit of help in reaching its full potential. VS .NET is a fine integrated development environment (IDE), but even Microsoft doesn't have the resources to make it perfect for every developer. In fact, it's impossible to make an IDE that's perfect for every developer, because different developers have different habits. Fortunately, there are a variety of ways in which you can make the IDE more useful for your own needs and working habits. These range from taking advantage of the options already present in the product, to writing macros to automate repetitive tasks, to installing third-party tools and add-ins that bring new functionality to the IDE.

In this chapter, rather than focus on the code of Download Tracker (which is still moving along), I'm going to turn my attention to the development environment. You'll see some more code, but the goal of this chapter is to demonstrate some of the ways that the IDE can help you write your own code.

Customizing Visual Studio .NET

I'm always surprised at the number of developers I find who are using VS .NET with everything set exactly as it came out of the box. There are hundreds of settings that you can tweak and adjust in VS .NET, and it's the rare developer who won't benefit from at least some customization. In this section, I'll show you some of the places where you might benefit from making your own changes to the IDE. I assume that you already know the basics: customizing toolbars via Tools ➤ Customize; rearranging, docking, and floating windows with the mouse; and opening new windows from the View menu. Instead, I'll concentrate on some of the more obscure things you can change.

Using Profiles

A good place to start is with the My Profile tab on the Start Page. If you've closed the Start Page, you can get it back by selecting Help ➤ Start Page (why this isn't on the View menu with all of the other windows remains one of the mysteries of VS .NET). You probably saw this page (shown in Figure 6.1) when you first installed VS .NET, but it's worth another visit now that you have some experience with the product.

The controls on the My Profile tab interact in ways that aren't immediately obvious. Choosing a setting from the Profile combo box is equivalent to choosing a particular group of settings in the Keyboard Scheme, Window Layout, and Help Filter combo boxes. If you then make any change in one of those other boxes (even one that matches an existing profile), the profile changes to "(custom)".

FIGURE 6.1
Selecting a profile

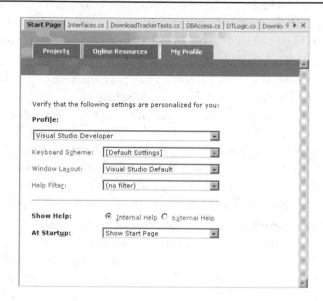

Changes to your profile take effect immediately, and there's no undo for them, so experiment with caution. If you've developed a custom window layout that you like, you may not want to make any changes to your profile.

The Keyboard Scheme combo box lets you set the keyboard shortcuts to be compatible with previous IDEs:

- Visual Studio .NET Defaults
- Visual Basic 6
- Visual C++ 2
- Visual C++ 6
- Visual Studio 6

The Window Layout combo box lets you choose among several standard ways to arrange the various tool windows:

- Visual Studio Default
- Visual Basic 6
- Visual C++ 6
- Student Window Layout
- No Tool Windows Layout

The Help Filter combo box lets you select a default subset of the help feature to search when you click F1. You can also choose whether to display help in a window within VS .NET (Internal Help) or in its own window (External Help). Finally, you can decide what to display when you launch VS .NET.

Although it's tempting to select a profile that corresponds to whatever tool you were using before VS .NET so as to get an immediate productivity gain, I personally prefer to use the default Visual Studio Developer profile. That's because many books and articles assume that you're using the default profile. If you're not using that profile, you may have trouble following specific instructions. As a simple example, if you're a Visual Basic (VB) 6 developer making the transition and you use the VB 6 keyboard shortcuts, your IDE will use F8 to debug the next statement. This can be confusing when you're reading a tutorial, book, or article that instructs you to click F11 to debug, because that's the default keystroke.

I also prefer to leave the Help Filter set to "(no filter)". That's because the indexing in the VS .NET help (and MSDN help in general) is not all that reliable, and I've found that setting the filter can keep me from finding help topics that seem perfectly applicable to my current search. You should experiment with the filter settings to see whether you prefer the focused search in the topics that VS .NET thinks apply, or the wider search that covers everything. The trade-off is between possibly missing something pertinent and having to wade through lots of irrelevant information.

NOTE The Start Page itself can be customized too, though many developers won't need to bother with this. Still, in a corporate setting you can use a custom Start Page to deliver content to all of your developers, just as Microsoft delivers updates to the Online Resources tab. See "Customizing the Visual Studio .NET 2003 Start Page" (`http://msdn.microsoft.com/library/en-us/dv_vstechart/html/vstchCustomizingVisualStudioStartPageEverett.asp`) for details.

Setting VS .NET Options

The Tools ➤ Options menu item is your gateway to hundreds of ways to customize VS .NET. It's impossible to be specific about how many customizations you'll find here, because this is a part of the extensible interface; third-party products can add their own property pages to the Options dialog box. Figure 6.2 shows this dialog box on my computer; as you can see, several products (such as Logidex and NUnitAddin) have added themselves to the list of folders at the left side of the dialog box.

Here are some of the specific settings that I've found it helpful to change:

Environment, General   Under this menu, increase the number of items in the most recently used lists from 4 to a more reasonable number, such as 10 or 15. Unless you have a very small screen or don't work with many projects, you'll find this the easiest way to locate your current work.

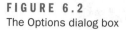

FIGURE 6.2
The Options dialog box

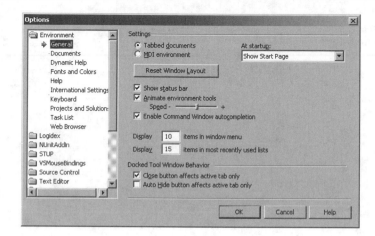

Environment, Documents   Under this menu, check the Auto-load Changes box. This will remove one of the annoying "Are you sure?" prompts that litter software today. This is especially useful if you're using an external source code control utility. Otherwise, you'll be prompted every time you get a more recent copy of a file that you have open.

Environment, Fonts And Colors   The default font for VS .NET is a 10-point Courier font. Depending on your monitor size and resolution (and your eyesight), you might find it useful to select a smaller font here. Also, in Courier New it can be hard to tell the difference between some characters (such as the numeral 1 and the lowercase l, or curly braces and square brackets), a problem that can be alleviated with specialized programming fonts. Figure 6.3 shows the same window using 10-point Courier and 8-point ProFont; as you can see, the ProFont version gets considerably more information into the same space. This is useful when you're trying to get a sense of the overall code flow, or you're reading extensive comments (as long as you don't reduce the font to the point of eyestrain). Of course, fonts are a matter of personal preference; if you like your source code in 24-point Garamond Bold, then by all means set that as your default font.

TIP   You can download ProFont and Sheldon (another excellent programmer's font) from www.tobias-jung.de/seekingprofont/.

Database Tools, Server Explorer   The default login timeout is 15 seconds. If you're working with a SQL Server across a wide area network (WAN) or the Internet, that will probably be too short. Increasing this value to 60 seconds can help avoid maddening connectivity problems.

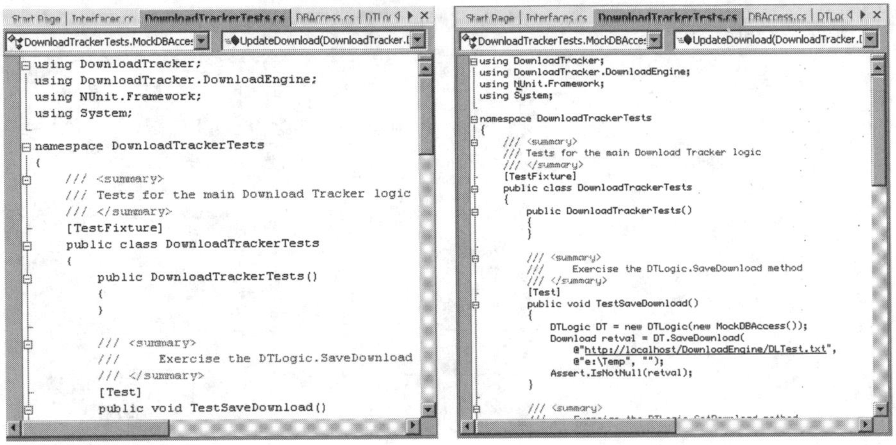

FIGURE 6.3
Comparing 10-point
Courier with 8-point
ProFont

Whether or not you agree with these recommendations, take a few minutes to explore all the choices in the Options dialog box. You'll probably find some control over the environment that you didn't know you had.

NOTE In addition to the general settings I've discussed that affect all of your development with VS .NET, each individual language has its own settings (under "Text Editor" in the options tree). You can, for example, control whether each language has line numbering displayed in the editor window, or how many spaces a tab is equivalent to.

Using VS .NET PowerToys

For even more customization possibilities, check out the VS .NET PowerToys. These are a set of utilities designed to work with VS .NET that are not part of the product, even though they have input and code from the product team. The PowerToys home page is at `www.gotdotnet .com/team/ide/`. The lineup continues to expand, but here are some of the PowerToys that I find useful:

VSTweak Just in case the Options dialog box doesn't offer enough settings for you, VSTweak adds control over more settings. The utility includes a manager for command window aliases, editing for most recently used (MRU) lists, and the ability to extend the list of file extensions that VS .NET recognizes.

VSWindowManager You've probably noticed that the IDE opens a different set of default windows when you enter debug mode. That's an example of a window layout.

VSWindowManager lets you define custom window layouts and apply them automatically or on demand. If there's a set of tools that you always want to see when editing Extensible Markup Language (XML) files, for example, you can create a window layout of those tools and then recall it with a single menu choice.

VSMouseBindings   This utility lets you assign commands to the buttons on your mouse, even if you have a five-button mouse.

VSEdit   By default, if you double-click a C# file (or any other file associated with VS .NET) in Windows Explorer, it will open in a whole new VS .NET session. If you use VSEdit, you can open the file in an existing session instead, which is much faster.

Writing VS .NET Macros

After you get the IDE set up the way you like it, take a look at the VS .NET macros. Many developers never discover (or never use) this facet of VS .NET, which is a shame. One of the things that separates the beginning coder from the seasoned developer is an attitude toward repetitive work. This applies not just to writing code but to performing repetitive actions in the IDE as well. Perhaps you need to apply a comment with a copyright notice to the top of every code module. You could do this using cut and paste, but there's an alternative. VS .NET lets you record and replay macros, collections of actions that can simulate almost anything that you can do with the mouse and keyboard.

Overview of Macros

If you've used macros in Microsoft Word or Excel, or worked with Windows Scripting, you should have a pretty good mental model of macros. A macro, in this case, is a series of actions saved in a scripting language. The group of actions can be stored and later replayed. The goal of macros is to simplify repetitive work by letting you do just one thing (run the macro) instead of an entire series of things (the actions contained in the macro).

VS .NET includes everything you'd expect from a modern high-end macro language:

- A macro recorder and playback facility
- A macro editor
- Keyboard bindings for macros
- An object model to let macros work with the IDE

Let's briefly look at each of these facets of VS .NET macros.

Alternatives to VS .NET

Although I'm focused on VS .NET in this chapter (and throughout the book), you should be aware that you have alternatives for developing .NET applications. Depending on your budget, other tools, and needs, one of these tools might be right for you.

Notepad   You don't actually need an IDE at all to build .NET software. The .NET Framework SDK (www.microsoft.com/downloads/details.aspx?FamilyId=9B3A2CA6-3647-4070-9F41-A333C6B9181D&displaylang=en) includes command-line compilers and tools that work just as well as VS .NET for developing .NET applications. You can use Notepad (or any other text editor, such as SciTE, www.scintilla.org/SciTE.html&e) to build your source code. I wouldn't recommend this approach, though, unless you have a favorite text editor that you simply can't bear to part with.

SharpDevelop   SharpDevelop (sometimes called #develop) is a free, open-source IDE for both C# and VB .NET projects. SharpDevelop offers an excellent environment for beginners who don't want to invest in VS .NET. You can download a copy from www.icsharpcode.net/OpenSource/SD/.

Antechninus C# Editor   The Antechinus C# Editor (www.c-point.com/csharp.htm) is a $35 program that provides a good deal of help if you're working in C#. Its features include IntelliSense, links to the .NET documentation, code-completion templates, a C# tutorial, and syntax coloring, just to name a few.

ASP.NET Web Matrix   ASP.NET Web Matrix (www.asp.net/webmatrix/default.aspx?tabIndex=4&tabId=46) is another free IDE, this one developed by the ASP.NET team and community. It's very small (1.3-MB download), but even so it includes some features that aren't present in VS .NET, such as a built-in web server and design-time rendering of user controls. It's definitely worth a look if you're doing mostly ASP.NET development.

C#Builder   C#Builder is Borland's entry into the .NET IDE world. The C#Builder home page is at www.borland.com/csharpbuilder/. The product comes in a variety of editions, including a free personal edition (which, however, is pretty feature poor). C#Builder is worth testing if you're using Borland's other software lifecycle tools or if .NET/ Java 2 Enterprise Edition (J2EE) interoperation is high on your list.

PrimalCode   PrimalCode, from Sapien Technologies (www.sapien.com/), is an IDE aimed strictly at the developer who prefers to work in source code; there are no visual designers at all. Its advantages are a small footprint, support for multiple web technologies (including Active Server Pages, PHP, and Java Server Pages in addition to ASP.NET), and a nice set of integrated tools. It's an interesting alternative if your primary needs are in ASP.NET and web services.

Eclipse   Eclipse (www.eclipse.org/) is a free, open, extensible IDE that has strong support in the Java world and an impressive array of features. Although Eclipse isn't a .NET IDE in its default configuration, Improve Technologies (www.improve-technol-ogies.com/alpha/esharp/) distributes a free C# plug-in that allows you to edit C# files in Eclipse. If you work mostly in Java, this may be the easiest way for you to dabble in C#.

Snippet Compiler   Although it's not a full IDE, Jeff Key's excellent Snippet Compiler is worth mentioning. Snippet Compiler (shown below) nestles down on your Windows Taskbar until you need it, when it presents you with a simple way to test code. This is great when you're trying to figure out how to do something and don't want the overhead of firing up VS .NET. You can get a free copy from www.sliver.com/dotnet/SnippetCompiler/.

IntelliJ IDEA   IDEA (www.intellij.com/idea) is a well-respected Java IDE. As of this writing, the company doesn't offer a .NET version, but it has announced that it's working on one (no delivery date has been announced, however). If it manages to bring the full suite of refactoring tools over, it could well be a force to be reckoned with.

The Macro Recorder

VS .NET makes it extremely easy to get started writing macros. That's because it includes a macro recorder that lets you create a macro simply by carrying out the actions that the macro should contain. After you've launched VS .NET and loaded your project, follow these steps to record a macro:

1. Select Tools ➢ Macros ➢ Record Temporary Macro or press Ctrl+Shift+R to start the Macro Recorder. This will open the Recorder toolbar, shown in Figure 6.4.

2. Carry out your actions just as you normally would. To create a macro to add copyright notices, I first pressed Ctrl+Home to move to the top of the window, typed the copyright notice, and pressed Enter to insert a blank line.

3. Click the Stop Recording button on the macro toolbar.

FIGURE 6.4
The Recorder toolbar lets you start, pause, finish, or cancel macro recording.

To prove that the new macro works, you can test it out. Open a new code module in the editor, and then select Tools ➢ Macros ➢ Run Temporary Macro. VS .NET will add the copyright notice to the new module.

The Macro Editor

Recording macros is simple, but sometimes recorded macros will need a bit of cleanup to be really useful. The tool for doing this cleanup is the Macro Editor. To see your new macro in the Macro Editor, follow these steps:

1. Select View ➢ Other Windows ➢ Macro Explorer. This will open the Macro Explorer window, which shows all of the macros that you have loaded. Macros are organized into projects, each of which can contain many modules. In turn, each module can contain many macros. You'll find your new macro in a module named RecordingModule in a project named MyMacros.

2. Right-click on the TemporaryMacro macro and select Edit. This will open the macro in the Macro IDE, shown in Figure 6.5. Alternatively, you can press Alt+F11 to open the Macro IDE.

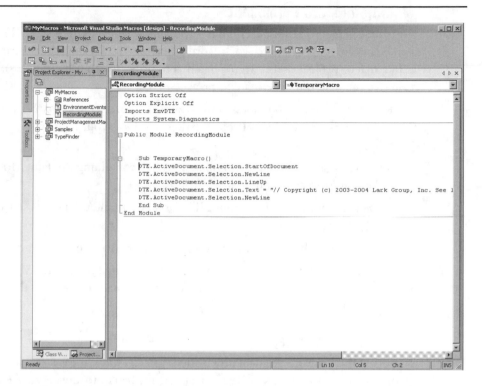

Here (slightly reformatted) is the code that the Macro Recorder produced for the copyright macro:

```
Sub TemporaryMacro()
DTE.ActiveDocument.Selection.StartOfDocument
DTE.ActiveDocument.Selection.NewLine
DTE.ActiveDocument.Selection.LineUp
DTE.ActiveDocument.Selection.Text = _
  "// Copyright (c) 2003-2004 Lark Group, Inc. " & _
  "See license.txt for licensing details."
DTE.ActiveDocument.Selection.NewLine
End Sub
```

As you can see, VS .NET macros are written in VB .NET (even if they're recorded in a C# project). The DTE (design-time environment) object is the root of an object model that encompasses the entire VS .NET IDE. This object model is far too complex to explain in detail here, but you'll find it documented in the VS .NET help files (look for the "Common Environment Object Model" section of the documentation).

Making a Macro Permanent

Of course, a macro is most useful if it's available whenever you need it. The temporary macro will be overwritten whenever you record a new macro. To keep the macro, you'll want to save it in a macro project of its own (or in a macro project with other macros). Follow these steps to move the macro to a permanent project:

1. Right-click on the root node in the Macro Explorer, and select New Macro Project. This will open the New Macro Project dialog box. Give your new project a name and save it in a convenient spot.

2. The previous step creates a new macro project containing a default Module1. Double-click on Module1 to open it in the Macro IDE.

3. Paste the macro into the module. This is a good time to give it a sensible name, such as AddCopyrightComment.

4. Click the Save button on the Macro IDE toolbar to save the changes.

Your new macro project will now be loaded every time you launch VS .NET. If you want to stop this automatic loading, you can right-click the macro project in the Macro Explorer and select Unload Macro Project.

Macros from the Keyboard

Now that the macro is permanently loaded, you can make it easy to run by binding it to a key-stroke combination. VS .NET lets you attach any macro to any keystroke through its Options dialog box. Follow these steps to bind the macro to a key combination:

1. Select Tools ➢ Options

2. In the Options dialog box, open the Environment folder and select the Keyboard node.

3. Scroll down the list of commands until you find the macro that you just saved. It will be located at Macros.MacroProjectName.ModuleName.MacroName.

4. Place the cursor in the Press Shortcut Keys box and press the key combination that you want to assign to the macro—for example, Ctrl+Shift+3. VS .NET will warn you if the key combination is already in use.

5. Click OK to make the assignment.

Now you can add the copyright comment to a new module with the press of a few keys.

NOTE   There's a lot more to know about macros, especially the details of the DTE object model (which is also used by add-ins, discussed in the next section of this chapter). An excellent reference is *Inside Microsoft Visual Studio .NET* (Microsoft Press, 2002), by Brian Johnson, Craig Skibo, and Marc Young.

Choosing Add-Ins

VS .NET was designed from the start to be extensible, and many utility vendors have taken advantage of this extensibility. In the remainder of this chapter, I'll look at a selection of ways to make your time writing code with VS .NET more productive (or more fun), and to improve the quality of the code that you write in this environment. This isn't intended to be a comprehensive survey by any means. I'm going to single out some add-ins that I've used myself and that show the range of capabilities that an add-in can bring to VS .NET.

> **NOTE** This chapter includes information on some general-purpose add-ins. You'll also find more specific add-in coverage in other chapters. For instance, I talk about NUnitAddin in Chapter 5, "Preventing Bugs with Unit Testing," and the CodeSmith add-in in Chapter 8, "Generating Code."

Some Simple Examples

Some add-ins exist that let you add a single missing function to the VS .NET IDE. For example, suppose you want to know how many lines of code you're written in your project. You could open up each code module separately, use Ctrl+End to get to the last line, note the line counter in the VS .NET status bar, and add up all the individual numbers using a spreadsheet—or you could download and install the free Project Line Counter add-in from WndTabs (www.wndtabs.com/plc/). This add-in has the simplest interface possible: a single toolbar containing a single button. Load your project, click the button, and you'll see a report similar to the one in Figure 6.6.

FIGURE 6.6
Project Line Counter

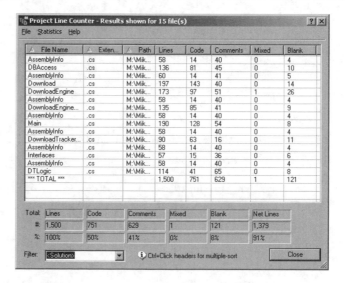

Of course, developers can seldom stop at a single feature, and the developer of Project Line Counter is no exception. In addition to displaying information on your project, this add-in lets you filter the report to show only information from a single project in your solution, or to export the report to a comma-separated value (CSV) or XML file for further analysis.

The sharp-eyed reader will notice that Figure 6.6 contains all of the various projects that make up Download Tracker, including all of the different code layers and the test projects. To make it easier to work on Download Tracker without having multiple instances of VS .NET open, I created an empty VS .NET solution and then added all of the individual projects to this solution.

Before moving on, it's worth taking a moment to think about when it's useful to know the number of lines of code in a project. Lines of code, sometimes referred to as LOC, is one of the earliest metrics developed for managing software projects. Over the past several decades, LOC has been largely discredited as a useful measure, for two reasons. The first problem is the explosion in computer languages. A single line of code in one language might be equivalent to hundreds of lines of code in another language. For example, writing code in C++ is often more verbose than writing the same code in VB, even when the functionality is identical. Second, even within a language different coders can use different numbers of lines of code for the same expression. Consider this snippet of code from `Download.cs`:

```
public string ProductName
{
    get
    {
        return _ProductName;
    }
    set
    {
        _ProductName = value;
    }
}
```

This code would work just as well written like this:

```
public string ProductName {
    get    {
        return _ProductName; }
    set    {
        _ProductName = value;    }
}
```

So, is it 11 lines of code or 6?

But the fact that LOC varies between languages and developers doesn't make it perfectly use-less. If you compare LOC between your own projects written in the same language, it's a reasonable way to confirm your own sense of which project is larger and which modules have involved the most effort. Keeping an eye on the relative percentage of comment and blank lines can also help you pick out modules that are underdocumented (or overdocumented, though that's much rarer).

Another simple and free add-in is QuickJump.NET (`www.codeproject.com/dotnet/ quickjump_net.asp`). With this little tool involved, you can click Alt+G and get a window showing all of the members in the current class. Type a few letters to filter the list, and you can jump right to the applicable declaration. Figure 6.7 shows this add-in in action.

FIGURE 6.7
QuickJump.NET

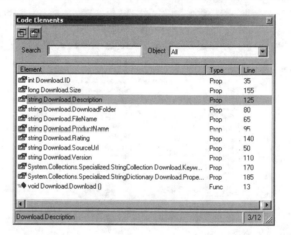

QuickJump.NET illustrates another reason for installing an add-in: Sometimes functionality is already present in VS .NET, but it doesn't work the way you would prefer. If you want to find a particular member in the current class, you can select it from the Members drop-down list at the top of the code editor. Alternatively, you can enter incremental search mode by pressing Ctrl+I and then typing the start of the member you're looking for until the search highlight finds it (press Enter to exit from incremental search mode). For a third alternative, you could open the Class View window and expand the tree to find the member that you want, and then double-click it. However, some people prefer the convenience of a list of members in a separate window, and for those people this add-in exists.

Navigating and Analyzing Your Code

VS .NET is a good platform for writing code, but sometimes it leaves a bit to be desired when it comes to managing large projects. For example, suppose you want to know where you've used a particular property. This is essential knowledge when you're thinking about changing the property's data type. You could just make the change and then build the project to see what breaks. But a better solution (at least for Visual Basic .NET and C# projects) is Total .NET XRef from FMS (`www.fmsinc.com/dotnet/xref/index.asp`). At $199, this tool keeps track of the structure of your projects. Place your cursor in any identifier, click the XRef button, and you'll get a window listing every place that identifier is used. You can see files, classes, lines, members, and even a preview of the usage. A single click takes you to the definition of the object, or you can double-click to see any usage line. Besides making it easy to navigate to everywhere that a member is used, Total .NET XRef, shown in Figure 6.8, is a good tool for quick-and-dirty impact analysis.

FIGURE 6.8
Total .NET XRef

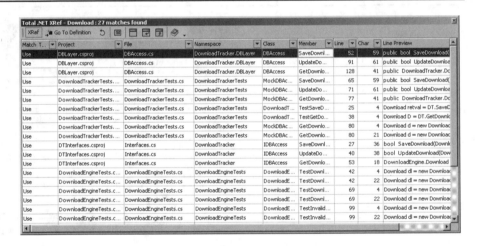

Speaking of FMS, you might also check out Total .NET Analyzer (`www.fmsinc.com/dotnet/Analyzer`). This $499 add-in leverages the same parser as Total .NET XRef to look over your code and warn you about deviations from best practices and likely errors. These range from using string concatenation where a StringBuilder would be a better choice, to unused code, to performance issues, to violations of generally accepted naming standards. All of the recommendations show up in a dockable window (shown in Figure 6.9), and you can click on any of them to go right to the line of code that the tool doesn't like. You can also customize the rules list to a certain extent, though there's no way to add your own rules to the product.

NOTE   Another tool that can help check the quality of your source code is FxCop, a stand-alone utility from Microsoft. I'll talk about FxCop in Chapter 7, "Digging into Source Code."

FIGURE 6.9
Total .NET Analyzer

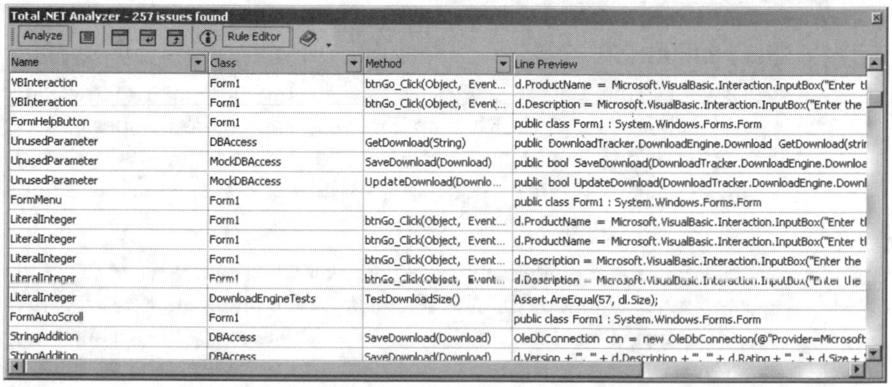

The Total .NET products (as well as other add-ins from other vendors) take advantage of a key feature of the DTE object model for add-ins. The add-in has access to every bit of code that you have loaded into a project. This makes it easy to catalog, cross-reference, analyze, or even modify code from an add-in.

Comparing Figure 6.6 with Figure 6.9, you'll see that Total .NET Analyzer found 257 issues in 1500 lines of code. Isn't that rather a lot? No, not really. I ran Analyzer with all of its rules turned on, including style rules (such as using camel case for variables) that I don't personally agree with. Also, there's a limit to how much intelligence you can build into this sort of static code analysis. For example, the tool properly suggests replacing literal strings with constants or resources as a general rule. But this rule fires multiple times when I build a Structured Query Language (SQL) statement using code like this:

```
cmd.CommandText = "INSERT INTO [Downloads]([ProductName], " +
    "[FileName], [DownloadDate], [Version], [Description], " +
    "[Rating], [Size])" +
    " VALUES('" + d.ProductName + "', '" + d.FileName +
    "', #" + DateTime.Now.ToShortDateString() + "#, '" +
    d.Version + "', '" + d.Description + "', '" +
    d.Rating + "', " + d.Size + ")";
```

There's not a lot of point to using string constants for strings that are used only once or to using resources for SQL strings (which, by definition, are never localized). Perhaps someday code analysis tools will be available that don't require thought on the part of the developer, but I haven't seen them yet.

TECHNOLOGY TRAP

The Ten-Ton IDE

Obviously, there are lots of VS .NET add-ins out there, at a variety of prices and with a variety of functionality. VS .NET has no particular limit on the number of add-ins that you can have loaded at one time. Many developers are a lot like magpies. We tend to collect every shiny thing that comes our way. Do this with .NET add-ins, and you may someday end up with a copy of VS .NET that has 30 or 40 add-ins installed.

If (like me) you're one of the developers with that tendency, try to restrain yourself. Having too many add-ins loaded at once can cause some problems with VS .NET. Chief among these is that startup time gets longer and the memory taken by the IDE increases, which can hurt your overall system performance. Paradoxically, too many laborsaving devices can make more work for you if you have to wait for the IDE to catch up. Also, the more add-ins you load, the greater the chance that they'll conflict in the shortcut keys they assign to various functions, at which point it becomes difficult to know which key will do what.

The best solution to this problem is to develop an explicit process for evaluating add-ins. Rather than installing an add-in and then just forgetting about it, install the add-in and set a reasonable period of time (a week works well for me) to evaluate it. Put a reminder in your Outlook tasks to make sure you remember when the week is up. Then think back over the past week and then decide whether the add-in really saved you time, made your code better, or had other benefits. If not, then uninstall it rather than just letting it sit there unused.

Switching Editors

VS .NET add-ins can have much more radical effects than just adding a new toolbar or window. For example, they can completely replace the built-in editors. Here are two products that do just that.

CodeWright for VS .NET (www.codewright.com/cwnet/default.asp) merges the Code-Wright programmer's editor directly into the VS .NET IDE. This lets you use CodeWright's keystrokes and color syntax (among other features) in your .NET source files, as well as making all of CodeWright's other high-end features (like the CodeMeeting chat window, which lets you edit documents collaboratively) available within the .NET interface. Especially if you're already a CodeWright user, spending $149 for this product will likely boost your productivity in VS .NET substantially. While the native VS .NET editor is good, it doesn't have the depth of keyboard tools and shortcut customization of a real top-end programmer's editor.

For XML files, you can get a similar plethora of tools by spending $999 for XMLSPY Enterprise Edition (www.altova.com) and then downloading the free package to integrate it with .NET. No more will you have the basic Microsoft XML-editing user interface for XML files in your .NET solution. Instead, XMLSPY's multiple views, debugging capabilities, and flexible interface will take over XML-editing duties. Given the cost, this probably makes sense only if editing XML is a frequent task for you, but if it is, this is a great way to merge two best-of-breed tools.

The Big Boys

Some add-ins are so all-encompassing that it almost seems silly to refer to them as add-ins. Products in this category include CodeSMART, Rational XDE, and Compuware DevPartner Studio.

CodeSMART 2003 for VS .NET ($189 from `www.axtools.com/index.htm`) is a sort of a Swiss Army knife of add-ins. In contrast to the single-purpose add-ins like Project Line Counter, CodeSMART does many things and does most of them very well.

It's unlikely that any developer will use all the functionality here, but you'll find your own favorites. One of mine is the Code Explorer, shown in Figure 6.10. It's a relatively easy concept to understand: Take the existing Solution Explorer, and tack the Class View functionality on to it. So you can drill from solution to project to class—and then on down into members. Each level maintains all of its existing context menu functionality, and then gains a bit more. For instance, the VS .NET Class View will let you quickly go to the definition of a member; Code Explorer also lets you go to the start or end of the member, or highlight it in code, or add it to the Workbench.

The Workbench is another CodeSMART tool window. It's a collection of nodes pulled off the Code View and kept as a flat list. This is a great way to focus on a subset of your project and to easily jump back and forth among the areas of your code that you're currently interested in.

Then there's the Find Type Reference facility, which helps you see where a particular type is used anywhere in your code; think of it as cross-reference on-the-fly. There are some other find and replace extensions as well, including the ability to search through all the files in your solution with one click (which Microsoft inexplicably left out of VS .NET).

CodeSMART also includes a number of code builders that range from simple (inserting a property with a particular name and return type, or inserting error trapping) to complex (implementing an entire interface). For other code construction tasks, CodeSMART includes an AutoText tool that can expand a few letters into an entire code snippet. There's also a sort of code repository to manage other chunks of code.

Code reformatting is another strength of CodeSMART. You can sort procedures in a class by type or name, split and otherwise automatically reformat lines, and even manage XML comments in VB .NET applications. CodeSMART includes a dialog box that lets you set the Name and Text properties of any control when you create the control, tasks you've probably done a million times in the Properties window by now.

FIGURE 6.10
CodeSMART Code
Explorer

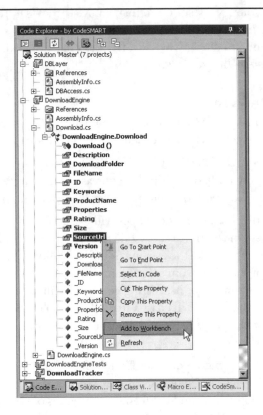

Even more ambitious is Rational XDE (more formally IBM Rational XDE Developer .NET Edition v2003.06). XDE makes the development environment even more complex by bringing modeling into the picture. With XDE installed, you continue to develop software inside the VS .NET shell. But now, in addition to writing code, you can design code with Unified Modeling Language (UML) diagrams (or with more abstract models, for that matter).

Key to making all this work is forward and reverse engineering support, as well as model-to-code synchronization. What that means is that you can make a change to your code, and XDE will update your model—or vice versa. If you've already got a project full of code, bringing it into the XDE world is as simple as loading your project and telling it to generate the model. Databases, too, can be engineered in both directions. Figure 6.11 shows a UML diagram of some of the Download Tracker classes, generated by XDE, together with the XDE Model Explorer and some of the options that it offers for building models.

XDE also supports repositories of patterns, so you can create reusable software assets and share them across your enterprise. It also supports runtime for trace sequence diagrams. Basically, you tell it that you want it to graphically monitor what's going on, and XDE builds a sequence diagram as the classes in your application interact in real time. It's cool to watch this process in action as your classes talk to one another. The sequence diagrams can be filtered easily to let you concentrate on the interactions you're interested in, making them a good debugging tool as well as a documentation tool.

NOTE   For more information on UML and patterns, see Chapter 2, "Organizing Your Project."

All this power comes at a cost in both complexity and money. You'll need to know the basics of UML before trying to use XDE, and you need to allow ample time to come up the product's learning curve (there's extensive documentation to help with that). As for the money, a single-user license with a year of support will set you back about $3500, putting it out of the range of projects like Download Tracker. But it's good to know about the high-end tools if you're in a setting where such things make sense on a corporate level.

FIGURE 6.11
UML model generated
by Rational XDE

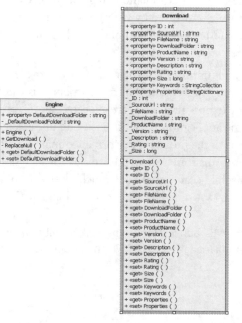
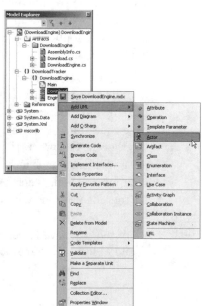

While XDE is directed at the architect, DevPartner Studio is aimed squarely at the developer. For $1495, it adds a number of high-end debugging and tuning capabilities to VS .NET. For starters, there's the Code Review facility. This is a rules-driven engine designed to help you locate dangerous parts of your code before they break down. It's something like Total .NET XRef, only with enhanced capabilities. In addition to warning you about dangerous code (and offering suggestions for fixes), it will also help you enforce naming conventions and calculate complexity for your methods. You can also edit and customize the rules used for the analysis, filter the results, and suppress rules in a given project.

DevPartner also contains an error-detection feature, which lets you run your application while DevPartner keeps an eye on the internals. This feature can detect COM API errors and memory leaks, deadlocks and unsafe threading code, and problems with dispose and finalize, among other issues.

DevPartner's code coverage analysis capabilities help you make sure that you're testing all of the code that you write. Like most of DevPartner's features, this one is pretty unobtrusive. Turn it on, run your application as you normally would, and exit the application. You'll get a code analysis report that shows which methods were called, what percent of lines of code were executed, and so on. Double-click a method and you get a color-coded view of the code showing exactly what was (and wasn't) exercised by your tests. Even better, if you're dealing with a distributed application, you can perform a joint and simultaneous code coverage analysis of both client and server pieces.

Runtime memory analysis and runtime performance analysis provide you with two other ways to track what's going on in a running application. The memory analysis will show you which methods used the most memory, where temporary objects are allocated, and so on. You can also force a garbage collection (GC) while the application is running—useful in cases in which you're not sure whether the GC process is part of the problem. Performance analysis will get you execution times, call graphs, and much more information. Both of these modes of analysis offer flexible ways to view their information, which is useful because there's so much information. Figure 6.12 shows a DevPartner memory analysis of the Download Tracker application in action.

NOTE   For the definitive list of VS .NET add-ins (and other .NET utilities), visit the SharpToolbox site at `http://sharptoolbox.madgeek.com/`, which is approaching 350 listed tools as I write this.

IDE Checklist

After a few years of working with code editors and drag-and-drop design tools, it's easy to just start using VS .NET without exploring it in any depth. But between the complexity and extensibility of the IDE, it's worth spending some time to see if you can make the development environment better for you. Consider these points:

- Select a profile that makes sense to you. I recommend the VS .NET default profile.
- Review the Tools ➤ Options settings to customize the IDE.
- Check out the VS .NET PowerToys for additional customization.
- Learn how to record and use VS .NET macros.
- As you have time and funds, test the various VS .NET add-ins to see which ones save you time or improve the quality of your code.

So far I've been talking as if you're going to write all of the code in your project yourself. But in the .NET world, that's never the case. Not only are there thousands of lines of code in the .NET Framework, there is a wide variety of reusable source code available for free. In the next chapter, I'll discuss some of the things that you can do to effectively use other people's code in your own projects.

FIGURE 6.12
Analyzing memory usage with DevPartner Studio

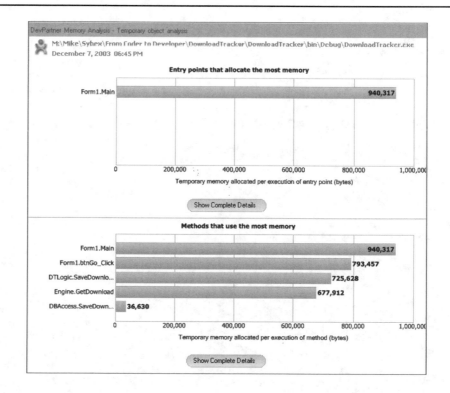

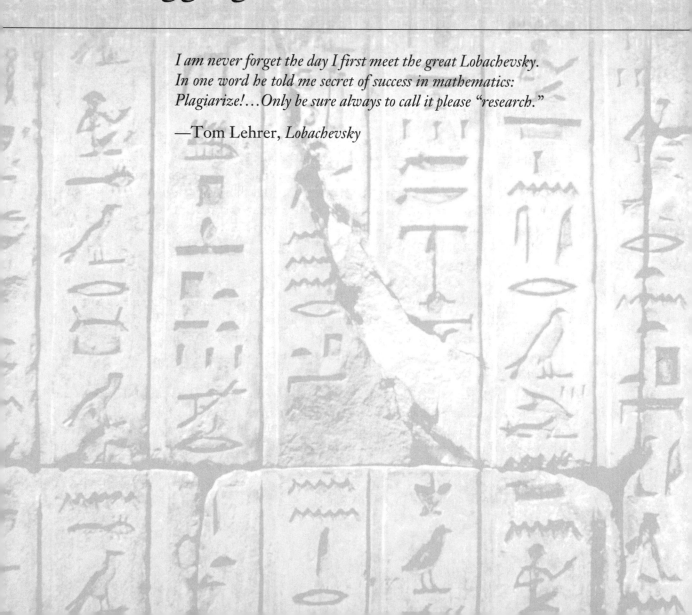

CHAPTER 7

Digging Into Source Code

*I am never forget the day I first meet the great Lobachevsky.
In one word he told me secret of success in mathematics:
Plagiarize!…Only be sure always to call it please "research."*

—Tom Lehrer, *Lobachevsky*

In software development, of course, we don't call it *plagiarism* or *research*, but finding reusable source code is an important technique because it increases our efficiency by relieving us of the need to "reinvent the wheel." That's one of the topics that I'll be discussing in this chapter. But before I look at sources of code that you can use in your own projects, I want to show you how to look more deeply at the code that you already have on your computer, by using a variety of spelunking utilities. Seeing how someone else (perhaps a member of Microsoft's .NET development team) solved a problem may be the fastest way to solve a similar problem yourself.

NOTE   One thing to keep in mind is that you should be sure you have the rights to reuse code before you actually do so. Just as you will probably apply license terms to your own code to spell out what others can do with it, you must respect the licensing terms of code owned by others. (I'll talk more about licensing in Chapter 14, "Protecting Your Intellectual Property.") If you're not sure that you can legally reuse code, don't do it.

Spelunking Utilities

One of the interesting things about the .NET Framework is that .NET code is very open. That is, even if you don't have the original source code for a library or an application, you can find out quite a bit about that source code. This can come in handy when you have a question about how something works. In the first part of this chapter, I'll show you a variety of ways to go exploring inside .NET code that's already on your computer. Later on in the chapter, I'll discuss some of the things that software publishers can do to make it harder to explore within their code; *obfuscation* can be an important tool in protecting intellectual property.

Ildasm

As you probably already know, all .NET code is executed by the Common Language Runtime (CLR). The CLR doesn't understand anything about the plethora of .NET languages—Visual Basic .NET (VB.NET), C#, managed C++, and so on. Rather, each of those languages is compiled into a single unified format named Microsoft Intermediate Language (MSIL). The CLR, in turn, can execute MSIL code.

The .NET Framework SDK includes several utilities that let you work with MSIL code. One of these, Ildasm, is a disassembler for MSIL code. That is, it can take a file full of MSIL and turn it into something at least moderately human readable. I'll demonstrate Ildasm by looking at one of the Download Tracker components. Here is a part of the source code for DBAccess.cs, in the DBLayer component of Download Tracker:

```
/// <summary>
///      Save a download in the database
```

```csharp
/// </summary>
/// <param name="d" type="DownloadTracker.DownloadEngine.Download">
///     <para>
///         Information on the download
///     </para>
/// </param>
/// <returns>
///     True on success, false on failure
/// </returns>
public bool SaveDownload(DownloadTracker.DownloadEngine.Download d)
{
    OleDbConnection cnn = new OleDbConnection(
     @"Provider=Microsoft.Jet.OLEDB.4.0; Data Source=" +
     this.DatabaseLocation);
    OleDbCommand cmd = cnn.CreateCommand();
    try
    {
        cmd.CommandType = CommandType.Text;
        cmd.CommandText = "INSERT INTO [Downloads]([ProductName], " +
         [FileName], [DownloadDate], [Version], [Description], " +
         [Rating], [Size])" +
         " VALUES('" + d.ProductName + "', '" + d.FileName +
         "', #" + DateTime.Now.ToShortDateString() + "#, '" +
         d.Version + "', '" + d.Description + "', '" + d.Rating +
         "', " + d.Size + ")";
        cnn.Open();
        cmd.ExecuteNonQuery();
        // Retrieve the new autonumber value into the download object
        cmd.CommandText = "SELECT @@IDENTITY";
        d.ID = (int)cmd.ExecuteScalar();
        return true;
    }
    catch (Exception e)
    {
        return false;
    }
    finally
    {
        if(cnn.State == ConnectionState.Open)
            cnn.Close();
    }
}

/// <summary>
///     Update a download in the database
/// </summary>
```

```
/// <param name="d" type="DownloadTracker.DownloadEngine.Download">
///     <para>
///         The download whose information is to be uploaded.
➥ The Download.ID property must be supplied.
///     </para>
/// </param>
/// <returns>
///     True on success, false on failure
/// </returns>
public bool UpdateDownload(DownloadTracker.DownloadEngine.Download d)
{
    OleDbConnection cnn = new OleDbConnection(
    @"Provider=Microsoft.Jet.OLEDB.4.0; Data Source=" +
    this.DatabaseLocation);
    OleDbCommand cmd = cnn.CreateCommand();
    try
    {
        cmd.CommandType = CommandType.Text;
        cmd.CommandText = "UPDATE [Downloads] SET [ProductName] = '" +
        d.ProductName + "', " +
            "[FileName] = '" + d.FileName + "', [Version] = '" + d.Version +
            "', [Description] = '" + d.Description + "', [Rating] = '" +
➥d.Rating +
            "', [Size] = " + d.Size + " WHERE [DownloadID] = " + d.ID;
        cnn.Open();
        cmd.ExecuteNonQuery();
        return true;
    }
    catch (Exception e)
    {
        return false;
    }
    finally
    {
        if(cnn.State == ConnectionState.Open)
            cnn.Close();
    }
}
```

To use Ildasm, select Start ➢ Programs ➢ Microsoft Visual Studio .NET 2003 ➢ Visual Studio .NET Tools ➢ Visual Studio .NET Command Prompt. This will open a command prompt with the environment variables and path set up to run .NET utilities. Type **ildasm** at the command prompt and press Enter to open the Ildasm window. Select File ➢ Open, browse to the DBLayer.dll file, and click Open. This will disassemble the MSIL file to a tree view. Figure 7.1 shows Ildasm with all of the tree view nodes expanded.

FIGURE 7.1
A .NET file in Ildasm

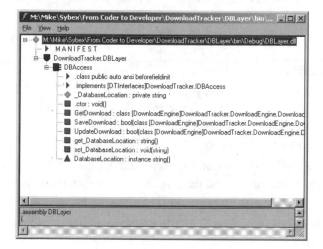

Each of the nodes in the Ildasm tree represents a particular piece of the source code—the constructor, methods, properties, and so on. Double-clicking any of the nodes without children will open a separate window that displays the relevant portion of the MSIL. Figure 7.2 shows the disassembly window for the SaveDownload method.

If you inspect the disassembly, you'll find that it includes all of the literal strings (though not comments) and objects from the original source code. In fact, it also includes all of the logic from the source code, though it can take some deciphering to figure out what's going on.

FIGURE 7.2
Disassembling a method with Ildasm

```
DBAccess::SaveDownload : bool(class [DownloadEngine]DownloadTracker.DownloadEngine.Download)
.method public hidebysig newslot virtual final
        instance bool  SaveDownload(class [DownloadEngine]DownloadTracker.DownloadEngine.
{
  // Code size       288 (0x120)
  .maxstack  5
  .locals init ([0] class [System.Data]System.Data.OleDb.OleDbConnection cnn,
           [1] class [System.Data]System.Data.OleDb.OleDbCommand cmd,
           [2] class [mscorlib]System.Exception e,
           [3] bool CS$00000003$00000000,
           [4] object[] CS$00000002$00000001,
           [5] valuetype [mscorlib]System.DateTime CS$00000002$00000002)
  IL_0000:  ldstr      "Provider=Microsoft.Jet.OLEDB.4.0; Data Source="
  IL_0005:  ldarg.0
  IL_0006:  call       instance string DownloadTracker.DBLayer.DBAccess::get_DatabaseLoca
  IL_000b:  call       string [mscorlib]System.String::Concat(string,
                                                              string)
  IL_0010:  newobj     instance void [System.Data]System.Data.OleDb.OleDbConnection::.cto
  IL_0015:  stloc.0
  IL_0016:  ldloc.0
  IL_0017:  callvirt   instance class [System.Data]System.Data.OleDb.OleDbCommand [System
  IL_001c:  stloc.1
  .try
  {
```

For most developers, Ildasm is mostly useful as a demonstration of the open nature of .NET code. But there are easier alternatives to learning MSIL if you just want to figure out what a class does or how it works.

Reflector

With enough practice, you could learn to translate MSIL to the original C# code. But why bother? That's the sort of routine task for which computers are well suited. Lutz Roeder's free Reflector for .NET (www.aisto.com/roeder/dotnet/) can take a .NET assembly and show you the source code that created the assembly.

Figure 7.3 shows Reflector with the DBLayer.dll file loaded. On the left you can see a tree view of the classes and members included in the file. On the right, Reflector is displaying the source code for the SaveDownload method, which it automatically decompiled for me.

Reflector has a bunch of other features to help you find your way around a .NET library: It can disassemble to MSIL as well as decompile to C# or VB.NET, it will show you call trees for a method, and it has flexible search features that let you quickly find classes and members of interest. Here is Reflector's version of SaveDownload. Although it differs from the original source that you saw earlier in the chapter, it's pretty easy to tell what's going on here, without needing to learn the details of MSIL.

FIGURE 7.3
Exploring with Reflector

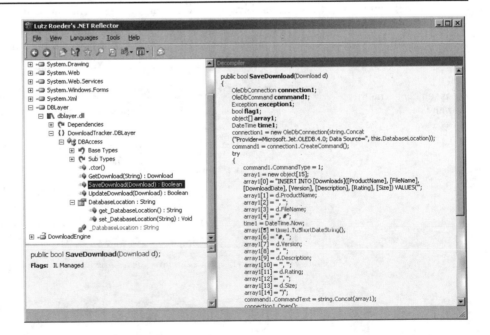

```
public bool SaveDownload(Download d)
{
    OleDbConnection connection1;
    OleDbCommand command1;
    Exception exception1;
    bool flag1;
    object[] array1;
    DateTime time1;
    connection1 = new OleDbConnection(string.Concat(
➥"Provider=Microsoft.Jet.OLEDB.4.0; Data Source=",
➥this.DatabaseLocation)));
    command1 = connection1.CreateCommand();
    try
    {
        command1.CommandType = 1;
        array1 = new object[15];
        array1[0] = "INSERT INTO [Downloads]([ProductName],
➥[FileName], [DownloadDate], [Version], [Description],
➥[Rating], [Size]) VALUES('";
        array1[1] = d.ProductName;
        array1[2] = "', '";
        array1[3] = d.FileName;
        array1[4] = "', #";
        time1 = DateTime.Now;
        array1[5] = time1.ToShortDateString();
        array1[6] = "#, '";
        array1[7] = d.Version;
        array1[8] = "', '";
        array1[9] = d.Description;
        array1[10] = "', '";
        array1[11] = d.Rating;
        array1[12] = "', ";
        array1[13] = d.Size;
        array1[14] = ")";
        command1.CommandText = string.Concat(array1);
        connection1.Open();
        command1.ExecuteNonQuery();
        command1.CommandText = "SELECT @@IDENTITY";
        d.ID = ((int) command1.ExecuteScalar());
        flag1 = true;

    }
    catch (Exception exception2)
    {
        exception1 = exception2;
        flag1 = false;
    }
```

```
        finally
        {
            if (connection1.State == 1)
            {
                connection1.Close();
            }
        }
        return flag1;
    }
```

You can do a lot more with Reflector than just look at your own source code, however. It's a great tool for answering questions about how the .NET Framework functions, and to help you write better code in your own classes. For instance, consider the tail end of the SaveDownload method:

```
    finally
    {
        if(cnn.State == ConnectionState.Open)
            cnn.Close();
    }
```

The intent here should be obvious: If the connection is open at the end of the method, close it. But as you may know, there's a second way to finish using an object: the Dispose method. The Dispose method takes a single Boolean parameter. If the parameter is True, then it releases unmanaged resources as well as managed resources. Depending on what your application is doing, this might be critical, because unmanaged resources will hang around until the garbage-collection process decides to destroy the object. If those resources are scarce, this might cause problems for your application, or for the rest of your system.

But the .NET Framework help is maddeningly nonspecific about whether the OleDbCommand.Dispose method actually has any unmanaged resources to dispose of. So, should I call Close, or Dispose, or both, when I'm done with a connection? Rather than speculating or guessing, I can use Reflector to actually decompile the relevant parts of the .NET Framework into C# code and find out for sure!

As Figure 7.4 shows, Reflector can drill into the Framework classes just as well as it can into code you write. You may notice that many of the members of the class are shown in lighter type. These are internal or hidden members, and they're not documented. But their decompiled code can make for interesting reading!

Here's the code that Reflector shows for the OleDbConnection.Close method:

```
    public void Close()
    {
        if (this.objectState != 0)
        {
            this.DisposeManaged();
            this.OnStateChange(1, 0);
        }
    }
```

FIGURE 7.4
Reflecting into the
.NET Framework

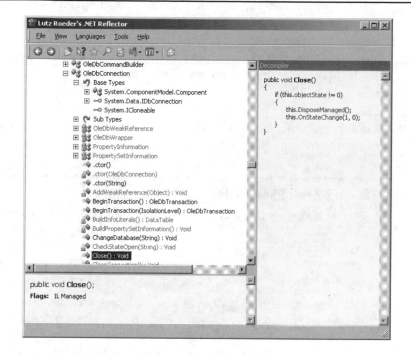

Similarly, I can use Reflector to discover the code for the `Dispose` method:

```
protected override void Dispose(bool disposing)
{
    if (disposing)
    {
        if (this.objectState != 0)
        {
            this.DisposeManaged();
            if (base.DesignMode)
            {
                OleDbConnection.ReleaseObjectPool();
            }
            this.OnStateChange(1, 0);
        }
        if (this.propertyIDSet != null)
        {
            this.propertyIDSet.Dispose();
            this.propertyIDSet = null;
        }
        this._constr = null;
    }
    base.Dispose(disposing);
}
```

It's apparent from this that the Dispose method is doing some work that the Close method is not, so if I want to minimize my application's resource usage, I should call Dispose when I'm done with OleDbConnection objects. But should I call just Dispose, or both Dispose and Close? Well, you'll see that all that Close does is call the DisposeManaged method, which is also called by the Dispose method. So there's no need to call both, and I can just replace the calls to Close with calls to Dispose.

RULE   When you're not sure what part of the .NET Framework does, don't speculate: Look at the source code and find out.

The .NET Arms Race: Reflection vs. Obfuscation

The feature of .NET that allows this sort of deep analysis of .NET code is called *reflection*. If you investigate the System.Reflection namespace, you'll find well-documented APIs to return information on classes and members. Between reflection and MSIL, it's possible to find out quite a bit of information about the structure of a .NET application, even without the source code.

While powerful, this facility can be a problem for the independent software vendor who wants to make a living. Many developers are worried that with all of their source code open for inspection they won't be able to maintain a competitive advantage. To combat this, another group of .NET utilities have grown up: obfuscators. *Obfuscation* is the process of taking source code and automatically changing it to make it harder to understand, before it's compiled.

For example, Visual Studio .NET 2003 includes a version of an obfuscation utility named Dotfuscator. Dotfuscator, among other things, changes the names of all classes and members in your application to arbitrary strings so that they don't give anything away. It also gives the same name to unrelated members, as long as they don't have identical signatures. The free version is somewhat limited, but the manufacturer will also sell you an upgrade to a more robust version. Other obfuscation utilities can even change loops or logical tests so that they have the same effect that they originally did but are harder to decipher.

Quite a few obfuscators are available for .NET applications. These include:

- Demeanor for .NET (www.wiseowl.com/products/Products.aspx)
- Dotfuscator (www.preemptivc.com/dotfuscator/index.html)
- Salamander .NET Obfuscator (www.remotesoft.com/salamander/obfuscator.html)
- Spices .NET (www.9rays.net/cgi-bin/components.cgi?act=1&cid=86)

Only you can decide whether your code is truly earthshaking enough to require obfuscation. If you do want to obfuscate your shipping code, though, you'll need to plan your process carefully. Ideally, you should build an unobfuscated version of your code to test and debug with, and an obfuscated version to ship. Of course, you should also make sure that the obfuscated version passes all of the unit tests, just in case the obfuscation utility does something unexpected.

Keep in mind, though, that obfuscation is only a way to increase the difficulty of understanding your code; it will not prevent a truly determined investigator from figuring out what's going on. Even if you come up with a scheme that encrypts your code on the drive, the code will have to be decrypted to run, and the curious developer could look at the copy in memory instead of the copy on the drive. The bottom line is that any code (.NET or otherwise) that you install on the customer's hard drive is susceptible to reverse engineering with enough effort. If an algorithm is truly top-secret and proprietary, the best bet is not to install it at all. Instead, implement it on your own servers and use a web service or other remote interface to let clients call the algorithm and get back results without ever running the code on their own computers.

I'll look more at obfuscators in Chapter 14, "Protecting Your Intellectual Property."

Experimenting with New Code

While looking at source code is a useful way to see how something works, there are times when you really need to run the code for a complete understanding. But writing a complete Visual Studio .NET solution to test the behavior of a single component is a lot of work. When you're just exploring, it's useful to have some tools that let you instantiate a new component and explore its behavior without a lot of overhead. I'll show you a pair of these tools in this section.

nogoop .NET Component Inspector

One of the best tools I've found for this is the nogoop .NET Component Inspector ($19.95 from www.nogoop.com/product_1.html). You might think of .NET Component Inspector as a generalized test bench for all sorts of .NET components and classes. By using this utility, you can find out what a new bit of code does without the bother of writing a dedicated test application.

Figure 7.5 shows the .NET Component Inspector in action. In this case, I've decided to investigate the SqlConnection object. The steps for doing so were easy:

1. Right-click the System.Data assembly on the GAC tab and select Open. This loads the namespace information for the particular assembly.

2. Drill down in the Assemblies/Types tree to locate the SqlConnection object. The object is shown in boldface to indicate that it's creatable. I dragged SqlConnection to the Objects pane to create a new instance of the object.

3. Right-click on the object and select Event Logging to log its events.

4. Click in the ConnectionString property. The Parameters window shows me that this property requires a string, so I type in the string and click Set Prop.

5. Click in the Open method. Then click the Invoke Method button in the Parameters window. This actually calls the Open method on a live copy of the object, and the property values and Event Log tab get automatically updated.

As you can see, the .NET Component Inspector also has a Control Design Surface pane. That's because it also lets you test .NET controls in either design mode or run mode. Figure 7.6 shows an instance of the Windows.Forms.ProgressBar control being tested in the .NET Component Inspector framework.

Snippet Compiler

Another useful tool for exploratory development is the free Snippet Compiler (www.sliver .com/dotnet/SnippetCompiler/). Unlike .NET Component Inspector, Snippet Compiler works by letting you write code to exercise a new component—but it does so with a minimum of overhead. When you install Snippet Compiler, it will locate an icon in the tray area of your Windows Taskbar. Double-click the icon to open the minimal integrated development environment (IDE) shown in Figure 7.7.

FIGURE 7.5
Using nogoop .NET Component Inspector

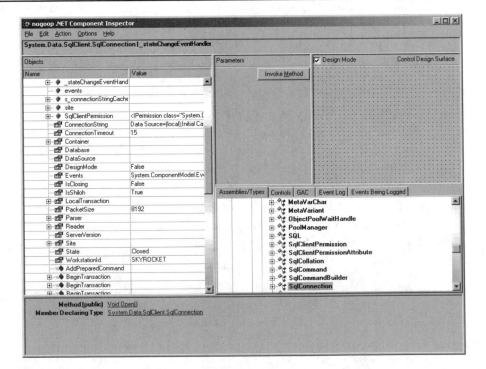

FIGURE 7.6
Testing a control

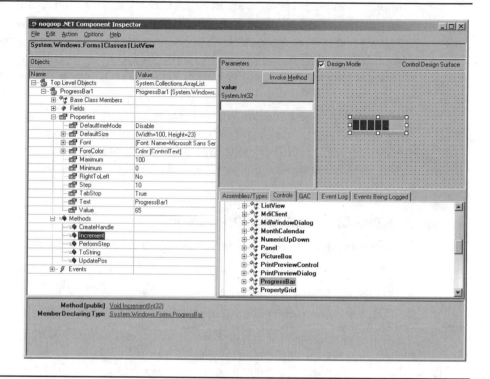

FIGURE 7.7
Snippet Compiler

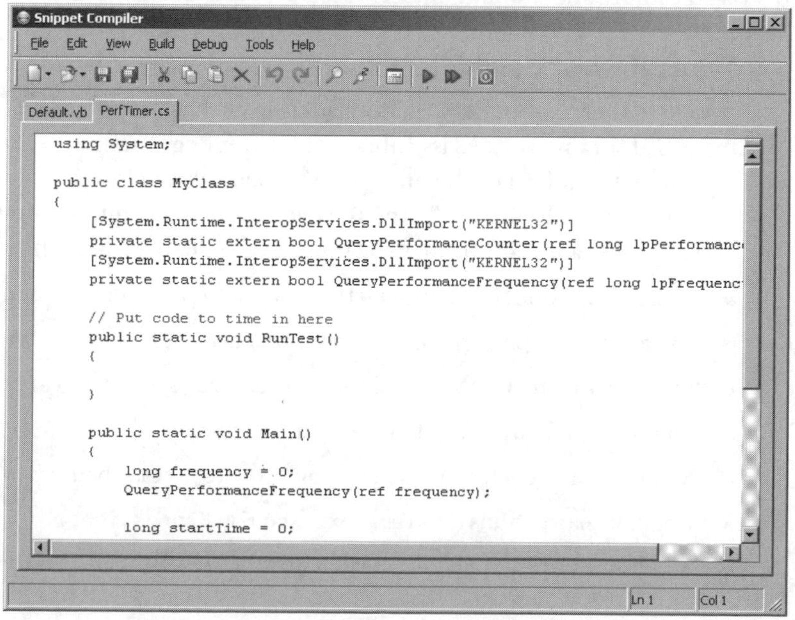

```
using System;

public class MyClass
{
    [System.Runtime.InteropServices.DllImport("KERNEL32")]
    private static extern bool QueryPerformanceCounter(ref long lpPerformance
    [System.Runtime.InteropServices.DllImport("KERNEL32")]
    private static extern bool QueryPerformanceFrequency(ref long lpFrequenc

    // Put code to time in here
    public static void RunTest()
    {

    }

    public static void Main()
    {
        long frequency = 0;
        QueryPerformanceFrequency(ref frequency);

        long startTime = 0;
```

Snippet Compiler lets you work in either C# or VB.NET, and it can handle console, Windows Forms, or ASP.NET snippets. It's got a reasonable selection of IDE features (like marking errors and color-coding), and it lets you get code up and running quickly. You wouldn't want to try to build an entire project with this tool, but for those times when you want to answer a simple question about how some code works, it's the perfect complement to a more full-featured IDE like Visual Studio .NET.

By using Ildasm or Reflector to inspect source code and .NET Component Inspector or Snippet Compiler to investigate the behavior of a control or component, you can easily evaluate new pieces of code that you're thinking of incorporating into your applications—whether they're supplied in source code form or as compiled components.

Sources of Reusable Source Code

For too many developers, the process of creating a new application goes something like this:

1. Figure out what you're going to build.

2. Figure out what the major components of the project are.

4. Pick one component, jump in, and start writing code.

You'll notice I left out step 3, and that's no accident. Before you start writing code for a new project, you should think about (and look for) all of the code that you *don't* have to write. For a .NET application, that might amount to quite a bit of code. If you know where to look, there is an astonishing amount of free, reusable, high-quality .NET code out there.

The Framework and Friends

The first source of reusable code is as close as the computer where you have .NET installed: the .NET Framework Class Library (FCL). A huge amount of functionality is already packaged in the hundred or so namespaces, thousands of classes, and hundreds of thousands of members of the FCL. You'll find the code for many common programming tasks in the FCL. Here are just a few of the many features available, together with their namespaces:

- Hashtables, queues, stacks, dictionaries, and other data structures (`System.Collections`)
- Event log and performance counter creation, reading, and writing (`System.Diagnostics`)
- Support for the COM+ services architecture (`System.EnterpriseServices`)
- Support for Windows Management Instrumentation (WMI) (`System.Management`)
- Symmetric and asymmetric cryptography (`System.Security.Cryptography`)
- Regular expressions (`System.Text.RegularExpressions`)
- Sending Simple Mail Transfer Protocol (SMTP) mail (`System.Web.Mail`)

- Support for Extensible Markup Language (XML), XPath, Extensible Stylesheet Language Transformations (XSLT), XML Schema Definition (XSD), and other XML standards (`System.XML`)

If you've never taken the time to sit down with the FCL documentation, you really ought to do so. I've seen developers waste a great deal of time writing code to perform functions that are already covered by the FCL. Not only does this take away from the time and energy you could have invested in your own custom work, but it's unlikely that you'll be able to test your own code under the many diverse circumstances that the FCL has been through.

For an overview of the FCL, you can start online at `http://msdn.microsoft.com/library/en-us/cpref/html/cpref_start.asp`. Unless you've got a speedy Internet connection, though, you'll probably find it easier to browse the documentation locally; it's installed when you install the .NET Framework Software Development Kit (SDK) or Visual Studio .NET. I recommend at least reading the top-level topic for each namespace. That will show you all of the classes in the FCL; when you can use one, with any luck you'll remember its existence.

If you prefer written documentation, a number of books have been published that try to provide an overview of the FCL. One good reference is *C# in a Nutshell*, by Peter Drayton, Ben Albahari, and Ted Neward (O'Reilly, 2003).

If the FCL doesn't contain the code that you need, check out some of the other .NET libraries that Microsoft has released. Today's extension might well be a part of tomorrow's Framework. Indeed, the `System.Data.Odbc` and `System.Data.OracleClient` namespaces started as downloadable extensions to version 1.0 of the FCL. Now they're incorporated seamlessly in the 1.1 FCL.

Here are some of Microsoft's other managed code packages:

- The Office Primary Interop Assemblies (PIAs) let you drive Microsoft Office applications from .NET code. For Office XP, you can download the PIAs from `www.microsoft.com/downloads/details.aspx?FamilyId=C41BD61E-3060-4F71-A6B4-01FEBA508E52&displaylang=en`. For Office 2003, the PIAs are part of the retail distribution (though you'll need to do a complete or custom installation, rather than a typical one, for them to end up on your hard drive).

- The SQLXML library (`http://msdn.microsoft.com/sqlxml/`) contains a great deal of add-on XML functionality for Microsoft SQL Server 2000. One of the things you'll find here is a set of .NET classes for directly retrieving SQL Server data as XML from your .NET applications.

- The Web Services Enhancements (WSE) are a set of implementations of web services specifications such as WS-Security, WS-Routing, and WS-Referral. I expect that most of these will show up in future versions of the FCL, but for now you can download the add-on library from `http://msdn.microsoft.com/webservices/building/wse/default.aspx`.

In general, Microsoft is committed to .NET as its development model for the foreseeable future. As Microsoft products are released in the next several years, I expect to see most of them include their own libraries for working with .NET code.

The Microsoft Application Blocks

As I mentioned in Chapter 2, "Organizing Your Project," Microsoft also has an increasingly active Patterns & Practices group. These people are putting out an immense amount of guidance on how to use .NET and other Microsoft products effectively in your own applications. The products of the Patterns & Practices group include a series of *application blocks*—libraries of reusable .NET code for common purposes. The list of application blocks will probably be longer by the time you read this book, but it currently includes these libraries:

- The Aggregation application block, for aggregating and transforming information from multiple sources (`http://msdn.microsoft.com/library/en-us/dnpag/html/ServiceAgg.asp`).

- The Asynchronous Invocation application block, for agent-based asynchronous processing (`http://msdn.microsoft.com/library/en-us/dnpag/html/PAIBlock.asp`).

- The Caching application block, for caching information in distributed applications. Note that for pure ASP.NET applications you should probably use the ASP.NET cache instead (`http://msdn.microsoft.com/library/en-us/dnpag/html/CachingBlock.asp`).

- The Configuration Management application block, for securely reading and writing configuration information from a variety of sources (`http://msdn.microsoft.com/library/en-us/dnbda/html/cmab.asp`).

- The Data Access application block, to simplify ADO.NET data access (`http://msdn.microsoft.com/library/en-us/dnbda/html/daab-rm.asp`).

- The Exception Management application block, which provides an extensible framework for handling exceptions (`http://msdn.microsoft.com/library/en-us/dnbda/html/emab-rm.asp`).

- The Logging application block, to enable distributed and asynchronous logging across an entire application (`http://msdn.microsoft.com/library/en-us/dnpag/html/Logging.asp`). For more details on this particular application block, see Chapter 10, "Logging Application Activity."

- The Updater application block, which provides a "pull model" for updating desktop applications over a network (`http://msdn.microsoft.com/library/en-us/dnbda/html/updater.asp`).

- The User Interface Process application block, a model for writing user interface (UI) and workflow processes as a distinct layer (`http://msdn.microsoft.com/library/en-us/dnbda/html/uip.asp`).

TECHNOLOGY TRAP

The Iceberg of Code

After a look at the list of application blocks, you may be tempted to incorporate most or all of them in your application. If you're writing a small utility or vertical market application, this might well be a mistake. Load in all the thousands of lines of code from the application blocks, and seven-eighths of your application will be Microsoft code, lurking beneath the visible tip of your own work. You can end up spending much of your testing time trying to figure out how all of the application blocks fit together, instead of exercising the code that you're getting paid to write.

When thinking about the application blocks, or other bits of reusable code, you need to keep costs and benefits in mind. You could, for example, incorporate the Logging application block into just about any application. But before you do, figure out what benefits you hope to gain from a distributed, asynchronous logging framework. If you can't think of any benefits, don't incorporate the code. Even if you can think of benefits, you need to balance them against the costs: the time spent to read and understand the documentation for the application block and the effort required to use it from your code.

Logidex .NET Library

With all of the content available on the Patterns & Practices and Microsoft Developers' Network (MSDN) websites, it can be hard to locate the samples that you need for a particular purpose. That's where Logidex .NET Library (`http://lab.msdn.microsoft.com/logiclibrary/logiclibrary.aspx`) can come in handy. Logidex is a commercial Software Development Asset (SDA) management tool. The Logidex .NET Library is a stripped-down version that is made available for free to .NET developers. It works as a Visual Studio .NET add-in, letting you locate and download .NET patterns and sample code from within Visual Studio .NET.

To use Logidex, you start with the main Logidex Explorer window. This window connects over the Internet to the Logidex repository at MSDN (in the commercial version, you can also have local repositories). After connecting, you can go to the Search Result window to search for SDAs. Searching for assets with the string "log*," for example, turns up 176 assets as I'm writing this. Double-clicking an asset retrieves its details to the Information window, as shown in Figure 7.8.

In the Information window, you can read about the asset, and then click over to a list of its artifacts. These might include a list of requirements, a usage guide, and sample code. You can easily download any of these artifacts to your machine to explore further, or to incorporate directly into a solution.

FIGURE 7.8
Information on a
Logidex SDA

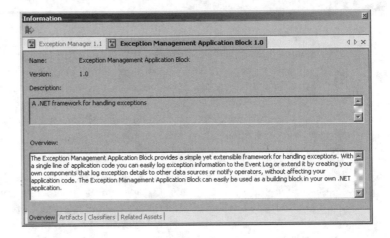

The final piece of Logidex is the Reference Models window. A reference model provides a sort of clickable picture of a group of assets—for example, the major Framework classes, or patterns based on tiers. Drilling into the picture with your mouse ultimately results in an asset search.

The free MSDN version is essentially a read-only subset of the full Logidex product. With the free version, you can search for SDAs, but you can't add to the database. The full version lets you put your own SDAs into a library so that other developers can search for them and reuse them in their own projects. The capture process is well integrated with Visual Studio .NET. For example, suppose you've created a new .NET class library that you want to add to the SDA library for your organization. Right-click in Solution Explorer and select Capture Project to launch the Asset Creation wizard (assuming you have rights to add to the library; there's role-based security in place). This works you through the steps of documenting your asset and then lets you edit it in depth, still within Visual Studio .NET. Logidex makes good use of the IDE, letting you link assets by drag and drop, or add them to reference models the same way.

There are other capture modes as well. If you want, you can even set up a rule-driven system that looks at check-ins to your source code control system and automatically pushes them into a library for reuse. There's also a browser-based interface for times when you don't have Visual Studio .NET loaded.

The full version of Logidex is out of the reach of most independent software developers. Expect to pay from $30,000 to $50,000 to set up a 10-user pilot program. But that's no reason not to try the free version as a good way to locate sample code and patterns on MSDN.

Other Sources of Free Code

Of course, not all .NET sample code comes from Redmond. When you consider that Microsoft handed out beta copies of Visual Studio .NET to every man, woman, child, and dog with the slightest interest in programming, it would be amazing if you couldn't find a lot of .NET source code out there. Indeed, there are dozens of websites containing freely downloadable source code. Of these, I think two in particular are worth bookmarking:

- The Code Project (`www.codeproject.com/`)

- GotDotNet User Samples (`www.gotdotnet.com/Community/UserSamples/`)

Between them, these two sites have thousands of code samples that you can search by topic or keyword. The quality is a bit uneven; this code doesn't go through the rigorous review process that Microsoft uses internally. But you can find quite a few gems lurking here.

> **TIP** Google is your friend when it comes to finding source code. But there's a trick: Don't use ".NET" as a search term, because it's too common in other contexts. For example, "queue .NET" turns up many hits that have nothing to do with .NET programming at all. Instead, use "C#" as a search term; "queue C#" will give you a much more focused set of results.

Evaluating Code: FxCop

You may have noticed that most .NET code from Microsoft follows certain patterns. For example, class names (such as `SqlConnection`) use Pascal casing, while parameter names (such as `connectionString`) use camel casing.

> **NOTE** Pascal casing capitalizes each concatenated word in an identifier. Camel casing capitalizes all concatenated words except the first, leading to a "camel's hump" in the middle of two-word identifiers.

While this sort of choice is arbitrary (camel-cased identifiers perform no better or worse than Pascal-cased ones), the .NET Framework developers argue that there's a benefit to consistency across all class libraries. This consistency in the FCL extends far beyond simple naming guidelines. The .NET Framework General Reference includes an entire section of "Design Guidelines for Class Library Developers" (it's also available online at `http://msdn.microsoft.com/library/en-us/cpgenref/html/cpconnetframeworkdesignguidelines.asp`) that covers 13 major areas:

- Naming guidelines
- Class member usage guidelines

- Type usage guidelines
- Guidelines for exposing functionality to COM
- Error raising and handling guidelines
- Array usage guidelines
- Operator overloading usage guidelines
- Guidelines for implementing Equals and the equality operator
- Guidelines for casting types
- Common design patterns
- Security in class libraries
- Threading design guidelines
- Guidelines for asynchronous programming

After you've worked with the .NET Framework for a while, you'll find that you expect class libraries to conform with these guidelines. For example, you'll expect to be able to invoke just about any method asynchronously, because that's just how .NET works in general.

Wouldn't it be nice to be able to check whether a new class library conforms to the design guidelines? The .NET developers think so too, which is why they've released a free tool named FxCop (`www.gotdotnet.com/team/fxcop/`). While FxCop doesn't check for conformity with every single design guideline, it does incorporate a database of more than 200 rules from the guidelines.

There are two main uses for FxCop. First, you can use it to get a quick feel for whether a class library that you're contemplating using conforms with the design guidelines. Second, you can use it to check your own code (if you're writing class libraries) to see whether you're doing things the .NET way.

FxCop organizes its work into projects. A project consists of one or more assemblies to be checked, and one or more rules to be used to check the assemblies. Figure 7.9 shows FxCop in action, in this case looking at the `DownloadEngine.dll` assembly with all rules enabled. As you can see, you can select which parts of an assembly to inspect, right down to the member level. Similarly, you can choose whether to enable or disable individual rules, and even to exclude individual warnings.

As you can see, even with the small number of members in `DownloadEngine.dll`, FxCop found some things to complain about. For more details, you can double-click on any of the rule violations. This will open the Active Message Details dialog box, shown in Figure 7.10.

FIGURE 7.9
FxCop in action

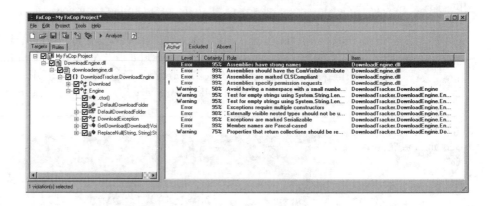

FIGURE 7.10
FxCop rule details

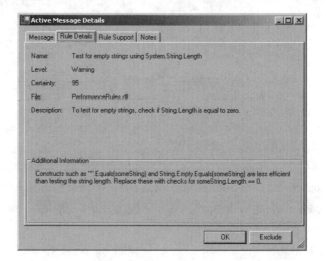

If you're going to use FxCop (or any similar tool, such as Total .NET Analyzer or Compuware DevPartner Studio, both of which I mentioned in Chapter 6, "Pumping Up the IDE"), I have two pieces of advice. First, start using the tool on a regular basis early in your development cycle so that you can correct any problems as they occur. If you wait until you're ready to release a class library to test for guideline conformance, you'll probably find hundreds of errors. Then you'll have to decide between delaying the software's release or ignoring the tool's recommendations. Second, use your judgment. There may be good reasons to ignore some or all of the rules in any particular library. Perhaps you're designing code to wrap a legacy API, for example, in which case you should probably conform to that API's naming rules rather than the .NET rules. Remember, the design guidelines exist to make life for developers easier, not harder.

RULE   Design guidelines are a means to an end, not an end in themselves.

If you do find yourself trying to automatically fix every single problem that FxCop finds, one quick cure is to run an FxCop analysis of one of the FCL assemblies. Figure 7.11 shows the result of running all of the FxCop rules against System.Data.dll. Obviously the Microsoft designers were not concerned with following every little guideline perfectly.

FIGURE 7.11
FxCop and the FCL

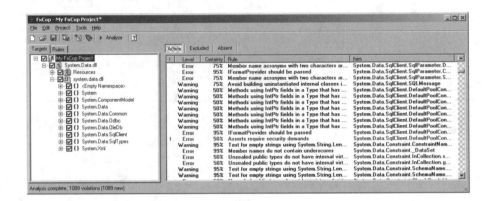

Source Code Checklist

Source code is at the heart of any application, and you'll be working with it every single day that you develop. It's worth learning about tools and techniques to make working with code easier:

- Use utilities such as Ildasm or Reflector to analyze the code when you're not sure what it will do.

- Use tools such as Snippet Compiler or .NET Component Inspector to experiment with new components without the overhead of building an entire project.

- Get to know the FCL and the classes that it contains so that you can avoid reinventing the wheel.

- Investigate other sources of reusable code when you want to incorporate common functionality in your projects.

- Use a tool such as FxCop to check code for conformance with design guidelines.

There's another alternative to writing your own code or incorporating someone else's code: using tools to automatically generate the code for you. I'll introduce this technique in the next chapter.

CHAPTER 8

Generating Code

> [F]or if you press a piece of underwear soiled with sweat together with some wheat in an open mouth jar, after about 21 days the odor changes, and the ferment coming out of the underwear and penetrating through the husks of the wheat changes the wheat into mice. But what is more remarkable is that mice of both sexes emerge (from the wheat) and these mice successfully reproduce with mice born naturally from parents.... But what is even more remarkable is that the mice which came out were not small mice... but fully grown.
>
> —Jean-Baptiste van Helmont

Software is not, unfortunately, as easy to generate spontaneously as mice. But it need not be as difficult as many developers make it, either. Every developer writes code from scratch, building new functionality out of thin air. Some write code using cut and paste, blithely ignoring good maintainability practices in their haste to finish a project. However, a growing number of developers these days are turning to code generators—programs that will write the code for you. Although code generators aren't new, they've become more popular in recent years, thanks in part to the ease of integrating them with modern development environments such as .NET. In this chapter, I'll briefly survey the code-generation landscape, and talk a bit about how this trend fits into the .NET landscape.

Understanding Code Generation

Perhaps you've never considered code generation as a viable way to build your own applications. In this section of the chapter, I'll show you a simple (and common) example of a situation where a code-generation tool can save you a lot of time and effort. Then I'll pass on a taxonomy of code-generation tools, and talk about some of the areas where code generation can be useful.

A Code-Generation Example

Let's suppose you have a SQL Server database containing a number of tables. For this example, the standard Northwind database will do just fine. Being a good developer and wary of SQL injection problems, you've decided to use stored procedures for all of your code's interaction with the database. It's relatively easy to sit down and write the first of these stored procedures—say, a procedure that adds a record to the Categories table:

```
CREATE PROCEDURE [dbo].procAddCategories
    @CategoryName nvarchar(15),
    @Description ntext,
    @Picture image,
    @CategoryID int OUTPUT
AS

INSERT INTO [dbo].[Categories] (
    [CategoryName],
    [Description],
    [Picture]
) VALUES (
    @CategoryName,
    @Description,
    @Picture
)

SET @CategoryID = @@IDENTITY
```

Easy enough—but of course the job doesn't end with one stored procedure. You'll probably want stored procedures to update existing records, delete records, return a single record, and return a list of records. And you'll want these stored procedures for every table in the database. With a dozen tables in the database, you're talking about 60 stored procedures here. Of course, they're all easy to write; it will just take you an afternoon of boring cut-and-paste work, at least if you don't make a mistake along the way.

RULE Before spending time doing repetitive work in development, think about whether you can automate the task instead.

This situation is ideal for code generation. Instead of writing 60 stored procedures by hand, here's how you could do it using CodeSmith (`www.ericjsmith.net/codesmith/`):

1. Launch CodeSmith and double-click the `AllStoredProcedures.cst` template to open its property sheet, shown in Figure 8.1.

FIGURE 8.1
CodeSmith template properties

2. Fill in the database connection and set other properties according to your preferences.
3. Click the Generate button. Figure 8.2 shows a portion of the output.
4. Copy the CodeSmith output to SQL Server Query Analyzer and execute it.

FIGURE 8.2
CodeSmith output

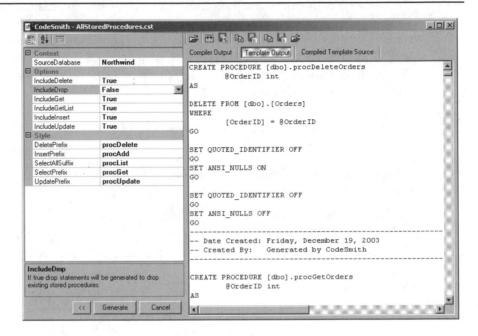

Now you can take the rest of the afternoon off, since the tool has done all the work that you'd planned to finish today.

CodeSmith works by using templates that are similar to ASP.NET pages. When you click the Generate button, the CodeSmith engine uses these templates, plus your inputs, to construct the desired output. The output can be any text at all, from a programming language to documentation to XML files. It's limited only by your cleverness in designing the template.

Code-Generation Taxonomy

Code-generation tools come in a variety of forms, from simple to complex, and are capable of tackling a variety of tasks. To understand where you might use code generation, it helps to have a breakdown of these tools into organized categories. Fortunately, someone has already done the hard work of creating such a classification. Jack Herrington's book *Code Generation in Action* (Manning, 2003) and his Code Generation Network website (www.codegeneration.net) provide much information and many links for the developer interested in learning more about this field.

Herrington identifies two basic kinds of code generators: active and passive. A passive code generator dumps code into your project and forgets about it. The Data Form Wizard in Visual Studio .NET (VS .NET) is a perfect example of a passive code generator: It asks you some questions, and then builds the form for you. If you want to change the form, you need to run

A Crash Course in SQL Injection

You may or may not be familiar with SQL injection, but as a developer, it's a problem that you should be aware of. While this is not a security book, I think it's worth a small amount of space to make sure that you understand the basics.

SQL injection is most typically a problem in web applications that build up a query based on user input. For example, an ASP.NET application might contain this line of code:

```
SqlString = "SELECT * FROM Customers WHERE CompanyName = \"" +
    txtName.Text + "\""
```

Later on, a SqlCommand object could be used to execute the specified SQL statement and return results. The problem arises because of the user input. A sufficiently malicious user could enter this text into the txtName control:

```
A";DELETE FROM Orders --
```

Because SQL Server sees the semicolon as a statement separator, this is interpreted as two statements. The first selects customers where the CompanyName column contains the value A. The second deletes every row from the Orders table! The trailing -- causes SQL Server to treat anything following as a comment.

You can choose among several strategies to prevent SQL injection in your own application. One approach is to attempt to validate user input to ensure that it doesn't contain dangerous characters. Another is to use stored procedures, which in general are not vulnerable to this problem.

For additional information on SQL injection, I strongly recommend you read these two white papers:

- SQL Injection: Are Your Web Applications Vulnerable? (www.spidynamics.com/papers/ SQLInjectionWhitePaper.pdf)

- Advanced SQL Injection in SQL Server Applications (www.nextgenss.com/papers/ advanced_sql_injection.pdf)

through the whole process again; you can't go back and tell the wizard to just make a few changes.

By contrast, an active code generator takes responsibility for maintaining the code. When you want to change the classes produced by an active code generator, you tweak the input file or the code generator itself; you never directly edit the output. Herrington identifies six basic types of active code generation:

- The *code munger* takes an input file, parses it, and creates an output file from some built-in or external template.

- The *inline-code expander* takes source code with some special markup and creates production code from it. Embedded-SQL generators, which allow you to drop SQL statements into C or Java code (for example), work this way.

- The *mixed-code generator* is similar to the inline-code expander, except that the results are written right back to the input file. For example, special comments might specify delegate code that needs to be created and added to the file.

- The *partial-class generator* reads some sort of abstract definition file and builds a base class source code file to implement the definition. The user can then create a derived class to get the final desired functionality.

- The *tier generator* builds an entire tier (typically, a data-access tier) from an abstract definition. UML products that integrate with your IDE can fall into this class.

- The *full-domain language* is a Turing-complete programming language created just for your problem. It gives you a general-purpose way to specify code that should be created.

Within this taxonomy are many, many code-generation tools for the .NET languages. Some, like the CodeSmith tool that I briefly demonstrated earlier in the chapter, are very general-purpose tools. Others are targeted at one specific area, such as creating business objects or building database-backed web applications.

Brainstorming Code-Generation Uses

Don't get the impression that code generation is only concerned with putting out source code that you can then feed into a compiler. It's better to think of code generation as a technology for automatically generating a variety of end products, only some of which fall into the traditional category of "code." Here are just a few examples of things that you might produce using code generation:

Database-access code   This includes stored procedures and data-access classes.

User-interface code   This might be your final production code, or it might be quickly mocked-up code that allows you to test classes in your project.

Documentation   Think about the XML comments in C#, which can be turned into HTML help by NDoc. You'll learn more about NDoc in Chapter 12, "Creating Documentation."

Unit tests   If you're going to generate code, why not generate tests for the code as well?

Web services   You could write a Web Services Description Language (WSDL) file and have all the code needed to implement it automatically generated.

DLL wrappers for legacy code   Indeed, the .NET Framework will do some of this for you when you set a reference to a COM library from your .NET project.

Configuration files or initialization files   For example, you might automatically generate an `app.config` file for your application based on a customer name and license key number.

Scripting files   You could use Windows Management Instrumentation (WMI) and VBScript to provision websites into a new installation of Internet Information Services (IIS), for example.

Installation files   The Windows Installer service works by looking at tables in a database, and there's no reason that you couldn't build some or all of those tables with a code-generation tool.

What it boils down to is this: If you can describe an output that you'd like to get, you can likely build a code generator to take the description to the actual output. (This leaves aside the question as to whether it's more work to write the output or build the generator.)

Code Generation for .NET

Several factors have combined to make .NET a good arena for code generation:

- The increasing popularity and visibility of code generation in software development
- The extensible nature of VS .NET, which makes it easy to integrate tools to the IDE
- The `System.CodeDom` and `System.CodeDom.Compiler` namespaces, which make it easy to generate source code

As a result, quite a few code-generation tools are available for .NET developers. After a brief look at the native code-generation features of VS .NET, I'll introduce some of these tools.

Code Generation in Visual Studio .NET

In some sense, all development environments are code generators; the code that ultimately runs on the computer is not precisely the code that you wrote, but a translation of that code into machine language. But VS .NET also includes built-in source code generation facilities, even though you might not have noticed them. In some cases, VS .NET takes your input and translates it into actual C# or Visual Basic .NET source code, which is then compiled into your project.

For instance, VS .NET offers the ability to build strongly typed `DataSet` classes, which add the benefits of design-time type checking and IntelliSense to the basic `DataSet`. You might not have used this feature, so here's an example to let you see how it works:

1. Launch VS .NET and create a new C# Windows application.

2. Right-click on the Project node in Solution Explorer and select Add ≻ Add New Item.

3. In the Add New Item dialog box, select the Data Set template. Name the new item **Customers.xsd** and click Open.

4. Open the Server Explorer window (by default, this window auto-hides at the left side of the VS .NET workspace).

5. Click the Connect to Database toolbar button. Use the Data Link Properties dialog box to connect to the Northwind sample database.

6. Expand the new database node in the Server Explorer tree view and drag the Customers table to the Customers.xsd design surface. This will create a picture of the table's schema, as shown in Figure 8.3.

FIGURE 8.3
Building a strongly
typed DataSet

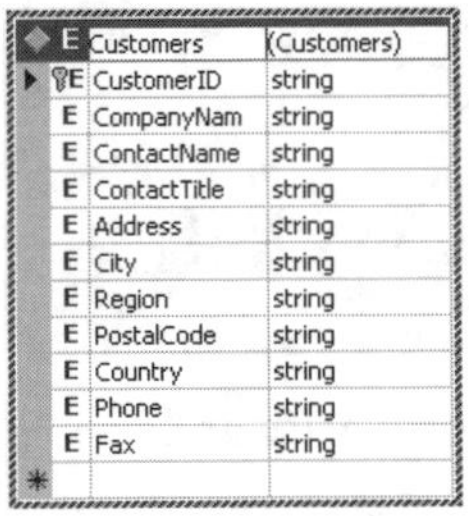

At this point, you can use the Customers class in code, with object properties representing the table and column names. For example, this code snippet would retrieve a particular customer ID to a text box:

```
SqlConnection cnn = new SqlConnection(connectionString);
SqlDataAdapter da = new SqlDataAdapter();
SqlCommand cmd = cnn.CreateCommand("SELECT * FROM Customers");
Customers cust = new Customers();
da.Fill(cust, "Customers");
txtCustomerID.text = cust.Customers[4].CustomerID;
```

Magic? Not quite. If you look at the properties of the Customers.xsd item, you'll see that it has a Custom Tool property with the value of MSDataSetGenerator. This is a code-generation tool supplied by Microsoft. When you save the Customers.xsd file, VS .NET automatically invokes the tool to generate code based on the XML schema that you specified. You can see the generated code if you like. To do so, click the Show All Files button on the Solution Explorer toolbar. Expand the node for Customers.xsd and you'll find two files, one of which is named Customers.cs. This file contains all of the C# code to build the strongly typed DataSet class, as well as a warning: "Changes to this file may cause incorrect behavior and will be lost if the code is regenerated."

VS .NET uses this method to generate some other types of code as well. For example, when you set a web reference to a WSDL file, behind the scenes a code generator is running to provide the proxy class for the web service. Independent software vendors can also ship their own code generators that integrate in this fashion.

.NET Code-Generation Tools

A wide variety of code-generation tools work with .NET languages. These range from general-purpose tools, such as CodeSmith, to full application generators that start with a database and give you back an entire ASP.NET application. There's no way for me to provide a complete list here; even if I could develop such a list, it would be out of date by the time this book was published. Instead, I'll briefly mention some of the ones that I've tried out, so you can get a sense of the market.

AlachiSoft TierDeveloper   This tool, with pricing starting at $1295, lets you go from a database (SQL Server, Oracle, or some others) to a full application. It integrates with VS .NET and builds data access classes, COM+ transaction–enabled components, and even complete web applications. It can also automatically generate a web services interface to the data objects. It's available from www.alachisoft.com.

Iron Speed Designer   This $495 package builds complete ASP.NET applications from a database and a set of "layout pages," which are HTML templates containing special tags that tell Iron Speed where to insert its code. The generated pages are completely reentrant (that is, they can be regenerated without losing your custom changes), and a variety of flexible examples are provided with the tool, which is itself an ASP.NET application. It's available from www.ironspeed.com.

m3rlin   This is a free and open-source project that uses the ASP.NET engine at runtime to generate code based on templates and XML. Although the documentation is minimal, you can look over the source code to see how it works, and you may find it a useful starting point for your own code-generation projects. You'll find it at www.gotdotnet.com/Community/UserSamples/Details.aspx?SampleGuid=dfef25fa-f545-4289-b9fc-05270ea41fb3.

Olero ORM.NET   At $495, ORM.NET is designed specifically to generate a data access object layer from your SQL Server database. Although you don't need to worry about stored procedures when using its object-oriented code from your own applications, it will also generate wrappers for any existing stored procedures in your database. It's available from www.olero.com/OrmWeb/.

Solutions Design LLBLGen Pro   Another code generator to get Visual Basic .NET or C# code from SQL Server or Oracle databases, LLBLGen Pro is a €170 tool. It features a lot of places where you can fine-tune the generated code, and it builds a variety of different classes to handle data access for you. It will generate either monolithic classes, or dual classes that separate your custom code from generated code so you can rerun the generation process without losing your customizations. It's available from www.llblgen.com/defaultgeneric.aspx.

Workstate Codify   This VS .NET add-in for templated code generation costs $75. It's unique among the code generators I've seen in that it can inject little bits of generated code into the middle of a class. For example, you can generate property syntax even while writing the rest of your class from scratch. It also includes an integrated template editor to make it easy to change templates while your project is still loaded. It's available from www.workstate.com/codify.

Yes! Software CodeCharge Studio 2.2   For $500, CodeCharge Studio provides a very flexible environment for generating web applications, hosted in its own IDE or optionally running as a Microsoft FrontPage add-in. It offers a lot of flexibility in code generation, letting you target ASP, JSP, PHP, Perl, ColdFusion, or ASP.NET. With its wizards and security features, CodeCharge Studio ends up feeling more like an alternative development environment than a code generator. It's available from www.codecharge.com/index2.php.

Code Generation in Download Tracker

One of the things that I need in Download Tracker, but have not yet implemented, is a collection of Download objects. You'll recall that an individual Download object in the Download-Engine project represents a file downloaded from the Internet, together with the metadata that Download Tracker allows the user to add. A matching collection will let me work with more than one Download object as a group. This will come in useful when I'm ready to return a set of search results from the core engine back to the user interface layer. Of course, I could just use a simple Collection class for this, but I'd like some other features:

- The collection should be sorted so that I can return it in a particular order.
- The collection should only accept objects of the Download type.

This second requirement is just good coding practice. If I use a strongly typed collection, then I'll get additional IntelliSense as I'm developing the application, and I'll be protected against a whole group of silly errors that can result from putting the wrong object into the wrong collection.

If you poke around the VS .NET help, you'll find a walkthrough on creating your own custom collection class. This ends up requiring a fair bit of code to do right. The code is also rather repetitive; once you've written one strongly typed collection class, it's not an exercise that you want to repeat every time you need another such class. This makes developing such classes an ideal situation for code generation.

Fortunately, CodeSmith already includes a template for a strongly typed, sorted collection. By using this template, I can create the collection that I need with little effort. I'll use Code-Smith's VS .NET integration to make this easier.

TECHNOLOGY TRAP

The Velvet Straightjacket

Many code generators available for .NET are all encompassing. They work by letting you specify things about your application, such as the tables where data is stored and the general layout of ASP.NET pages, and then build the entire application for you from your specification. While this can save you a tremendous amount of time and repetitive programming, it can also lock you in to a particular tool if you're not careful.

When you're using one of these comprehensive code-generation systems, make sure you understand the extent to which you're committed to keep using it. What happens if you need to add another developer to the project? What happens if you have to make custom changes to the user interface? What happens if you're ready to upgrade to a new version of .NET but the tool hasn't been revised yet?

Considering the expense of these tools, it's worth doing a serious evaluation before purchasing. When you do so, look not just at whether the end product fits your needs but at how it's implemented. To avoid getting trapped in the future, the generated code should let you make changes easily—and should be easy to remove from the tool if you later decide that the project should stand on its own.

The first step is to add the template, `CSSortedList.cst`, to the DownloadEngine project. You can add any file you like to a project in VS .NET (though of course the program doesn't really know anything about .cst files, which means you won't get color-coding or IntelliSense if you work with the file in this interface). This particular template comes from a source that I trust, but even so, I spent a few minutes reading through it to get a sense of how it works.

The template is a necessary part of the process, but there are also some properties that I need to specify when building the actual `Downloads` class. CodeSmith handles this by letting you define a property set as an XML file. I added a new XML file, `Downloads.xml`, to the project with this content:

```xml
<?xml version="1.0" encoding="utf-8" ?>
<codeSmith>
    <propertySets>
        <propertySet>
            <property name="KeyType">string</property>
            <property name="ItemType">Download</property>
            <property name="ClassName">Downloads</property>
            <property name="ClassNamespace">
            DownloadTracker.DownloadEngine</property>
        </propertySet>
    </propertySets>
    <template path="CSSortedList.cst" />
</codeSmith>
```

Note that the CodeSmith XML syntax allows you to define multiple property sets within a single XML file. If I needed several strongly typed collections in this project, I could define them all with a single file. The property set itself is simply a list of values that the template needs to do its work; these are the same values that I would fill in manually if I were using the CodeSmith user interface.

The key to making this work is to set the `CustomTool` property of the `Downloads.xml` file to `CodeSmithGenerator`. This tells VS .NET to invoke the CodeSmithGenerator tool every time that the file is saved, and to use the file as input. The result is that as soon as I save the `Downloads.xml` file, I get `Downloads.cs` as a hidden file in my source code tree.

The final step is to get the correct files into my source code control system. In this case, I've checked in `CSSortedList.cst` and `Downloads.xml`, but *not* `Downloads.cs`. That's because the first two files contain all of the information necessary to rebuild the third, so there's no point in putting the third file into the system separately.

RULE   Put code-generation source files, but not code-generation result files, under source code control.

Deciding Whether to use Code Generation

Like many other things in software development, code generation is a bit of a balancing act: there are good reasons to use it, but there are also good reasons to avoid it. Ultimately, you need to decide on a case-by-case basis whether code generation makes sense for individual projects. That said, I can provide some general guidelines.

The list of reasons not to use code generation starts with vendor worries. If you choose to let your project depend on a tool from an independent software vendor, then you need to take into account what might happen if the vendor goes out of business or fails to support its product. At the very least, you should have a backup plan: Can you simply continue to use the already-generated code, even if you have to abandon the tool? If not, how long will it take to replace it with other code, whether from another tool or written by hand? Another way to avoid this problem is to write your own code-generation tools. That can be an attractive alternative if your team is large enough to support a dedicated toolsmith, but it's less feasible for a small team or a lone wolf developer.

You also need to worry about the quality of the generated code. It probably won't be exactly the code that you would have written yourself, which may be a good thing or a bad thing depending on your own level of experience. But if you have to go into the code and fix it, it's useful to understand what's going on. Comments and documentation are your friends here. Products that let you edit a template to customize the generated code (as opposed to those that lock everything up in compiled logic) have an advantage here.

Also, beware: With many code-generation products, any fixes you make will vanish if you need to regenerate the code later on. This makes it more important to focus on products that generate the code you want the first time, or that let you edit the template rather than the generated code.

Here's a final cautionary note: You need to realize that these tools don't quite provide something for nothing. Depending on the complexity of the tool, a substantial learning curve may be involved in using it effectively. You should use the tool often enough that the time spent learning it is outweighed by the time it saves. Otherwise, why bother?

On the positive side, saving labor is usually the most attractive reason for adopting a code-generation tool. If you're faced with writing wrapper classes for a thousand database tables, for example, it's difficult to imagine that you'd spend less time doing it by hand than you would learning to use a tool for the same purpose. And the more projects you use the tool with, the more savings it can deliver for the same amount of effort.

Equally important as a reason to use these tools is the impact of code generation on the quality of the final code. If you use it right, code generation can help prevent errors that might otherwise creep into your source code. The `Downloads.cs` class, for example, includes over 1500 lines of code and comments. How many mistakes might I have made writing that by hand? Instead, by using a thoroughly debugged template together with a code generation tool, I can have high confidence in the mechanics of the collection class.

Code-Generation Checklist

Code generation is an underutilized tool for many developers, and that's a shame. Rather than charging into writing code by hand, it's worth considering whether a code-generation tool can help. Follow these guidelines to help evaluate code generation for yourself:

- When faced with large quantities of repetitive code to write, consider using a code-generation tool instead.

- Evaluate multiple code-generation tools to find the one that works best for your own situation.

- Have a plan for moving beyond the tool if necessary.

- Place code-generation inputs, but not outputs, under source code control.

- Balance the learning curve against the time saved.

In the next chapter, I'll move on to a topic that applies to all code, whether you write it by hand, import it from another project, or generate it: tracking and dealing with bugs.

CHAPTER 9

Tracking and Squashing Bugs

[God] must have an inordinate fondness for beetles.

—J.B.S. Haldane

By the same token, we software developers must dearly love bugs—we create so many of them. Okay, so perhaps we don't lavish the same gentle affection on our bugs that those shiny new beetles presumably get, but that doesn't cut down on their number. Author Steve McConnell (in his book *Code Complete* [Microsoft Press, 1993]) cites an industry average of 15 to 50 errors per thousand lines of code, and suggests that some projects have 10 times that many. Imagine trying to deal with 500 errors in a thousand lines of code!

In this chapter, I'm going to introduce you to some strategies designed to lower those numbers. I won't try to teach you how to use the debugger or analyze running code. Rather, this chapter is about a whole constellation of factors that surround the hunt for bugs: managing risk, testing code, working with hardware, and tracking the bug activity.

Risk Management

Pop quiz: What's the biggest threat to the chance of your application shipping on time and within budget? If your answer is that you don't know, then how in the world do you know whether it's worth spending time and effort fixing that bug you just found? If the entire application is doomed because Widgets Inc. isn't going to ship the "dripping wax"—style user interface components that your users demand on time, what's the point of worrying about the calculation error in the fifty-sixth decimal place? In the memorable words of Rogers Morton, you might as well be rearranging the furniture on the deck of the Titanic. That's why I'm opening a chapter on bug tracking with a discussion of risk management.

You're probably at least vaguely aware that software development is a risky business, but you might not have thought about those risks in a structured fashion. To give you a framework for thinking about risks, I'll discuss risk assessment and risk control, as well as tools for controlling risk in the overall project, and then specifically in your bug-tracking and -squashing efforts.

Risk Assessment

The first step in risk management is simply to understand the risks to your project. The easiest way to do this is simply to brainstorm a list of things that might go badly wrong. These need not be risks that will derail the project entirely. You should also include ones that could have a substantial effect on cost, schedule, or quality (because those factors are interrelated, most risks will have an impact on all three). To come up with such a list, you first need to define the desired outcome of your development project. For Download Tracker, I'd like to have a finished version of the application available on the book's website by the time that you buy a copy of the book. Here are a few of the things that could torpedo that plan:

- I discover a requirement that I can't figure out how to implement.
- I have so much consulting work that I don't have time to finish the code.

- I am unable to register the website at the URL I want to use.
- I can't arrange a source code control system license.
- I can't finish all the planned features in the time allowed.
- I lose the program's source code due to a hardware failure.
- The book schedule slips far enough to conflict with other planned projects.
- My code quality is too low to share without embarrassment.

Because this list is the product of brainstorming, it isn't in any particular order, and not all of the risks are serious. Note also that the risks will vary from project to project. For example, while I'm working on this book, I'm also helping commercialize some vertical market applications. For those applications, one very real risk is that someone else might put a similar application on the market before my team can finish its work. For Download Tracker, though, that risk doesn't bother me; because I'm not particularly trying to commercialize this application, it doesn't matter to me whether someone else beats me to market.

NOTE   Keep in mind that there are some risks you can't foresee. A bus could hit your lead developer, or an asteroid could land on your office. Risk management can reduce risk and make you better able to cope with risks both expected and unexpected, but it can't eliminate the risks entirely

Having a list of risks is better than having no list at all, but it still doesn't answer the question as to which is the most important risk. Ordering the list of risks is the next step in risk assessment. To do so, you need to come up with a numeric measure of each risk. Normally this is done by assigning a probability and a cost to each risk; the expected impact of the risk is then the probability of the risk occurring multiplied by the cost if it does occur. Of course, the probability must lie somewhere between zero (the risk will never come to pass and can safely be ignored) and one (the risk will certainly happen). Often it's convenient to express costs in terms of the project's schedule, but you can just as well use monetary costs if you can come up with them.

A common objection at this point is that it's impossible to quantify either the probability or the cost. Actually, it's quite possible to assign numbers to both; the question is whether the numbers will be accurate. The best answer I can give to that objection is that the numbers will be accurate enough to work from. Once you've got some experience developing, you can also consult your gut feelings as to the relative importance of risks; if your gut disagrees with the costs you've assigned, it's time to review your work. Table 9.1 shows my assessment of the risks for this project.

TABLE 9.1 Risk Assessment for Download Tracker

Risk	Probability	Cost in Weeks	Impact
Too much other work	0.25	12	3.0
Low quality	0.2	12	2.4
Too many features	0.50	4	2.0
Schedule slip	0.1	12	1.2
Can't get SCC license	0.3	4	1.2
Hardware disaster	0.05	20	1.0
Impossible requirement	0.1	8	0.8
Can't get URL	0.05	1	0.05

In this case, I've chosen as my measure of cost the number of weeks that it would take me to work around the problem if it crops up. Having gone through this exercise, I can now order the risks by priority, from the highest-impact risk to the lowest-impact one.

RULE   Focus your attention by developing a risk assessment for every project you work on.

Risk Control

Unless you want to imitate a cartoon ostrich by sticking your head in the sand, assessing risks is only half of risk management. The other half is controlling the risks. Although you may feel that the risks to your application are completely out of your control, that's very seldom the case (unless you've chosen to include low-probability risks like "asteroid strike" on your list). Normally, even if you can't completely control a risk, you can take actions to lower its probability, or its cost, or both.

After you've identified and prioritized your list of risks, you can formalize the risk control process by creating a written risk management plan. Table 9.2 shows my risk management plan for Download Tracker.

With a risk management plan in hand, you can avoid finding yourself reacting in emergency mode if a risk does materialize. Having decided in advance how you'll react to a risk means you can simply execute your plan. Also note that many of the management steps I've listed are aimed at making sure that the risk never materializes, instead of reacting to it if it happens.

TABLE 9.2 Risk Management for Download Tracker

Risk	Management Steps
So much consulting work that I don't have time to finish the code	Avoid work with deadlines until safely after the book is ready to print. Reserve time in schedule to work on book code.
Code quality too low to share without embarrassment	Implement unit tests and track bugs.
Too many features to finish in time allowed	Rewrite Chapter 1 in galleys to remove features if necessary.
Book schedule slips far enough to conflict with other planned projects	Get chapters in by originally scheduled dates. Use vacation time if necessary to get back on track.
Can't arrange source code control system license	Contact vendor well before the end of the project, so as to have time to switch vendors if necessary.
Hardware failure destroys source code	Keep source code on mirrored drives and in source code control repository on a separate computer.
A requirement that I can't figure out how to implement	Keep in touch with C# experts; don't be shy about asking for help.
Unable to register website at the URL I want to use	Register URL well in advance of project end, brainstorm alternatives.

Maintaining the Top Five Risks List

On a project involving several developers, or one that's going to occupy you for an extended period of time, you may find it useful to maintain a formal Top Five Risks List. As the name implies, this is a list of the most important risks to the project. It's usually helpful to include some other information, as shown in Table 9.3.

TABLE 9.3 Top Five Risks List for Download Tracker

Rank This Week	Rank Last Week	Weeks on List	Risk	Management Steps
1	2	11	So much consulting work that I don't have time to finish the code	Avoid work with deadlines until safely after the book is in galleys. Reserve time in schedule to work on book code.
2	3	9	Code quality too low to share without embarrassment	Implement unit tests and track bugs.

TABLE 9.3 CONTINUED Top Five Risks List for Download Tracker

Rank This Week	Rank Last Week	Weeks on List	Risk	Management Steps
3	1	11	Too many features to finish in time allowed	Rewrite Chapter 1 in galleys to remove features if necessary.
4	-	1	Book schedule slips far enough to conflict with other planned projects	Get chapters in by originally scheduled dates. Use vacation time if necessary to get back on track.
5	4	3	Can't arrange source code control system license	Contact vendor well before the end of the project, so as to have time to switch vendors if necessary.

The goal of the Top Five Risks List is to give you a single place where you can immediately and easily review the most serious threats to your project, and you can tell which ones are growing or shrinking in importance. If you're working with a project team, this is information that you should review at weekly status meetings. For larger projects, you may want to expand the list to the top 10 or 15 risks, and review it at the management level on a daily basis.

Bug Triage

But what's the relationship between risk management and bugs in your software? There are two connections. First, if you're in imminent danger of being seriously affected by one of the risks on your list, you probably have more important things to do than fixing bugs. Second, the mindset of risk management is the same mindset that you need to have when you're performing bug triage. Just as not all risks are created equal, not all bugs are created equal.

Triage is a term borrowed from emergency medicine, where it refers to the prioritization of patients for treatment based on the extent of their injuries and chances of survival. In the context of software, it refers to prioritizing bugs based on their seriousness and deciding what to do about each one.

If you learn computer programming in a classroom environment, you may not be exposed to the concept of triage at all. Bugs in your homework assignments are considered mistakes, and you are penalized for each one. Your goal is to create perfectly bug-free programs.

In the real world, things are very different. Every once in a while there's a news story reporting breathlessly that, for example, Microsoft Windows 2000 contains 63,000 unfixed bugs. That's not because the developers at Microsoft are incompetent fools. Rather, it's the reverse;

it's because the developers at Microsoft are very good at what they do, and they know that almost no substantial software project is going to go out the door without bugs. Rather than focus on a zero-bug goal, they focus on having zero unfixed bugs that require fixing—quite a different matter. A bug might be placed on the "don't fix" list because it's so minor that no user will ever notice it, or because it doesn't prevent the application from functioning, or because you know the feature will be completely replaced in the next version. It's up to you to decide where the quality bar is for your own applications.

NOTE   In some areas, such as developing software for the manned space program or for use in medical devices, the goal is still zero bugs. The rough-and-ready techniques I've been describing in this book don't apply to projects with such a stringent goal.

When you're triaging bugs, you need to focus on resolving the bugs rather than fixing them. You might resolve a particular bug in one of several ways. Bug-tracking products vary somewhat in terminology, but this is a typical set of alternative resolutions:

By design   At times, testers will report as a bug something that works exactly the way that you designed it. For example, you might design an inventory application to not allow withdrawals of more material than is available, and to change the requested amount to the maximum available amount in such cases. A tester could report the change of the number he or she entered to another number as a bug in your application. Be careful when using this resolution, though; if something works as you designed but not as end users expect, it might be time to change your design. Alternatively, you might make a note to explicitly spell out this bit of design in the application's documentation.

Duplicate   Particularly if you have many beta testers, you might find the same bug being reported two, three, or more times. When you spot this situation, resolve the extras as duplicates. Good bug-tracking software will let you link the duplicate bugs to the one that you choose to leave open, so that the ultimate resolution of the issue can be tracked.

Postponed   Sometimes you'll agree that something is a bug but will not want to fix it right away. For example, you might be planning to add support for Unicode in version 2.0 of the application, in which case you should simply postpone all Unicode-related bugs until you're ready to work on that version. Resource constraints can also force you to postpone bugs; in this case, you need to find the bugs with the least impact on end users and postpone those. A bug that shows up only when your application is run under the Turkish version of Windows 98 with a particular obsolete CD-ROM drive installed, for example, is a good candidate to be postponed, because such a bug may never affect a real user of the software.

Not reproducible   Testers are not infallible, and sometimes you'll get bugs that you simply can't reproduce on your system. Resolve such bugs as not reproducible. Good testers will treat this resolution as a request for more information rather than as an insult, and you may well get the same bug back with additional explanation that makes it possible for you to reproduce the bug. When you're thinking of resolving a bug as not reproducible, try to figure out how the tester could have seen such a thing happen. Is it something that you fixed in a more recent build? Is it an artifact of a particular data file that you don't have? "It works on my machine" is a very unsatisfying explanation for resolving a bug as not reproducible, because, as every tester knows, you're not going to ship your machine to the customer.

Won't fix   Resolving a bug this way is the same as postponing it forever. You are acknowledging that the bug exists but at the same time claiming that it's not worth the resources to fix it. Perhaps it's a problem with a feature that you've decided to cut, or a case that you never expect an end user to see. Be cautious about resolving bugs this way; if you refuse to fix too many, testers may wonder why they're even bothering to test your application.

Reassigned   Depending on your bug-tracking system, this may or may not be seen as a resolution, but it has the same effect: it gets the bug off your desk. You might reassign a bug to another developer if you determine the bug is actually in his or her code rather than yours. You might even reassign it to your subcontractors or suppliers by opening a bug against their code instead of yours.

Fixed   Sometimes, the best way to resolve a bug is just to fix it. In fact, for many projects this will be the most common resolution for bugs.

This is a good place to put in a few words about the "politics" of bugs. In many organizations, the bug-tracking workflow goes something like this:

1. A tester finds a bug and reports it.
2. The bug is assigned to a manager for initial triage.
3. The manager resolves the bug if possible or assigns it to a developer.
4. The developer resolves the bug (by fixing it or otherwise resolving it).
5. Resolved bugs are returned to a tester. Usually this is the same tester who reported the bug, but this isn't always the case. Bugs reported by external beta testers, for example, may be reassigned to internal testers.
6. The tester either closes the bug or reopens it with additional information or comments, in which case the process starts over at step 2.

With several people involved, bug resolution can become a very political activity. I've seen bugs in large organizations ultimately involve dozens of people, as multiple bug reports get duplicated to a single underlying bug, which then wanders from developer to developer in search of someone to claim responsibility. I've seen bugs bounce back and forth from tester to developer a dozen times as they argue over whether "postponed" or "won't fix" is a reasonable resolution ("But we have dozens of customers using that CD-ROM drive in Turkey!"). I've seen developers mark a dozen bugs as "won't fix" without even reading them, as a passive-aggressive protest against having too much work. I've seen testers spend their time on the most stable part of a product, because at least the developer of that portion doesn't ignore their bug reports.

At the end of the day, a bug-tracking system will work only if all concerned keep in mind that their ultimate goal is to ship a high-quality project. If you're a manager, you need to keep an eye on the bug-tracking system for these political games, and figure out how to rearrange resources or smooth relations between strong egos to keep them from getting out of hand.

QA and Testing

Where do bugs come from? Or, more precisely, how do they get identified (since whether or not you want to admit it, you know quite well where they come from; they're inserted into the product by your own efforts and those of the rest of your development team).

If you're fortunate enough to be working in a medium or large organization, bugs are normally found by people working in the quality assurance (QA) department—the testers. As a developer, you shouldn't view testers as the enemy. Rather, they're your allies in making a better product. In this section, I'll give you a brief overview of the activities of a good software tester, and talk about how to be your own tester.

Types of Software Testing

Here are some of the types of testing that might go on with any given application. This overview won't give you enough information for you to actually work as a software tester, but it should be sufficient to help you speak the same language.

Unit testing   In unit testing, a single component or function is tested to make sure that it's bug free. Typically, unit testing is done by developers rather than by testers, as I discussed in Chapter 5, "Preventing Bugs with Unit Testing."

Functional testing   This involves testing the application to make sure that it conforms to the requirements and specifications. A tester can carry out thorough functional testing only if there is a written specification for the product, which is one more good reason for committing specifications to writing. Even if there is no written specification, though, testers can perform functional testing simply by exercising the application and deciding whether its behavior makes sense.

Conformance testing   The purpose of conformance testing is to ensure that the application conforms to industry specifications. For example, if the application outputs Extensible

Markup Language (XML) files, conformance testing would check whether these files conform to the World Wide Web Consortium (W3C) XML specification.

Compatibility testing   The goal of compatibility testing is to check that the application runs in as wide a variety of computing environments as possible. This might involve using different sets of hardware, different versions of the operating system, different user interface languages, or different browsers. Compatibility testing is often quite challenging due to the sheer number of possibilities involved.

Performance testing   This testing involves identifying performance issues or creating benchmarks under normal operating conditions. The goal of performance testing is to check that the application's performance will be acceptable to users.

Stress testing   Stress testing identifies how the application fails when it is subjected to excessive stress. Stress testing often involves using software to simulate a large number of users, low RAM, CPU contention, and other unusual conditions. The goal is to make sure that the application failure doesn't result in damage to the operating system, data loss, or other undesirable consequences.

Regression testing   When a new build of the application is made available to testers, one of the first things they normally do is run a suite of regression tests—tests that were passed by previous builds of the software. This is an easy way to make sure that new features didn't break existing functionality. Developers can also perform their own regression testing by maintaining a suite of unit tests.

Smoke testing   This involves running "quick and dirty" tests that exercise major features without which it's pointless to continue testing. If the smoke tests fail, the build is considered completely broken and testers normally wait for the next build.

Black-box testing   This testing of components is based strictly on their external interfaces, treating the implementation as a "black box." Most testing done by QA departments is black-box testing.

White-box testing   Here the internal behavior of components is tested, with full knowledge of the implementation. Unit testing by developers tends to be white-box testing.

Many books, tools, and other resources are available to help software testers do their jobs. This book isn't primarily about testing, so I won't try to review this literature here. One good starting point if you'd like to learn more is the Software QA/Test Resource Center (`www.softwareqatest.com/index.html`). A critical piece of testing software in many organizations is a test framework that allows saving and consistently executing a set of tests. One excellent .NET-aware framework is TestComplete, from AutomatedQA Corp. (`www.automatedqa.com/`).

QA for the Lone Wolf

At many software companies, the software development staff breaks down something like this:

- One third management and architects
- One third developers
- One third testers

But when you're working by yourself, it's hard to saw off an arm and a leg and call them your QA department. You will likely need to spend time being your own tester. Unfortunately, the plain fact is that many good developers are lousy testers. It's difficult to take code that you've just written and then systematically attempt to prove that you haven't finished with it after all. Here are a few tips for the developer who doesn't have a testing department to call on:

- Use unit tests to keep bugs from creeping into your code in the first place.

- Create a list of critical requirements so you can perform a "smoke test" on each new build.

- Set code aside for a few days before performing functional testing on it.

- If at all possible, get someone else to test your application. Perhaps you can send it to external beta testers, swap-test with another independent developer, or convince your teenagers that your application is a video game in disguise.

- Keep a written list of requirements, and test to make sure the application meets each one.

- Use a bug-tracking system to keep track of past bugs. This will help you learn which types of bugs you are most prone to introduce.

- Be sure to check absurd input: 0 where you know only positive numbers should be entered, letters in place of numbers, dates with meaningless years, and so on. Even if your users don't try to mess up your application this way, they'll make typing mistakes with the same effect.

- If you think of something that might go wrong while you're in the middle of coding, enter it as a bug in your bug-tracking system. This will help you remember to test the problem when you're not wearing your coding hat.

As the developer of the code, you do have one advantage: All of your testing can be white-box testing. You should make full use of the source code to help prevent bugs, by coding defensively (see Chapter 4, "Coding Defensively") and by reading over your work to make sure you've thought of everything. When you do discover a bug in functional testing, take one step beyond fixing the bug and think about how you could have prevented it in the first place—more unit tests? Better checking of input conditions? More thorough code review? Over time, you should be able to identify the most common sources of bugs in your own code and eliminate them.

RULE   Treat bugs as a learning experience, not as a threat to your coding skills.

Finally, keep in mind that it is extremely difficult to be an effective tester of your own application. It's quite common to develop blind spots where you simply don't notice how an application is subtly failing, or to avoid testing something absurd because you know that it doesn't make sense. Even if you have to do the majority of your own testing, try to find someone, whether it be spouse, best friend, or next-door neighbor, to at least try out your application a few times.

Building a Test Network

For the most part, books on software development treat software as pure stuff of the mind, sprung from the efforts of our intense concentration on some kind of ethereal being. In reality, of course, CPUs and RAM and monitors and lots of other hardware are involved. Although I've been ignoring the subject of hardware myself, this is a good point to bring grubby reality into the discussion. To test your software effectively, you need a network of computers. The more hardware resources you can put into testing, the more likely it is that you can duplicate peculiar configurations of hardware and software that shake out bugs in your product. For that reason, I'm going to put some thoughts about hardware for developers into this chapter.

Consider the sections that follow as guidelines, not hard-and-fast rules. What works for me in the hardware arena may not work quite as well for you.

Buy preassembled machines.   Purchase preassembled machines, not a basket of parts. Yes, you're a smart person and could build your own computer—but other people do that for a living, and they buy in bulk. You won't save more than $100 or so by buying parts, and you'll waste a lot of evenings. In the worst possible case, you'll also blow up something expensive, like a CPU. I have.

Buy name brands.   Buying from established vendors is always best. If you're in a decent-sized city, it's okay to buy from the local "white-box" shop if you get a good feeling when you walk in the door. (A "white box" is a no-name computer assembled from parts that have likely been imported from Taiwan.) If you're in the hinterlands and working by mail, you don't want to take that chance.

Buy serious development hardware.   For your main development box, buy as much as you can afford: RAM, hard drive, CPU speed, video resolution, monitor. You should be billing a high enough hourly rate that the productivity is worth it. Of course, if you're not doing hourly work, you may have to make some compromises here. In my own work, I've found that the most important factor is plenty of RAM, followed by a fast-enough CPU and a good-enough video card.

Skip the tape drive.   You can safely skip the tape drive; most developers never find time to set up a proper tape rotation schedule, or to take the tapes offsite. Instead, buy fast hard drives and store your data on a pair of mirrored drives. This protects you against drive failure. It does not protect you against house fires. If you're worried about that, use external USB 2.0 or FireWire drives for your data, and rotate them offsite frequently. I figure I'll have so many other things to worry about if the farm burns down that it's not worth the hassle for me. (I also back up critical files to a colocated server at my ISP's facility, and have collaborators on most of my coding projects who have full copies of the source code in other states.)

Store data separately.   I find that I *repave* (reformat and install everything from scratch) my development box about once every six months. This used to involve copying off all the data files, formatting, and putting on all the programs, then copying back the data files. I finally realized that at least some of that was pointless work. Now my main development box is actually two machines. One is the spiffy fast Athlon with all the RAM. This box has all of my programs installed but none of the data. The second box has a reasonable amount of RAM, a midrange CPU, and a ton of mirrored hard drive space. It stores all of my data: e-mail, source code, book chapters, articles, and so on. The two boxes are connected by a pair of fast network cards and a crossover cable, with addresses outside my main network space. Net result: I can completely reformat my program box without touching the data box. When I'm done reinstalling, I just map the drive back from the data box, and my data is there ready for me to get back to work. Of course, I don't install anything other than the inevitable Windows patches on the data box in order to keep it stable.

Keep drive images.   After you set up your computer the way you like it, but before you start working, consider using an application such as Norton Ghost (`www.symantec.com/sabu/ghost/ghost_personal/`) to store a snapshot of the drive, either to another hard drive or to a CD-ROM or DVD-ROM. This will speed up the inevitable rebuilds immensely. Of course, because they won't have the latest security patches, such snapshots do age to the point of uselessness eventually, but if you have to rebuild relatively soon they'll save you lots of time.

Use virtual machines.   Virtual machines are your friend. As a developer, you're likely need to test all sorts of crazy software that you don't want to run on your main box. That's what VMware Workstation (`www.vmware.com/products/desktop/ws_features.html`) or Microsoft Virtual PC 2004 (`www.microsoft.com/windowsxp/virtualpc/`) is for. With virtual machine software, you can create an entire computer inside a window on another computer, without installing anything on the real hardware. You can use virtual machines for setting up Bulgarian Windows 98 SE, or installing the latest Firebird beta so you can see how broken your CSS is, or testing at 640×480 screen resolution. My recommendation: Get another box just to run the virtual machines. Yes, you could run them on your main box, but these products suck down lots of CPU time, especially when you're starting and snapshotting and stopping machines. I personally don't care to wait for that.

Treat yourself to a good monitor or two.   A good monitor is a great productivity booster—multiple monitors are even better. I like lots of pixels. LCD screens are sleek and sexy, but they don't have enough pixels to suit me. I'm running a Sony Trinitron real CRT monitor on my development box. If I had enough physical desktop room, I'd probably put two of them side by side.

Use KVM switches.   I have 21 computers in my home office network at the moment. I do not have 21 monitors. I use Terminal Services or Remote Desktop to manage some of them. Most, though, are on a keyboard-video-mouse (KVM) switch, so I can have a nice keyboard and monitor no matter which system I'm trying to work with. If you're buying a KVM switch, make sure you get one that passes the mouse wheel signal through and that uses standard cables rather than hideously expensive proprietary ones.

Get your own domain.   If you're working with Internet technologies at all, I recommend you get your own domain routed to your house and learn to set up your own web server. This will give you a handy test bed, and teach you much about what will go wrong. If you're working with databases, set up your own database server. If you're developing against servers, you need to have ones that you can crash without upsetting anyone else.

Use a firewall.   When you're connected to the network full time, you must install a firewall. I personally prefer to use a hardware firewall, rather than complicate my software setup. Life is too short to spend a lot of time eradicating viruses and dealing with security holes.

Set aside test machines.   If you can afford a spare computer or two (check eBay for deals on not-so-new business computers), set them aside for use in testing. You really shouldn't test your own software, or new tools, on your main development computer. It's much safer to use a computer without anything important installed, so that if something goes terribly wrong, you can just reformat and reinstall your disk image rather than struggling to recover critical data or reinstall the programs that you use every day.

Use a mix of machines for testing.   It's unlikely that all of your users will have brand-new hardware. Test on a variety of systems: new, old, and ancient. Fortunately, older computers can often be had for little or nothing from friends or relatives who are upgrading (though they may expect you to help set up their new system in return!).

Set aside a build machine.   It's also useful to set aside one computer, with a carefully controlled configuration, to act as the build machine for your project. By building every version of the application on a single machine, you can eliminate problems, such as newer libraries creeping in because you upgraded some piece of software on your development machine. Alternatively, you can configure and use a virtual machine for this process. I'll talk more about the build process in Chapter 13, "Mastering the Build Process."

Bug-Tracking Tools

At last I've arrived at the portion of the chapter that you might have been expecting right from the start: using a tool to track bugs. Tracking bugs is one of those best practices that every developer should use on every application of any size or complexity. Keeping track of bugs—and their resolutions—is essential for two reasons. First, it's the best way to make sure that a bug actually gets resolved, rather than merely being forgotten. Second, it gives you a way to see what common mistakes have plagued your work in the past, and helps you figure out where to concentrate your code-improvement efforts. In the final part of this chapter, I'll show you how to choose and use a bug-tracking tool in your own development.

Choosing a Bug-Tracking Tool

There are dozens of bug-tracking tools available; indeed, if you include tools that are used within a single company, I'm sure there are thousands. These tools range from freeware applications to enterprise-level applications that will cost you hundreds of dollars per user. Some are cross-platform, some run as Windows applications, and some run as web applications. One list of bug-tracking applications is at `http://testingfaqs.org/t-track.html`; a search on Google will turn up even more alternatives.

Given this overwhelming variety of tools, how do you choose the one that's right for you? To some extent, it's going to be a matter of random chance. Few of us can afford the time to test out dozens of alternatives for a single tool. By asking developers you trust and reading reviews, you can probably come up with a shorter list to take a look at. When you do, here are some issues you might consider:

- Can you afford this particular tool? Consider not just the price of licensing, but also the cost of possibly needing a dedicated server or a database to go with it. If it's out of your price range, regardless of how good the tool is, it's not worth evaluating.

- Do you need to pay a license fee for each user, or is there a onetime price? Will there be additional costs as your company grows and you hire more developers and testers?

- Do you need to be able to track bugs on more than one platform (such as Linux and Windows)? If so, you'll want to limit your search to cross-platform or web-based solutions.

- Do you need to share bug-tracking information with a distributed team? If so, make sure your solution for bug-tracking includes a web or other remote component so that team members in remote locations can share in the process.

- Does the tool send e-mail notifications to users when they are assigned a bug? If not, you're going to have to find some other way to force developers to actually keep an eye on the bug list.

- Does the tool have a web-based or other interface that allows people outside your organization to enter bugs? If not, you'll have to retype any bugs you get from beta testers in order to get them into the system.

- Does the tool allow adding custom pieces of information to each bug? If not, you're at the mercy of the tool developers as far as what information you can track. This is fine, as long as you can't think of anything that you critically need to know that's not on the list.

- Does the tool distinguish visually between bugs and feature requests (or sort them)? If not, you'll probably end up using two different tools to track bugs and feature requests, which means developers need to look yet another place to do their jobs.

- Does the tool integrate with your other management tools? In particular, integration with requirements management tools and source code control tools can be useful as you attempt to trace exactly what happened with a particular feature.

- Does the tool allow a flexible workflow where, for example, a bug might be closed and then reopened when the tester discovers that it wasn't fixed after all? If not, you're going to be trying to adopt your process to the tool rather than the other way around, which is usually a bad idea.

- Where does the tool store information? If it's in an XML file or a SQL Server database, for example, you have some assurance that you can get the data back out if you ever switch tools (perhaps because the original vendor went out of business). If it's all in some proprietary format, you're staking your ability to remember history on the vendor's continued existence.

TECHNOLOGY TRAP

The Burden of Process

For some reason, bug tracking seems to attract people who believe that life is best structured with a very detailed process. I've seen some bug-tracking systems that made entering a bug a 30-minute process, by the time you collected all of the required information (library versions, operating system version, amount of RAM, other applications running at the same time...) and looked up the responsible developer so you could properly assign the bug.

Loading too much process on top of your bug-tracking system is dangerous. If you make the process of entering a bug difficult, people will not react by being more diligent about collecting the "necessary" information. Rather, they simply won't enter bugs at all. Instead, bug reports will come to developers via e-mail, telephone calls, and hallway conversations. The bug system will deteriorate into a sham, used only by managers and those testers too new to know any better.

If you're working with a team and you discover that the bug-tracking system isn't getting used, find out why. Most likely you'll discover that it's too cumbersome to enter a new bug. Get rid of the excess process, or find a tool with less process, to make your team happier and better track your bugs.

Beyond considering this list and looking at feature comparisons, it's important to spend a bit of time trying out any bug-tracking tool you're going to use. That's the only way to make sure that it's not an impediment to your workflow. Ideally, you want entering and tracking bugs to be so easy that testers and developers are never tempted to work around the tool. Fortunately, most vendors in this area offer some sort of trial version so that you can get a feel for functionality.

Using a Bug-Tracking Tool

For my own projects, I'm currently using FogBUGZ (`www.fogcreek.com/FogBUGZ/index.html`) as a bug-tracking tool. FogBUGZ suits my requirements well (being web-based, it's useful with the far-flung network of partners I have, and it integrates directly with my SourceGear Vault source code control system), though it's hardly the only package I could be using.

Figure 9.1 shows a typical FogBUGZ bug report. In this case, it's a closed bug from a vertical-market application that I helped develop (I'm not using Download Tracker for this example because I haven't yet started building up a database of Download Tracker bugs).

The first thing to notice here is the workflow. The bug was opened by someone testing the application and then assigned to me, since I was the developer of the feature in question. I fixed the bug, resolved it as fixed, and FogBUGZ automatically assigned it back to the person who originally entered it. He then tested the software again, agreed that the bug was fixed, and closed the report. It's important that developers not close their own bugs (indeed, good bug-tracking software won't even allow this). Otherwise, the temptation is simply too great to implement a quick-and-dirty "fix" that doesn't address the entire problem, and to sweep any problems back under the rug.

The bug report itself, while short, includes the three essential pieces of information that should be identified for every bug:

- What happened
- What the tester thinks should happen instead
- Steps to reproduce the problem

Without these three pieces of information, it's difficult or impossible to fix bugs (or even to know if they *are* bugs). Sometimes you don't need to be explicit about what should happen; if a particular series of steps causes your software to erase the user's hard drive, it's pretty obvious that "not erasing the hard drive" is the desired outcome (unless you're writing disk-partitioning software). But when in doubt, a good tester will be explicit when entering a bug report. Reproduction steps are especially critical. The easier it is for a developer to see the code actually failing, the more likely they are to be able to fix the problem.

FIGURE 9.1
A sample bug report

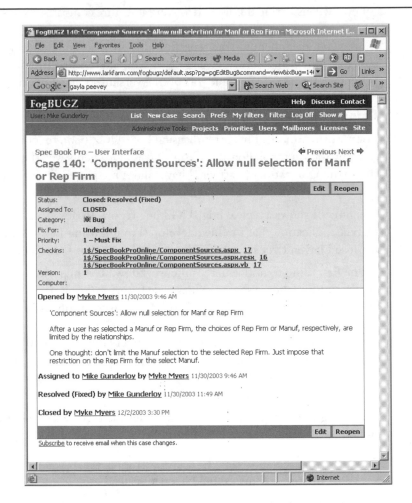

You can also see the effect of FogBUGZ-Vault integration in this example. Because I entered the bug number when I checked the fixed files into Vault, those files are listed on the bug report together with the appropriate version number. The hyperlinks in the bug report let me see the history of the affected file or the actual affected code.

This particular bug went through its entire life cycle in a matter of days, with most of the work being concentrated in a few hours. That's not unusual for bugs in applications that I work on. With tiny bugs, the temptation will always be there to just e-mail or phone the developer to get it fixed. Resist the temptation! By putting *all* bugs and feature requests in the bug-tracking system, no matter how trivial, you'll gain two big advantages. First, managers can be sure that there's a single place to go that contains every potential work item, and use it to monitor the workload. Second, developers can use the bug-tracking system to prioritize their work, because everything they need to do is stored in that single place.

RULE   Integrate bug tracking with your daily planning routine.

Bug-Squashing Checklist

Nobody writes perfect code. But with the right set of bug-tracking practices, you can make the code you release much better than the code you initially wrote:

- Develop a list of risks to your project, and assess their relative importance.
- Maintain a top-five risks list.
- Triage bugs to stay focused on the important things.
- Get help testing your code.
- Build a network of test hardware and software.
- Obtain and use bug-tracking software.

You can also make some changes to your software to make it easier to find and diagnose bugs. In particular, adding logging capabilities to an application can help you figure out exactly what went wrong. That's the subject of the next chapter.

CHAPTER 10

Logging Application Activity

Completed provisioning ship, having received the following:

1200 lbs. celery; 2000 lbs. oranges; 760 lbs. grapefruit from G. & W. Lambert; 1008 lbs. of butter, 30,150 lbs. potatoes; 2000 lbs. onions from the Producers Co-op Dist. Society, Ltd.; 3000 lbs. beef, 600 lbs. yeast; 2400 dozen eggs; 2000 lbs. apples; 1200 lbs. cabbage, from Cervetto & Co.; 1006 lbs. pork from Hutton & Foggit Jones; 500 lbs. cheese from Maxam Cheese Products.

Inspected as to quality by Jacoby, James M., Lt.(jg) (MC), USN, & as to quantity by Davis, A. G., CCstd, USN.

—Deck log of the USS Salt Lake City (CA25), May 25, 1942

There's no record that I can find of anything being wrong with the provisions of the *USS Salt Lake City*, but suppose there had been? In case of an outbreak of food poisoning, it could have been critical for the ship's medical personnel to know which food items came from which suppliers. Software application logs are similar to this sort of routine deck log entry. For the most part, you'll never need to refer back to the information in the log. But when something goes wrong, detailed logging can be incredibly useful. In this chapter, I'll look at a variety of tools and techniques for keeping track of your application's activity.

Logging Strategies

Before I discuss particular tools for logging application activity, I'm going to take a look at the general idea of logging. If you've never set up comprehensive logging for an application before, you might not be sure what this entails. The basic idea is simple: An application log is designed to provide a permanent record of activity within the application. The log might be saved to a text file, a database, or even an instant messenger session. The important thing is that the log provide the clues that you need to tell what happened while the application was running—particularly if something went wrong.

Logging during Development

Logging is typically not all that critical during development. That's because as the developer you have the comparative luxury to drop into the debugger when something goes wrong, so you may not have to analyze crashes based on the application's history. Yet there are still some circumstances where maintaining a log can be important:

- When internal testers are working with your application, a log can help you understand the actions that led to a particular bug.

- If the application depends on asynchronous input (such as financial data from an external web service, or events from an analog-to-digital converter), a log can help clarify the order of events.

- Some bugs only manifest themselves when the application isn't running in the debugger. For those bugs, a log can provide vital clues.

- Some bugs may occur only after hundreds or thousands of calls to a particular function. In such a case, it can be helpful to log what's happened during an automated testing run so you can look for patterns.

The basic goal of logging during development is to collect information that you can't get by running the code in the debugger.

Logging after Shipping

Logging is usually more useful after the product has actually shipped to end users. Generally speaking, you can't trust the ultimate users of an application to write a good bug report. (See Chapter 9, "Tracking and Squashing Bugs," for a discussion of good bug reports.) It's much easier to ask them to submit the log along with their description of the problem.

When the application is with end users, though, you need to pay attention to the potential overhead of logging. Depending on the amount of information you save and the form that you save it in, this overhead can be substantial. This leads to a simple rule:

RULE   In a shipping application, it should be easy to turn logging on and off.

Rather than implement continuous logging at all times, you need to implement a scheme that lets the end user turn logging on, perhaps by editing an XML file or a Registry key. That way, the logging code can be dormant and not affect application performance until it's really needed. Typically, you or (if you're lucky) your customer support staff will instruct the end user to turn on logging, re-create the problem, send you the log, and then turn logging back off.

When you do turn logging on in a shipping application, what should you log? Here are some ideas:

- Error messages and information, including a stack trace of the error
- The state of internal data structures at key points in the application
- User actions, such as button clicks and menu item selections
- The time that significant actions were performed
- Important information about the environment, such as variable settings and available memory

In general, you want to make sure that the application log includes enough clues that you can tell what went wrong when something goes wrong. If you think about how you debug your application when it's running on your computer, you should be able to come up with a good list of information to log.

RULE   Log the information that you use when debugging.

Logging Tools

As a developer, you have several good choices for implementing logging in your applications:

- The `Trace` and `Debug` classes
- The `EventLog` class
- The Logging Application Block

- The Enterprise Instrumentation Framework
- log4net

With these choices available, it's unlikely that writing your own logging code is the best bet. Take the time to evaluate these packages before you decide to set off on your own. You'll probably find that your logging needs have already been anticipated. In this section of the chapter, I'll review some of the features of these logging packages.

The *Trace* and *Debug* Classes

I mentioned the System.Diagnostics namespace, and the Trace and Debug classes that it contains, in Chapter 4, "Coding Defensively." Now it's time to look at the Trace class in somewhat more detail, because it provides basic runtime logging functionality. If your needs are simple, you might be able to use the Trace class in your own logging strategy. In this section, I'll dig into the Trace class in a bit more detail, showing you how to use the TraceListener and TraceSwitch classes to implement a configurable logging strategy.

Mechanics of the *Trace* Class

So far, you've seen the use of the Trace.Assert method during coding. But the Trace class is much more flexible than that. Table 10.1 lists some of the members of the Trace class.

TABLE 10.1 Selected Members of the *Trace* Class

Member	Type	Description
Assert	Method	Checks a condition and displays a message if the condition evaluates to False
AutoFlush	Property	If set to True, specifies that the Flush method should be called on the Listeners collection after every write
Close	Method	Flushes the output buffer and then closes the Listeners collection
Fail	Method	Displays an error message
Flush	Method	Flushes the output buffer and causes buffered data to be written to the Listeners collection
Listeners	Property	Specifies a collection of Listeners that will receive the trace output
Write	Method	Writes the given information to the trace listeners in the Listeners collection
WriteIf	Method	Writes the given information to the trace listeners in the Listeners collection only if a specified condition is True
WriteLine	Method	Same as Write, but appends a newline character after the information
WriteLineIf	Method	Same as WriteIf, but appends a newline character after the information

For application logging, the key methods here are the four `Write` methods, which can be used to write arbitrary information to the members of the `Listeners` collection. What can go in this collection? Just about anything, as you'll learn in the next section.

The `Debug` class has the same members as the `Trace` class, and uses the same communications channels. I won't use the `Debug` class in this chapter because it's generally not useful in logging after an application ships, because the debug code is disabled at that time.

Using Trace Listeners

Trace listeners are classes (derived from the abstract `TraceListener` class) that can receive messages from the `Trace` class. The `Trace` class can have any number of trace listeners in its `Listeners` collection, and all output from the `Trace` class (for example, the string sent with a call to `Trace.Write`) is received by every listener in the collection. The .NET Framework includes three standard implementations of the `TraceListener` class:

DefaultTraceListener A `DefaultTraceListener` object is automatically added to the `Listeners` collection of the `Trace` and `Debug` classes at startup. Its behavior is to write messages to the Output window.

TextWriterTraceListener A `TextWriterTraceListener` object writes messages to any class that derives from the `Stream` class. You can use a `TextWriterTraceListener` object to write messages to the console, to a file, or even to a network connection.

EventLogTraceListener An `EventLogTraceListener` object writes messages to the Windows event log.

You're also free to create custom trace listeners by creating your own class that inherits from the base `TraceListener` class. If you create such a class, you are required to implement at least the `Write` and `WriteLine` methods.

Controlling Tracing with Switches

To use the `Trace` class for runtime application logging, you'll also need to know about trace switches. Trace switches allow you to control the amount and detail of tracking done in a program. These switches are set in an external XML configuration file. Since XML files are plain text, this gives you an easy way to let the user turn on tracing (probably at your instruction). There's no need to recompile the application. The application will automatically pick up the changes from the configuration file the next time you run the application.

Trace switch classes derive from the abstract `Switch` class. There are two predefined classes for creating trace switches: the `BooleanSwitch` class and the `TraceSwitch` class. Both of these classes derive from the abstract `Switch` class. You can also define your own trace switch class by deriving a class from the `Switch` class.

The `BooleanSwitch` class lets you simply turn tracking on or off. Its default value is 0, which indicates that the `Trace` class should not produce any output. If you set the value of a `BooleanSwitch` class to any non-zero value, it turns tracing on.

The `TraceSwitch` class provides for five levels of tracing. These values are defined in the `TraceLevel` enumeration, with a default of 0:

- Off (0): No tracing
- Error (1): Error messages only
- Warning (2): Warning and error messages
- Info (3): Warning, error, and informational messages
- Verbose (4): All messages including extra detail

The `TraceSwitch` class has a set of properties that you can check at runtime to determine the specified tracing level, as shown in Table 10.2.

TABLE 10.2 Selected Properties of the *TraceSwitch* Class

Property	Description
Level	Returns one of the `TraceLevel` enumeration values to indicate the tracing level that's currently set
TraceError	Returns True if `Level` is set to `Error`, `Warning`, `Info`, or `Verbose`; otherwise, returns False
TraceInfo	Returns True if `Level` is set to `Info` or `Verbose`; otherwise, returns False
TraceVerbose	Returns True if `Level` is set to `Verbose`; otherwise, returns False
TraceWarning	Returns True if `Level` is set to `Warning`, `Info`, or `Verbose`; otherwise, returns False

Logging with the *Trace* class

Now that you've seen all the pieces that provide configurable tracing with the `Trace` class, let me show you how they fit together. Here's how I can use the `Trace` class to add some configurable logging to the `DownloadTracker` test program. First, I've declared a `TraceSwitch` class at the class level, so it's available throughout the application:

```
// Switch to control runtime application logging
static TraceSwitch ts = new TraceSwitch("MainLog",
    "Control application logging");
```

With the switch declared, I can use its properties to control the rest of the logging logic. For example, here's some code from the Load event handler for the main form:

```
private void Form1_Load(object sender, System.EventArgs e)
{
    // Add a listener if the user has requested tracing
    if(ts.Level>0)
    {
        TextWriterTraceListener tl = new TextWriterTraceListener(
            File.CreateText(Path.Combine(
            System.Environment.GetFolderPath(
            Environment.SpecialFolder.ApplicationData),
            "DTLog.txt")));
        Trace.Listeners.Add(tl);
    }
    // Write an informational message
    if(ts.TraceVerbose)
        Trace.WriteLine("Started DownloadTracker", "DTInformation");
}
```

This code adds a new trace listener to handle logged messages—but only if tracing is actually turned on in the application's configuration file. Then, if the tracing level is set to Verbose, it writes a message. The second argument to the WriteLine method is an arbitrary category for the event; this is mostly useful if you're using an EventLogTraceListener.

TIP   Note the use of the System.Environment.GetFolderPath method to make sure that the code writes the log file to a folder where the user is guaranteed to have the right to create files.

Whenever something significant happens in the application, it makes another call to the Trace.WriteLine method after checking the trace level:

```
private void btnGo_Click(object sender, System.EventArgs e)
{
    // Write an informational message
    if(ts.TraceInfo)
        Trace.WriteLine("User clicked the Go button", "DTInformation");

    // other code omitted

    // Write a log message
    if(ts.TraceError)
        Trace.WriteLine("Downloading " + d.ProductName, "DTAction");
    DT.UpdateDownload(d);
}
```

The final step is to set up the application configuration file, which is just an XML file named with the application's name plus the `.config` extension (for example, `DownloadTracker.exe.config`). Here are the contents that I'd ship that file with, with a trace level that disables all tracing:

```
<?xml version="1.0" encoding="utf-8" ?>
<configuration>
    <system.diagnostics>
        <switches>
            <add name="MainLog" value="0" />
        </switches>
    </system.diagnostics>
</configuration>
```

If you run the application with this configuration file, you'll find that it doesn't even create a log file. However, if you change the value attribute of the add tag, then events will be logged depending on the value that you set. For example, a value of 4 will produce a file similar to this:

```
DTInformation: Started DownloadTracker
DTInformation: User clicked the Go button
DTAction: Downloading Newdownload.zip
```

> **TIP**   If you add a configuration file named `App.config` to the root folder of your application, Visual Studio .NET will take care of making a copy with the correct name at runtime.

The *EventLog* Class

There's another logging option in the `System.Diagnostics` namespace: you can use the `EventLog` class to write directly to the Windows event logs. This has the advantage that most users already know how to use the Event Log Viewer to look at event log entries. It also puts your logging messages into a repository that's not likely to be damaged or deleted accidentally.

Keep in mind, though, that there is no event log on Windows 95 or Windows 98, so you'll need to find a different solution if your target market includes those operating systems.

Table 10.3 shows some of the important members of the `EventLog` class.

TABLE 10.3   Selected Members of the *EventLog* Class

Member	Type	Description
Clear	Method	Removes all entries from the specified event log
CreateEventSource	Method	Creates a custom event source that you can use to write to an event log
Log	Property	The name of the event log to use with this instance of the class

TABLE 10.3 CONTINUED Selected Members of the *EventLog* Class

Member	Type	Description
MachineName	Property	The name of the computer where the event log is located
Source	Property	The event source to use when posting events
SourceExists	Method	Checks to see whether a specified event source already exists
WriteEntry	Method	Writes a new entry to the event log

Writing to the event log is easy. Here's how you might instrument a click event:

```
private void btnGo_Click(object sender, System.EventArgs e)
{
    EventLog el = new EventLog("Application");
    el.Source = "DownloadTracker";
    // Write an informational message
    el.WriteEntry("User clicked the Go button", EventLogEntryType.Information);

    // other code omitted

    // Write a log message
    el.WriteEntry("Downloading " + d.ProductName, EventLogEntryType.Error);
    DT.UpdateDownload(d);
}
```

This code first sets up a reference to the standard Application log, and then uses the WriteLine method to pass messages to the log. Figure 10.1 shows one of these messages in the Event Log Viewer application.

If you like, you can create your own custom event log instead of using the standard Application log. This requires only a little more code. First, you need to check whether the log already exists, and create it if it does not. Second, you just use the new log name when writing events:

```
private void Form1_Load(object sender, System.EventArgs e)
{
    // Create the new event log and the corresponding source if need be
    if(!EventLog.SourceExists("DownloadTracker"))
        EventLog.CreateEventSource("DownloadTracker",
          "DownloadTrackerLog");

    // Write an informational message
    EventLog el = new EventLog();
    el.Source = "DownloadTracker");
    el.WriteEntry("Started DownloadTracker", EventLogEntryType.Information);
}
```

```
private void btnGo_Click(object sender, System.EventArgs e)
{
    EventLog el = new EventLog();
    el.Source = "DownloadTracker";
    // Write an informational message
    el.WriteEntry("User clicked the Go button", EventLogEntryType.Information);

    // other code omitted

    // Write a log message
    el.WriteEntry("Downloading " + d.ProductName, EventLogEntryType.Error);
    DT.UpdateDownload(d);
}
```

One nice thing about the event log methods is that they all take an optional parameter that specifies a computer name whose log should be used. If you're testing your application on an intranet, this gives you an easy way to consolidate events from many test machines to a single place.

Using an event log to handle your logging also means that you can take advantage of the standard Windows management infrastructure for events. For example, the user can specify a maximum size for the event log, and have newer events overwrite older ones when the log threatens to grow beyond that size. The Event Log Viewer application also supports filtering event logs to make it easier to find particular events.

FIGURE 10.1
An event log message
from Download Tracker

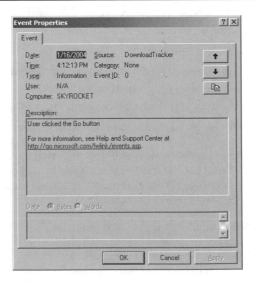

But the `EventLog` class doesn't have the ability to choose at runtime whether or not to write a particular event. If that's important to you, you'll need to use the `Trace` object to check for a trace level, and then call the `EventLog.WriteEntry` method depending on the current trace level.

NOTE I didn't want to load up the actual Download Tracker code with a bunch of different logging mechanisms. So unlike the other code in this book, you won't find most of the code from this chapter in the sample project.

The Enterprise Instrumentation Framework

The `Trace` class provides all the basics you need for application logging, but sometimes you'll need to move beyond the basics. For example, correlating application logs between multiple tiers of a distributed application can be difficult. One way to overcome this difficulty is to use the Enterprise Instrumentation Framework (EIF), a set of classes and utilities that work with the .NET languages to provide monitoring for distributed applications. Microsoft has released the EIF as a free download at `www.microsoft.com/downloads/details.aspx?FamilyId=80DF04BC-267D-4919-8BB4-1F84B7EB1368&displaylang=en`. Although it's presented as an event-monitoring solution, you'll see that it's well suited as the core of a logging strategy. The key features of EIF are

- A single model for raising and recording tracing and diagnostic events across all parts of a distributed application

- Windows Management Instrumentation (WMI) compatibility for integration with existing enterprise-monitoring tools

- A flexible runtime configuration layer that's designed to be modified by simple scripting code for "on-the-fly" changes to your monitoring configuration

- Windows Event Tracing, a new service for high-speed kernel-mode tracing that's capable of recording hundreds or thousands of events in rapid succession

- Event correlation across distributed applications

NOTE EIF was originally released with Visual Studio .NET 2003, but it will work with the .NET Framework 1.0 as long as you install SP2 for the Framework.

For the sort of small applications that I'm focusing on in this book, the EIF may be too complex. Nevertheless, it's worth having an overview of its architecture so that you can have it in mind as you move to more complex development.

The EIF Architecture

Figure 10.2 provides a high-level overview of the EIF architecture.

The overall idea of EIF is to define *event sources*, which post events from any tier of an application, and *event sinks*, which can receive events. EIF's own instrumentation API works as a routing layer between sources and sinks, and is controlled by XML configuration files. Those files themselves can be modified by scripting code, creating a convenient way for testers or administrators to manage the details of event logging. If your application begins to fail, for example, you can start capturing detailed information to a Windows event log, a trace log, or a WMI listener, simply by running a configuration script and without recompiling or stopping any tier of your application. Of course, you have to build in the event sources when you create the application. Note that this is an even more powerful way of configuring logging than the Trace class offers, because you can change the logging level on-the-fly while an application is actually failing. The price for this is that you need to deal with a more complex architecture.

FIGURE 10.2
EIF architecture

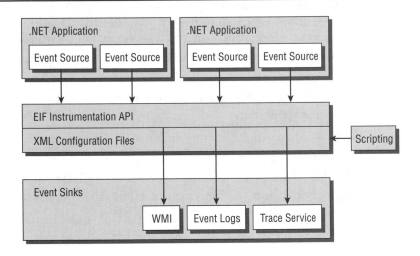

Event Sources

When you're using EIF, an event source is an instance of a particular class. When you hook up EIF to your application (by setting a reference to the Microsoft.EnterpriseInstrumentation namespace, which is available after you install the EIF download), it automatically adds a default event source with the reserved name Application. To raise an event, you call the static Raise method of one of the classes contained in the Microsoft.EnterpriseInformation.Schema namespace. If you don't specify a source, the default application source is assumed. The Microsoft.EnterpriseInformation.Schema namespace defines a number of event classes, which you can use to indicate different types of events. For example:

```
TraceMessageEvent.Raise("Tracing message");
AuditMessageEvent.Raise("Recording an audit record");
AdminMessageEvent.Raise("An administrative event");
```

To define your own event sources, in addition to those built into the EIF, you just create new instances of the EventSource class. For example, you might want to distinguish events raised by a user interface component from events raised by a database component. These user-defined event sources are known as SoftwareElement event sources. In code, it works this way:

```
class UserInterfaceComponent
{
    public static EventSource es = new EventSource("UI");

    // code somewhere in the component
    public void ConfigurationMethod()
    {
        // raise an EIF event
        TraceMessageEvent.Raise(es, "A message from the UI component");
    }
}

class DatabaseComponent
{
    public static EventSource es = new EventSource("Database");

    // code somewhere in the component
    public void DatabaseMethod()
    {
        // raise an EIF event
        TraceMessageEvent.Raise(es,
            "A message from the database component");
    }
}
```

Event Sinks

The EIF supplies three standard event sinks. You don't have to write any code to make use of these sinks, beyond the code that raises EIF events:

TraceEventSink   This sink uses the new Windows Trace Session Manager to write to a trace log. The sink can handle hundreds or thousands of events per second, and uses a custom binary log file format.

LogEventSink   This sink writes to the Windows Application event log. By default, it writes to the local machine, but you can also specify a computer name (useful for consolidating events to a central location).

WMIEventSink   This sink uses Windows Management Instrumentation (WMI) for output. It's the slowest of the three alternatives, and so should be reserved for infrequent or critical events. But it's also the one that will plug into third-party monitoring frameworks most easily.

You can also define custom event sinks. To do so, you derive a class from the abstract base class EventSink, writing code to send events wherever you like by implementing the Write method. Custom event sinks must be compiled with a strong name and installed into the Global Assembly Cache (GAC). For end-user logging, you'd probably want a custom event sink that simply saves events to a disk file. However, for an application that only runs on a single PC, EIF is probably overkill; for a distributed application, a more central sink such as the TraceEventSink or WmiEventSink is probably a better bet.

> **NOTE**   For more alternatives, see the discussion of the Logging Application Block later in this chapter.

> **NOTE**   If you need more information on assigning a strong name to an assembly a good place to start is with the Patterns & Practices chapter "Building Secure Assemblies" (http:// msdn.microsoft.com/library/default.asp?url=/library/en-us/dnnetsec/html/ THCMCh07.asp).

Configuring EIF

When you're using the EIF, your code won't contain any explicit connections between event sources and event sinks. Instead, a set of XML configuration files controls these connections at runtime. This has the great advantage that you can customize the configuration to save more or fewer events depending on circumstances. In a routine operation, you might not hook up any event sources to event sinks at all; in this case, all of the events are discarded with minimum overhead. To catch infrequent errors, you could connect all of the sources to a TraceEventSink for later analysis. Or, if there's a critical failure happening on a mission-critical server, you can quickly tie the components from that server into WMI for real-time monitoring.

Most of this plumbing is set up with an individual application's EnterpriseInformation.config file, which is stored in the same folder as the application's executable file. Sections in this file include:

<instrumentedApp>   Contains overall information about the application.

`<eventSources>` Includes definitions of each event source in the application.

`<eventSinks>` Defines the event sinks available to the application.

`<eventCategories>` Contains groups of event types that can be enabled or disabled as a unit.

`<filters>` Includes associations between event sinks and event categories.

`<filterBindings>` Contains associations between event sources and filters.

As you can see, the flexibility of EIF results in a pretty complex configuration file. Fortunately, you can start with the sample configuration files installed with EIF and adapt them to your own applications quickly.

The Logging Application Block

You probably noticed that some of the logging-oriented features of the Trace class are absent from the EIF. For example, there's no concept of levels of tracing in the EIF, nor is there any way to format events for easy reading. Microsoft addressed these and added some other features in another free download, the Logging Application Block, which is available at www.microsoft.com/downloads/details.aspx?FamilyId=24F61845-E56C-42D6-BBD5-29F0D5CD7F65&displaylang=en.

The Logging Application Block adds several features to the EIF. From the perspective of maintaining an application log, these are the most important:

- Support for a set of logging levels similar to those that the Trace class defines.

- A new event sink that accepts events into a Microsoft Message Queue (MSMQ) to provide reliable asynchronous logging. This is useful if part of your application is disconnected from your central event repository at times.

- A new event sink that accepts events into a SQL Server database.

- An event transformation engine that can add information to events (for instance, common settings that apply to all events in a class), delete unwanted information, and flexibly format the results using Extensible Stylesheet Language Transformations (XSLT). There's also an interface that allows you to write your own formatting classes.

Other features are included as well, such as support for tracing and metering within web services, that are less important for application logging.

Of course, if the EIF is complex, the EIF plus the Logging Application Block is even more complex. Still, if you're faced with a need to maintain correlated logs on the pieces of a distributed application, I recommend implementing the combination rather than using the EIF alone.

log4net

Another alternative directed specifically at logging is the open-source log4net project (based on the existing log4j open-source project from the Java world). log4net provides a wide range of features aimed directly at application logging:

- Support for the Microsoft .NET Framework 1.0 and 1.1, as well as the .NET Compact Framework, Microsoft's shared-source implementation ("Rotor"), and the open-source Mono implementation

- Output to an extremely wide variety of targets:
  - Databases via ActiveX Data Object (ADO)
  - The ASP.NET trace context
  - The console
  - Event logs
  - Disk files, with or without rolling overwrites
  - An in-memory buffer
  - Windows Messenger (net send) service
  - The Debugger
  - A remoting sink
  - E-mail
  - .NET trace listeners
  - UDP datagrams

- Multiple targets for a single log entry
- Level-based logging to pare events down
- As many different loggers as you like, arranged in a hierarchy for configuration purposes
- Dynamic runtime configuration via XML files
- Static configuration via assembly attributes
- Filtering on a per-target basis, so a target can decide which events it wants to log
- Flexible layout and rendering classes
- A plug-in architecture for easy extension

You can download log4net from `http://log4net.sourceforge.net/`. Like many open-source projects, it seems to be perpetually in beta; as I write this, you can download a beta build of version 1.2 or a release build of version 1.1.1. Either way, don't let the beta status scare you;

this is a mature product that has been under development in the .NET and Java worlds for quite a while now.

As you might guess from the list of features, quite a bit of complexity is available in log4net. But a simple example should give you the flavor of using log4net. For starters, here's what a log4net configuration file (by convention, named with the extension .log4net and the name of the application's executable) might look like for Download Tracker:

```
<?xml version="1.0" encoding="utf-8" ?>
<log4net>
  <!-- Define the logging target -->
    <appender name="FileAppender" type="log4net.Appender.FileAppender">
      <param name="File" value="DTlog.txt" />
      <param name="AppendToFile" value="true" />
    </appender>
    <!-- Set the default logging level and hook up the file -->
    <root>
        <level value="DEBUG" />
        <appender-ref ref="FileAppender" />
    </root>
</log4net>
```

As you can see, the configuration is all contained in XML. Just about everything about log4net can be set in the configuration file. This particular file defines a file to hold the output of logging operations, and sets the default logging to DEBUG, which means that all logging of DEBUG level or higher will be saved to the file.

There are several ways to associate this file (saved as DownloadTracker.exe.log4net) with the actual code being executed, but probably the easiest is to use a .NET attribute. Adding this attribute anywhere in the assembly will do the trick:

```
[assembly: log4net.Config.DOMConfigurator(
 ConfigFileExtension="log4net", Watch=true)]
```

Specifying true for the Watch attribute tells log4net to actively monitor the file, and reload it if it changes. This lets you make on-the-fly changes to things like the logging level, or even the logging target, without restarting the application.

log4net relies on *loggers* to actually provide the information to be logged. You can have any number of loggers in your application, arranged hierarchically. For example, Download Tracker might have a logger named DownloadTracker and another named DownloadTracker.Database. For simplicity, a small project will probably only use a single logger. This can be defined at the class level as a static object:

```
private static readonly log4net.ILog log =
 log4net.LogManager.GetLogger(
 System.Reflection.MethodBase.GetCurrentMethod().DeclaringType);
```

Note the use of reflection here to automatically assign a name to the log, based on the enclosing class. Using this code to declare your loggers means you automatically get a logger hierarchy that matches your class hierarchy. Table 10.4 shows the members of the ILog interface.

TABLE 10.4 Members of the *ILog* Interface

Member	Type	Description
Debug	Method	Logs a message with the DEBUG level
Error	Method	Logs a message with the ERROR level
Fatal	Method	Logs a message with the FATAL level
Info	Method	Logs a message with the INFO level
IsDebugEnabled	Property	Returns True if the logger will save DEBUG messages
IsErrorEnabled	Property	Returns True if the logger will save ERROR messages
IsFatalEnabled	Property	Returns True if the logger will save FATAL messages
IsInfoEnabled	Property	Returns True if the logger will save INFO messages
IsWarnEnabled	Property	Returns True if the logger will save WARN messages
Warn	Method	Logs a message with the WARN level

With these methods, I can rewrite the example of logging in the btnGo event procedure:

```
private void btnGo_Click(object sender, System.EventArgs e)
{
    // Write an informational message
    if(log.IsInfoEnabled)
        log.Info("User clicked the Go button");

    // other code omitted

    // Write a log message
    if(log.IsErrorEnabled)
        log.Errors("Downloading " + d.ProductName);
    DT.UpdateDownload(d);
}
```

Overall, log4net provides an extremely fast and flexible way to log just about anything in a proven, high-performance framework. If you're willing to incorporate an open-source dependency in your development, it's an excellent choice.

Diagnostic Tools

Despite your best intentions, you may some day ship an application to customers without including any logging capabilities. While I'd recommend against doing this, there are other ways to collect the information that you'll need if a problem occurs. In addition to depending on what your customer can tell you about the error, you can run diagnostic software to help you find the reasons for any failure.

Fortunately, Microsoft provides several diagnostic tools that you can use for your own purposes. The first of these is the System Information utility, shown in Figure 10.3.

FIGURE 10.3
The System Information utility

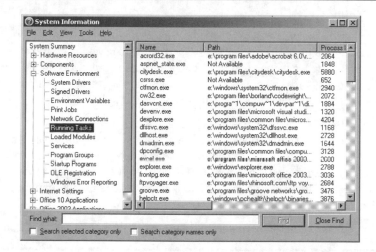

The System Information utility is available on all of the recent Microsoft operating systems, and collects all manner of system information into a single interface. For example, if you want to know the screen resolution and color depth that your users are running with, as well as their video driver details, they can find all of that collected in the System Information tree under Components/Display. To launch the utility, select Start ➤ Programs ➤ Accessories ➤ System Tools ➤ System Information. Alternatively, select Start ➤ Run and launch MSINFO32.EXE. Particularly if you want to collect a variety of information, users will find this utility easier to use than opening a dozen other windows.

If you need a truly comprehensive collection of diagnostic information, try the Microsoft Product Support Reporting Tools (www.microsoft.com/downloads/details.aspx?familyid= cebf3c7c-7ca5-408f-88b7-f9c79b7306c0&displaylang=en). These are a set of scripts from Microsoft designed to collect information without making changes to the system where they're run (beyond leaving some files on the hard drive). A variety of separate scripts are available; for general-purpose use, try the `Base/Setup/Storage/Print/Performance` script. On my Windows XP test system, this script collected several megabytes of information and compressed it into a single cabinet file. The information ranges from event log dumps to the group policy entries for the current user to Registry entries enumerating hot fixes to selected Registry keys. One caution, though: It can take 15 minutes for this script to complete its work, so be sure that your users have a block of time open and have saved their work before running it.

TECHNOLOGY TRAP

Think First!

Now that you've got logging on your mind, it's time to take a step back. It's all too easy to rush into a morass of detail when a bug pops up in your code. Whether this involves dropping into the debugger and setting watches and interrogating the values of variables when you're developing the software, or poring over log files and diagnostic information after the software has shipped, the detail is not the place that you should start.

Before diving into the details, take at least a few moments to think about what happened. Perhaps you can deduce the cause of the error simply by realizing what you've done wrong, or at least narrow down the portion of the code where it's likely to be. Does the error message tell you exactly what happened? Did the user try something that you never considered during testing? These can be much more important clues than a ream of step-by-step logging.

It's good to have logging available as a way to collect information when a truly mysterious bug occurs. But don't forget to look at the forest before you focus on the individual trees.

Logging Checklist

Just about any application should ship with a way to collect runtime logs. When equipping your application for logging, consider these points:

- Use logging during development to collect information that you can't get by running the code in the debugger.
- Use logging after shipping to collect the same information that you'd look for in the debugger.
- Provide an easy way to turn logging on and off at runtime, to avoid the overhead of continuous logging.
- Use the `Trace` class or the log4net package to implement logging for stand-alone applications.

- Use the Enterprise Instrumentation Framework and the Logging Application Block to implement logging for distributed applications.

- Be prepared to replace or supplement logged information with diagnostic information.

One good use for logs is to share information among the members of a team, particularly when the entire team is not located in the same place. In the next chapter, I'll look at some of the other issues involved with small development teams.

CHAPTER 11

Working with Small Teams

We trained hard . . . but it seemed that every time we were beginning to form up into teams we would be reorganized. I was to learn later in life that we tend to meet any new situation by reorganizing; and a wonderful method it can be for creating the illusion of progress while producing confusion, inefficiency, and demoralization.

—Falsely attributed to Petronius Arbiter; more likely Robert Townsend

Although Petronius Arbiter never said that, the sentiment still rings true: If you don't pay attention to the dynamics of teamwork, a team can be a horribly wasteful thing. But if you do pay attention, a good development team can be a marvelously productive entity, turning out high-quality software in record time. In this chapter, I address some of the issues involved in managing a software development team, with particular attention to geographically distributed teams.

Why Work with a Team?

Before thinking about effective teamwork, it's worth considering why you might want to work with a team in the first place. After all, no matter how well your team functions as a unit, there's going to be some overhead incurred in communicating with team members, assigning work, integrating different people's efforts, and so on. Here are some good reasons for undertaking development as part of a team rather than as a lone wolf:

Labor pool   Some projects are simply too large for a single developer to undertake. You might be able to easily develop a project with a dozen classes, and after some time you could extend that to include a hundred or so classes. But what do you do when your initial analysis indicates that you need five hundred classes? A thousand? Ten thousand? At some point, even with the best organization and code generation tools, you'll need to bring in additional help simply to get the job done.

Deadlines   Even if you can finish the hundred-class project, can you finish it soon enough to do you any good? Whether it's the market pressure of wanting to be the first one selling software in a new niche, or the client pressure of delivering a business application by an arbitrary contractual deadline, you usually won't have the luxury of working on a software project for as long as you might like. Sometimes you'll need additional hands just to get the job done in time for it to make a difference.

Skills   If there's one thing you should learn from this book, it's that creating a successful software application involves more skills than just writing code. Someone needs to create documentation and help files, graphics, a website, an installer application, and so on. While you could master all of the necessary skills in time, it may be a better use of your energies to focus on just a few of the necessary areas and find partners who can help with the rest.

The bottom line is that whether or not you're a lone wolf at heart, there are times when working with a team to produce high-quality software makes sense. For the rest of this chapter, I'll assume that you're trying to write software with a team and want to do an effective job. And, since it's *your* application I'm talking about, I'll assume that you're most likely the manager of the team as well.

Why Work Alone?

Although this is a chapter about working with teams, I want to spend a little while talking about working alone first. Not every software project can be effectively done by a team, and not every developer can work effectively on a team. While I encourage you to be flexible, and to consider a development team when it makes sense, here are some reasons why you might choose to work alone instead:

Small projects Some projects are small enough that they don't require a team to finish. In such cases, you might well choose to go it alone, just to avoid the overhead of introducing a team to the process. But before making a decision strictly based on size, remember that even small projects can benefit from a good team.

Psychology Did your report card consistently say "doesn't play well with others"? Do you feel like that's still the case, and you don't see anything wrong with this state of affairs? In that case, you might not be good team material yourself. Or perhaps you've been burned by a bad team experience in the past (for example, being stuck with team members who wouldn't pull their weight). If the very thought of teamwork makes you ill, you might have to concentrate on finding projects that you can do alone.

Opportunity If you're the only software developer in Left Flank, Missouri, your opportunities for building a successful team may be pretty limited. Don't be too quick to make this assumption, though; later in this chapter I'll talk about strategies for building a geographically distributed team.

NOTE When you have multiple people involved in building software, you also need to worry about the proper legal structure for your business. This is a separate question from whether to use a team at all, of course. You wouldn't take software design advice from your lawyer or accountant (I hope!), and you shouldn't take legal or accounting advice from me. I recommend consulting a competent professional in those areas. If you're strapped for cash, Nolo Press (www.nolo.com) sells some excellent legal self-help books.

Managing a Team

To get started thinking about teams, I want to touch on a few of the "soft" (nontechnical) issues involved in team management. I'm not going to try to cover the management field in general. Instead, I'll just mention a few areas that have been important on my own small teams: choosing a structure, tracking progress, and avoiding your own incompetence.

> **NOTE**   If you get interested in this subject, much has been written about managing people in the software business. The classic in the field (and a book well worth reading) is Tom DeMarco and Timothy Lister's *Peopleware* (Dorset House, 1999).

Choosing a Team Structure

One of the decisions that needs to be made early in the team-building process is how the team will be structured. Two of the most common alternatives for small teams are to set up a community of equals or a hierarchy. Each of these has its own pros and cons.

In a community structure, each person on the team is recognized as being equally capable. While different team members will work on different tasks, team members are expected to be able to step in and work on whatever area of the project needs the most attention. Decisions on a community project are typically made by consensus and may require extensive discussion before everyone is in agreement.

A hierarchical structure is more typical of for-profit software development by established companies. Such a structure has one manager (most often with a title such as "program manager," though there's no reason that the manager can't be a developer or a tester) who makes the major decisions and to whom everyone else on the team reports. Hierarchical teams are often structured with people in non-interchangeable roles; there will be a tester, for example, who does nothing but test even when development is lagging.

> **NOTE**   Are there other potential structures? Sure! For example, you might have a community of experienced developers, each managing a hierarchy of less-experienced developers. But these more complex alternatives tend to be used with larger projects than I'm focused on.

My own personal preference for small project teams is to set up a community of equals. Such teams can be harder to set up, but I find working in them to be more fun. However, there's no reason why your preferences need to match mine in this area. What's more important is that the entire team be clear on how things are organized.

> **RULE**   If team members can't agree on a basic structure, the team is unlikely to be able to produce any software.

Tracking Progress

Whatever your preference for team structure, it's important to keep track of what everyone is doing and whether they're running into any problems. Depending on the tools that you're using in your development, you may get some tracking as a side effect. For example, you can configure some source code control systems to automatically send e-mail whenever a new module is checked in. Similarly, some build tools can update a web page on your intranet whenever a new build is successfully tested.

In addition to these moment-by-moment updates (if they exist), it's helpful to get a sense of the big picture on a regular basis. For small teams, I like to keep the level of formal process to a minimum. One method that's worked well for me in the past is the 3×3 report. This report might go to all team members or only to the project manager, depending on how the team is organized. The key is to have each team member produce such a report on a regular basis; I find that weekly is usually the right frequency. As its name suggests, a 3×3 report contains three lists of three items each:

- Three accomplishments for the previous week
- Three obstacles to progress from the previous week
- Three plans for the coming week

There's no need to be completely dogmatic about the number of bullet points in each section. If you've got four accomplishments, or only two obstacles, that's fine. The important thing is to make time to step back once a week and be sure you're still on track. In a community team, you should also commit to watching everyone else's 3×3s and offering suggestions when you have them. In a hierarchical team, the team manager can watch for trouble signs. For example, if the same obstacle appears week after week, the team member may need some help in moving forward. Having items appear in plans for one week and then never show up in accomplishments for the next week can also be a problem.

The Peter Principle

The Peter Principle is a bit of satirical sociology from the late Dr. Laurence J. Peter: In a hierarchy, every employee tends to rise to his or her level of incompetence. Dr. Peter managed to get several books out of this sentence, but while his books are enjoyable, you can understand the principle without reading them. In most organizations, people are promoted when they do their job well, but never demoted unless they do something truly dastardly at the company Christmas party. The end result is that people stop getting promoted when they stop doing their job well, and languish in a position that they can't really fill.

In many software organizations the Peter Principle is evident at work. Successful developers get promoted and turn into unsuccessful managers of developers. In fact, the problem may be worse in software than in many other industries, simply because of the gap between what developers do and what their managers do.

If you find yourself managing a software development team, it's worth taking some active steps to avoid falling afoul of the Peter Principle yourself:

- Don't take on a big team as your first management task. Start small.

- Set aside part of your time to handle management chores, such as reviewing the weekly 3×3 reports, settling disputes among team members, and providing guidance for any team members who appear lost or confused. Don't assume things will just take care of themselves.

- Pay attention to the natural authority distributed around the team. If you're working with good people (and you should be), they will have good ideas that you never thought of.

- Take advantage of the literature on software project management to learn how to be a better manager. An excellent (and not too long) starting point is Jim McCarthy's *Dynamics of Software Development* (Microsoft Press, 1995).

Of course, as a developer-turned-project manager, you do have one big advantage: You understand the development process, so you're likely to be able to understand what the rest of the team is telling you. Just don't let the attraction of actually writing code keep you from doing the necessary management tasks.

TECHNOLOGY TRAP

Big Process in Little Teams

As you're reading about software project management, there's one thing that you should be aware of: Much of the literature presents processes and methodologies as if one size fits all. That is patently not true. Small teams have a different dynamic than big teams do, and can get by with far less process. In fact, too much process (defined as rules to follow, paperwork to fill out, and required tools and procedures) can be fatal to a small team's chances of actually shipping a product.

There are any number of formal processes out there for developing software, from the Microsoft Solutions Framework (MSF) to the Software Engineering Institute's Capability Maturity Model (CMM). Each of them specifies a method for developing software, often with a set of design documents that need to be produced, specific modeling requirements, and so on. While these methods can produce excellent software, they can also impose a tremendous overhead on the development organization.

It's worth browsing through the software management literature to look for practices that might apply to your team. A good starting point is Steve McConnell's *Rapid Development* (Microsoft Press, 1996), which presents a smorgasbord of practices. But implement new bits of process carefully and gradually, and try to measure whether they're actually helping or hindering your team.

Tools for Distributed Teams

With the ubiquitous presence of the Internet, it's become possible to develop software with a team even when the team members are distributed among diverse geographical locations. As I write this, I am located in rural Eastern Washington, where software developers are not precisely thick on the ground. But that's not keeping me from working on several software projects as a team member. I've got partners in Georgia, Seattle, Southern California, Florida, and Israel, just to name a few places.

Assuming you can get a decently high-speed connection to the Internet, remote collaboration is easier than ever. In this section, I'll review some of the tools available for distributed teamwork, with my thoughts on how to use them effectively.

E-mail

Is there any reader of this book who's not already using e-mail? I doubt it. The question is not whether you're using e-mail but whether you're using it efficiently. Here are a few tips:

- Make sure you have some form of spam protection to cut down on junk mail in your inbox. The built-in junk mail filtering in Outlook 2003 is pretty good. If you're using an older version of Outlook, I recommend a Bayesian filter such as SpamBayes (`http://spambayes`
`.sourceforge.net`) or Spam Bully (`www.spambully.com`).

- Save all e-mail related to your project. Use whatever filing capabilities your e-mail client offers to organize it. With hard drive space being extremely cheap these days, there's no reason to discard e-mail that you may want to refer back to in the future.

- Treat e-mail as a tool, not an interruption. There's no reason to interrupt what you're doing by reading each e-mail message as soon as it comes in. Set aside time each day to deal with e-mail messages in a batch. If you can't avoid looking as soon as the little message icon flashes, consider not even launching your e-mail client until you're ready to answer messages.

- Don't send copies of everything to everyone. You can always forward a message later if someone else needs to be brought in to a discussion. E-mail works best for focused exchanges. For open-ended exploration of a topic, consider a conference call or meeting instead. Alternatively, try a Microsoft Exchange public folder or a private news server, where participants can read a discussion without having it all show up in their inbox.

E-mail tends to be the first choice for many developers to use for communication within a team, and it works well for this purpose. But don't let your collaboration stop with e-mail. There are lots of other ways to share information online, as you'll learn in the rest of this section.

Instant Messages

Instant messaging is, in my opinion, another excellent tool for keeping team members in touch with one another. Of course, not everyone feels this way. Usability expert Jakob Nielsen has gone so far as to call instant messaging "toxic" and to declare that it "destroys productivity." I can only conclude that he and I have different approaches to dealing with instant messages, because for me, it's a real productivity enhancer.

As with e-mail, I find the key to effective use of instant messaging is to not let it dominate your schedule. When a new instant message comes in, you're not required to answer it immediately (though you may want to take a quick glance, just in case the subject is urgent). Instead, wait until you have a pause in your other work to deal with the message. If both parties take this approach, a single conversation can stretch out over hours or days, but that's OK; you can always scroll back to remind yourself what's gone before. One thing that I find helps take the sting of urgency out of instant messages is to run the instant messaging client on a secondary computer, rather than on the one where I'm actually writing software. That way, incoming messages don't take the focus away from what I'm doing.

A big problem with instant messaging is the proliferation of instant messaging services. If at all possible, try to get everyone on a project to agree on the same service, whether that be Jabber, MSN Messenger, Yahoo! Instant Messenger, or what have you. Failing that, you might want to investigate a client that can connect to multiple services, such as Trillian (www.trillian.cc/).

I find that it also helps to have a permanent record of instant message conversations automatically saved to my hard drive where I can easily search it in the future. Some instant messaging software can do this automatically; Yahoo!'s messenger client is an example. In other cases, there is add-on software to do the job, such as Messenger Plus, which extends MSN Messenger. Messenger Plus is available from www.msgplus.net/. One word of caution on this particular piece of software: Always do a custom installation so you can decide whether to install the accompanying sponsor software.

RULE   The key to using instant messaging and e-mail effectively is to manage them, rather than letting them manage you.

Online Workspaces

In some cases, you might consider anchoring your entire project at an online workspace. The two leading contenders in this category are SourceForge and GotDotNet.

SourceForge

SourceForge (`http://sourceforge.net/`) is a free repository for open-source code and applications that hosts over 70,000 projects. Projects hosted on SourceForge have access to a variety of services:

- A web-based administration tool to manage the entire project
- Web hosting for project-related content
- A suite of tools to manage bugs and feature requests
- Mailing lists
- Web-based discussion forums
- A file release system, including distributed high-speed download servers
- Access to compile farm hosts running various open-source operating systems
- MySQL database hosting
- A dedicated Concurrent Versions System (CVS) repository for source code control

To host a project at SourceForge, you must first create a SourceForge user account, which is a straightforward process requiring little personal data (though you must supply your legal name). The project must be an open-source project, as defined by the Open Source Initiative (OSI) at `http://opensource.org/docs/definition.php`. Among other things, the project must be licensed for free redistribution, including source code under a license that the OSI finds acceptable. These requirements make SourceForge hosting an unacceptable choice for most commercial projects, unless you're planning to make money only from ancillary services such as training and support.

NOTE   I'll discuss software licenses in Chapter 14, "Protecting Your Intellectual Property."

After creating your user account, you can submit a project registration to become hosted on SourceForge. This entails filling out a series of web forms, and may take half an hour or so even if you have all of your answers together before you start. You'll need to agree to the SourceForge terms of use and provide details on the project and the license you're using with it. All SourceForge project registration submissions are reviewed by the human staff before being approved, so it can take a couple of days for your new project to become active.

Figure 11.1 shows the SourceForge project home page for a typical project (in this case, the ndoc code documentation generator for .NET code). This is the public face of the project, and provides access to releases, news, mailing lists, bug reporting, the CVS repository, and so on.

FIGURE 11.1
A SourceForge project
home page

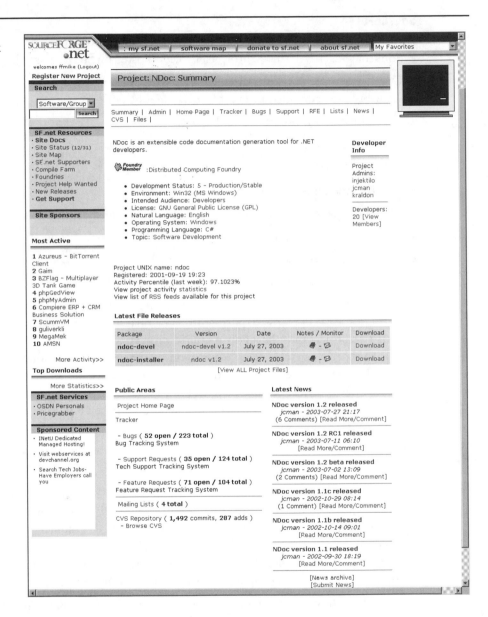

GotDotNet

Microsoft has also gotten into the online project hosting business, with the addition of Got-DotNet Workspaces to its GotDotNet community site for .NET developers (www.gotdotnet.com/community/workspaces/). Being much newer than SourceForge (and appealing to a much smaller number of developers), GotDotNet Workspaces has many fewer projects—about 5000, as of this writing. Projects hosted on GotDotNet have access to these services:

- Source code control that integrates with Visual Studio .NET
- Tools to manage bugs and feature suggestions online
- Web-based discussion feeds
- Hosting for release downloads
- RSS Feeds for project-specific news

As you can see, the services at GotDotNet are somewhat sketchier than those at Source-Forge, but (especially on the source code control front) they're more aimed at .NET developers. GotDotNet uses Microsoft Passport for authentication; as a result, you must have a Passport in order to participate in or download code from a workspace. The site supports both public and private workspaces. Although the default license is based on Microsoft's own shared source license, there is no requirement to adhere to a particular licensing scheme to host your code at GotDotNet.

To create a workspace, you must first register your user account using Microsoft Passport. You can then work through the workspace-creation steps, which are simpler than those at SourceForge. After agreeing to the site's use agreement, you must then submit the license agreement for your code, which is entirely under your control. The final step is to provide basic details about your project (name, description, language, and so on) and to specify whether you'd like a public or a private workspace. The process is completely automated; as soon as you submit the workspace details, it's automatically created for you.

Figure 11.2 shows the GotDotNet Workspaces home page for the .Text blogging engine. Like SourceForge, GotDotNet provides access to all of its essential features via a web interface.

Should You Use an Online Workspace?

Online workspaces are a good fit for projects that need to have their code and releases widely available to both developers and users. I must admit, though, that I don't find them a good fit for my own projects. The trade-off for the easy web availability tends to be a somewhat anemic feature set. Yes, you can manage your source code and track bugs and releases through either GotDotNet or SourceForge. But I think you can do a better job with a few simple tools that will cost you less than a few hundred dollars. If you're in a particularly resource-limited situation, an online workspace may let you get started with team development without a large investment. Even then, I'd suggest you plan for a future when you can move your project to more powerful tools.

FIGURE 11.2
A GotDotNet Work-
spaces home page

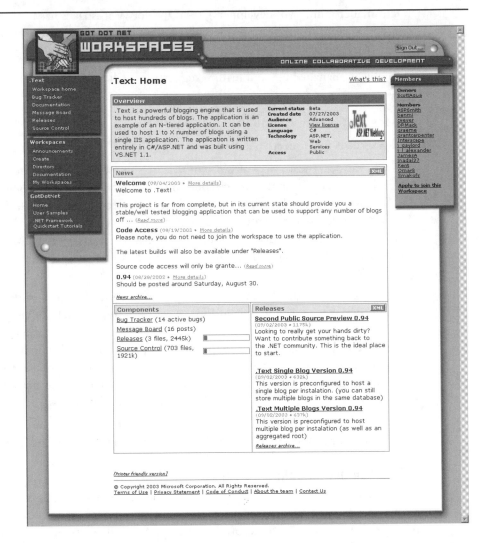

There's another factor that makes me hesitate to recommend an online workspace: You lose control of your code repository when you opt to host a project with one of these systems. While both the Open Source Developers Network (OSDN)—the parent of SourceForge—and Microsoft have said they plan to maintain these workspaces indefinitely, this is a fickle industry. If the business climate changes, you could suddenly find yourself about to lose your online project hosting. In the absolute worst case, you could lose your code without warning. Although that's not a probable outcome, it's not one that I care to risk at all.

Wikis

Another interesting tool for collaboration is the *wiki*. A wiki is a website that's written by its visitors; every page can be edited directly in the web browser by anyone who can view it. You might think this would lead to an avalanche of spam and pornography, but wikis keep track of the history of each page, and successful public wikis tend to breed a community of people dedicated to keeping things well organized. Two good examples are the original WikiWiki-Web at `http://c2.com/cgi/wiki` and the open-source Wikipedia encyclopedia at `http://en.wikipedia.org/`. Figure 11.3 shows a page from the original wiki. As you can see, the layout is plain but the editor does allow users to format the text and insert hyperlinks to other pages.

Wikis are a simple but powerful idea. Although the original software was written as a Perl script, the idea is simple and powerful enough that it's been implemented dozens of times in various languages (there's a page with links to many implementations at `http://c2.com/cgi/wiki?WikiEngines`). Here are some versions that play well with Microsoft software:

Open Wiki (`http://openwiki.com/`) IIS/ASP based; uses Access or SQL Server for storage.

FpWiki (`http://www27.brinkster.com/bleuciel/fpwiki/`) IIS/ASP/FrontPage based; uses Access for storage.

SushiWiki (`http://sourceforge.net/projects/sushiwiki`) C# code ASP.NET implementation; uses SQL Server, MSDE, or XML files for storage.

FlexWiki (`http://www.flexwiki.com/`) Implemented in C# and ASP.NET; uses the file system for storage.

DotWiki (`http://hcorrea.no-ip.com/dotwiki/default.aspx?topic=DotWiki`) Implemented in VB .NET and ASP.NET; uses SQL Server or MSDE for storage.

You can set any of these wiki versions up on an IIS server with a minimum of effort. Although the thought of tracking your project on publicly editable pages may give you pause, that's easily remedied by using IIS's security features to require a login with password to access any of the pages in the wiki folder.

Because they're editable by anyone on the project team, wikis are well suited to project teams organized as a community of equals. Such a team can use a wiki as a central repository for everything from design documents, to notes on bugs, to future plans, to everyone's pizza preferences for the celebratory party when the product ships. The only major drawback to this scheme is that there's no easy way (at least in the wiki software I'm familiar with) to link the data with richer document-oriented applications such as Microsoft Word or Microsoft Excel.

FIGURE 11.3
A page from a wiki

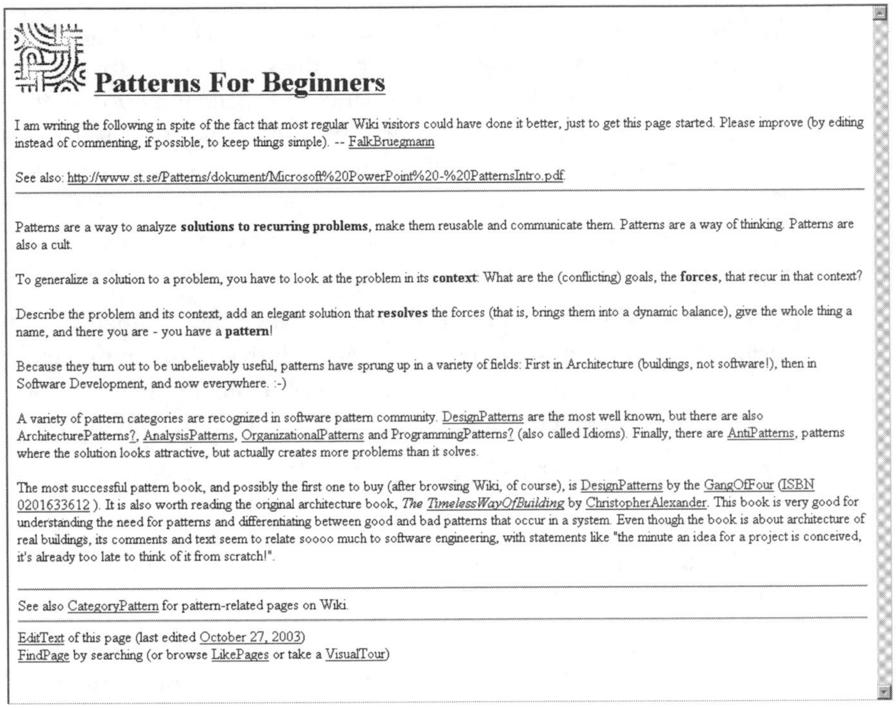

Patterns For Beginners

I am writing the following in spite of the fact that most regular Wiki visitors could have done it better, just to get this page started. Please improve (by editing instead of commenting, if possible, to keep things simple). -- FalkBruegmann

See also: http://www.st.se/Patterns/dokument/Microsoft%20PowerPoint%20-%20PatternsIntro.pdf

Patterns are a way to analyze **solutions to recurring problems**, make them reusable and communicate them. Patterns are a way of thinking. Patterns are also a cult.

To generalize a solution to a problem, you have to look at the problem in its **context**: What are the (conflicting) goals, the **forces**, that recur in that context?

Describe the problem and its context, add an elegant solution that **resolves** the forces (that is, brings them into a dynamic balance), give the whole thing a name, and there you are - you have a **pattern**!

Because they turn out to be unbelievably useful, patterns have sprung up in a variety of fields: First in Architecture (buildings, not software!), then in Software Development, and now everywhere. :-)

A variety of pattern categories are recognized in software pattern community. DesignPatterns are the most well known, but there are also ArchitecturePatterns?, AnalysisPatterns, OrganizationalPatterns and ProgrammingPatterns? (also called Idioms). Finally, there are AntiPatterns, patterns where the solution looks attractive, but actually creates more problems than it solves.

The most successful pattern book, and possibly the first one to buy (after browsing Wiki, of course), is DesignPatterns by the GangOfFour (ISBN 0201633612). It is also worth reading the original architecture book, *The TimelessWayOfBuilding* by ChristopherAlexander. This book is very good for understanding the need for patterns and differentiating between good and bad patterns that occur in a system. Even though the book is about architecture of real buildings, its comments and text seem to relate soooo much to software engineering, with statements like "the minute an idea for a project is conceived, it's already too late to think of it from scratch!".

See also CategoryPattern for pattern-related pages on Wiki.

EditText of this page (last edited October 27, 2003)
FindPage by searching (or browse LikePages or take a VisualTour)

Microsoft SharePoint

Another option for collaboration is Microsoft Windows SharePoint Services 2.0, the latest release of the software formerly known as SharePoint Team Services. As an optional (but free) component of Windows 2003, SharePoint provides a rich collaborative layer that any application is free to use. If you're running Windows 2003, you can download the installer for SharePoint from www.microsoft.com/windowsserver2003/technologies/sharepoint/default.mspx.

SharePoint is built on the twin foundations of Microsoft SQL Server (or MSDE), and ASP.NET. SharePoint is implemented largely as a set of *web parts*, which are ASP.NET controls that run on the server. Web parts can display lists or images, retrieve stock quotes or weather forecasts, and perform a host of other tasks. Web parts are grouped into web part pages, which can be built and modified in an HTML editor, FrontPage, or directly in the browser. A typical SharePoint site might have sections for announcements, events, news, and so on, all of which can be edited in the browser.

SharePoint 2.0 introduces "Meeting Workspaces" and "Document Workspaces." These are SharePoint sites organized around particular tasks and accessed mainly through Office 2003 documents instead of websites. A Meeting Workspace lets you organize the documents and tasks surrounding a meeting, while a Document Workspace provides you with a document-centric collaboration model. Document workspaces run inside a task pane interface as a part of Word, Excel, or PowerPoint documents.

SharePoint is at its best for intranet scenarios; it's not designed to function well in limited-bandwidth situations. If your work involves organizing and sharing many Microsoft Office documents, you may find it a useful tool.

Groove

Another interesting collaborative tool is Groove Workspace, available from `http://groove.net/`. Groove is a general platform for collaborative content of all sorts: files, messages, project plans, notes, instant messages, you name it. Because Groove provides a variety of public APIs, it's extensible to include more tools. The plumbing behind Groove is fairly complex, but the result is simple: All members of a workspace get synchronized copies of the entire workspace on their local computers (synchronization is carried on as a background task over the Internet, and does not require everyone to be online at the same time). Figure 11.4 shows a Groove workspace that I used to organize article publishing for a newsletter; I've also successfully used it to coordinate several software projects.

Groove comes in several editions, including a free Preview Edition (limited to creating three workspaces) and several paid editions, including a $199 Project Edition with Microsoft Project synchronization and other project-management features. You can experiment with the Preview Edition to decide whether the Groove way of working appeals to you, and then upgrade easily to one of the other editions if you like it.

Among other features, Groove is well integrated with Microsoft applications, including Office (imagine collaborative real-time editing of Word documents), Outlook, and SharePoint. You can use a Groove workspace as an extension of a SharePoint website to make it easy to share intranet content with partners outside your company. The major drawbacks of Groove in practice are that it doesn't have much market penetration (so you'll have to convince potential partners to install a copy) and its nonstandard user interface seems to be very resource intensive (requiring a powerful computer for good performance).

FIGURE 11.4
Groove Workspace

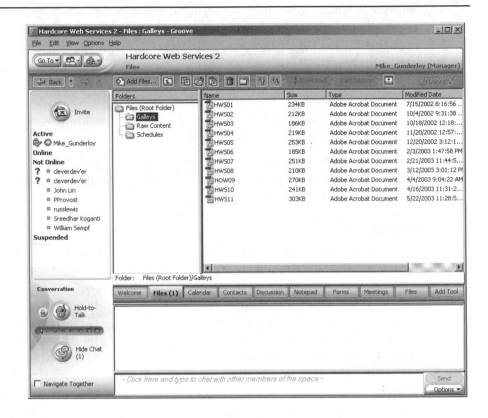

Programmer's Tools

Finally, I'd like to mention two collaborative tools that don't fit in anywhere else: CodeWright and CodeReview.

CodeWright (www.codewright.com/) is a programmer's text editor that's now owned by Borland. In addition to many of the features that you'll find in other programmer's editors (such as a flexible macro language and Visual Studio .NET integration), CodeWright includes an innovative feature that I haven't seen anywhere else: CodeMeeting. CodeMeeting acts as an instant messenger client embedded directly in the CodeWright interface, allowing you to chat over TCP/IP with any other CodeWright user. Even better, CodeMeeting enables collaborative editing for documents open in CodeWright. Either user can edit the document, and both users will see the changes. This opens up the possibility of doing long-distance pair programming, with two developers working on the same code, which is one of the practices recommended by Extreme Programming advocates. There's a free evaluation version available for download; a full CodeWright license will cost you $299.

Another interesting product is Macadamian's $39 CodeReview (`www.macadamian.com/products/codereview/`). CodeReview adds a toolbar that lets you manage the entire code review process without ever leaving Visual Studio .NET. You can send out a chunk of code for review, add comments and suggestions to code under review, and accept or reject suggestions with a single click. If your entire team uses this add-in, you get the benefit of many eyes without needing a separate code review process or a separate code review application.

Teams Checklist

Developing software as part of a team can be a real challenge, or a very rewarding experience. Here are some tips to make your team development experiences easier:

- Don't be afraid to work with a team when it's the only way to finish the project.
- Make sure the whole team agrees on the team structure.
- Track the progress of each team member to keep the team on target.
- Set aside time to handle the inevitable overhead of managing a team.
- Don't use a heavyweight process for a small team.
- Use collaborative software wisely to help team members work together.

Whether you're working as part of a team or strictly on your own, there are still some basic activities that have to take place as part of turning out high-quality software. One of these is creating documentation, which is the subject of the next chapter.

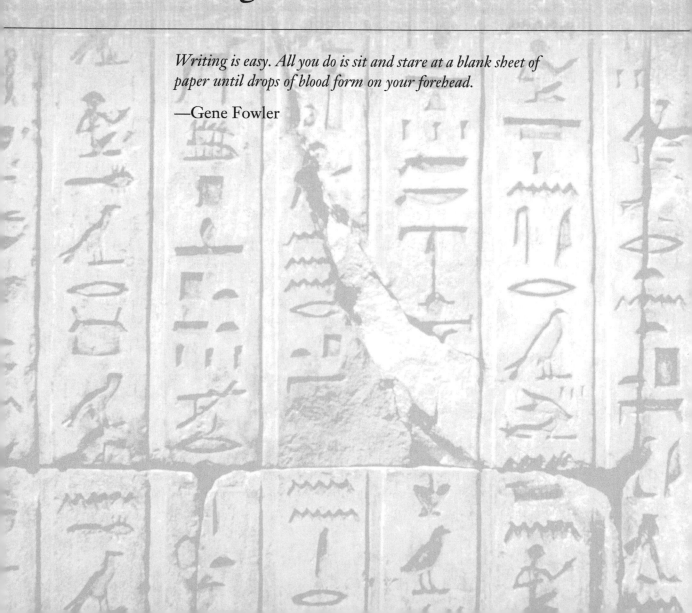

CHAPTER 12

Creating Documentation

Writing is easy. All you do is sit and stare at a blank sheet of paper until drops of blood form on your forehead.

—Gene Fowler

Apparently software authors as a group don't have the fortitude to actually dab blood off their foreheads. At least, that's one possible explanation for the generally abysmal state of software documentation today, from small freeware applications to large commercial shrink-wrapped products. Nevertheless, even if you find it difficult, writing documentation is a necessary part of the process of producing a product. No matter how good your code is, if people can't figure out how to use it, they won't be interested in your product—or you'll be inundated with complaints and tech support requests.

In this chapter I'll look at some tools and techniques for producing your own documentation. I'll start with the most difficult part of the job (help files for end users) and then touch on help for developers, help for teams, and other issues.

Writing End-User Help Files

If you're working with a large team, you may have the luxury of dedicated user-assistance professionals, whose entire job is to design and create such things as help files and manuals. But on small projects you'll probably find that you need to be your own help designer. All too often, this task gets relegated to the end of the process, after the code is finished. The result can be a slapped-together help file that's not really any help—and that doesn't do more than annoy users.

Rather than treat the help file as an annoyance to be tacked on to an already-finished project, you need to consider it as you're developing the application. Providing effective help to end users requires you to build hooks for help right into the application, as well as to decide how to expose the help in the user interface. For all but the simplest applications, the strategy of just opening a general help HTML page whenever the user presses F1 won't be sufficient.

In this section of the chapter, I'll discuss some of the thinking that goes into an effective help system, and then look at some of the tools that can help you build such a system.

Understanding User Needs

When you're ready to start developing a help file, keep one cardinal rule in mind:

RULE   You are not the intended user of your own help files.

Presumably you know your own application and its functions quite well, and won't be the one asking for help. But other people aren't as fortunate as you in this regard. When you're ready to start writing help files (or other documentation), you need to think about the needs of the end user. If you watch real users at work with a new application, you'll find four general reasons why they turn to the help system:

They just started using the application, and want to know what it does and get an overview of making it do those things.   Perhaps they're not sure whether your application can export data in a format that they need, or they want a step-by-step approach to getting started.

They're in the middle of some particular task and need help with that task.   Perhaps the user just opened a dialog box for the first time and finds it to be confusing, or can't quite figure out which choice to select in a combo box.

They want to perform a particular task but don't know how to begin.   This can happen, for example, when the user has been told that the application contains an embedded web search facility but has no idea how to get to it. If there's no obvious control on the user interface for this functionality, they're stuck.

Something is broken, and they want to fix it.   If an error message shows up on screen, or the user gets frustrated and wants to contact technical support, your help should supply useful answers.

If you keep these four reasons in mind, you'll be able to make your help system more effective. For the first, it's worth having an overview be the default topic in your help file so that it's the first thing users see when they open help. If your application is especially complex, you may even want to place a separate menu item on the Help menu to open an overview or a tutorial. The overview topic should also offer easy links to other information of interest to new users, such as tutorials.

For the second reason, context-sensitive help is your friend. If the user clicks the Help button in a dialog box, they're almost certainly looking for help on how to use that dialog box, not a general help topic. Fortunately, any modern development system will let you build context-sensitive help so that you can take users to the appropriate help topic for their current location in the application.

You need to realize, though, that even writing help for a dialog box takes some thinking. It's not enough to just describe what each control on the dialog box does. That's like trying to teach someone to drive by explaining the name and appearance of each control on the dashboard, without telling them how to use the controls. Dialog-box help also needs to contain general advice on what information you're expecting the user to supply.

For the user who doesn't know how to undertake a task, you need to take advantage of the index. People tend to look in the index when they don't know where to find something. That's because the table of contents organization often doesn't make it clear what's located where, and search technology is often confusing to use.

Of course, building an index is also a bit of an art. When you're creating your help index, be sure to consider all reasonable (and maybe even some unreasonable) synonyms for key terms.

For example, you might want to index a topic on searching under "search," "find," and "locate." The problem is that the user won't know which term your application uses until they find the page in the help system that uses the term. A good index is the best way to break this chicken-and-egg cycle. A glossary can also help the user locate the terms you use quickly, without needing to read through the entire index.

You should also beware of the easy-to-make assumption that you know what your user really wants to do. The phrase "It looks like you're writing a letter..." wasn't originally intended as a joke, but it sure worked out that way. Do your best to display the perfect topic when the user asks for help, but do it unobtrusively, and make it easy to get to the rest of the help file if you guessed wrong.

Finally, when the user runs into a snag in your application, do the best you can to be helpful. Your help file should contain examples of all the errors that you expect the program to generate, as well as advice on how to recover from them. If all else fails, make it easy to contact technical support; either the help file or the Help menu should include a clear link to your online support resources, or a phone number if you provide telephone support.

Choosing Help Topics

Users are likely looking at the help file because they want to do something. You can respond to this by making sure that your help is task oriented. In many cases, a step-by-step set of instructions will work better than a long block of text, even if the same details appear in the text. When you're laying out the page with the instructions, leave plenty of white space and number the steps. Figure 12.1 shows a sample help topic from the Download Tracker help file. Note that the topic opens with step-by-step instructions and postpones some detailed information until the bottom of the page.

Deciding which help topics to include in a help file is something of an art. Here are two rules of thumb that I use to decide which help topics to include:

1. If users invoke help from within the application, they should get help relevant to the task at hand.

2. Major topics that users should understand to make effective use of the application deserve their own help topics.

Showing task-specific help requires determining with the greatest possible specificity what users were doing when they pressed F1 or invoked the Help menu. This is easy to do in dialog boxes but not so easy when the help request comes from your application's main interface. Knowing which control has the focus provides some clues. In complex cases, you may find it useful to build some history tracking into the application itself. If the user has been working with parts of the application that are related to performing a mail merge, you might want to show a help topic on performing mail merges if you can't come up with anything more specific.

FIGURE 12.1
A task-oriented help
topic

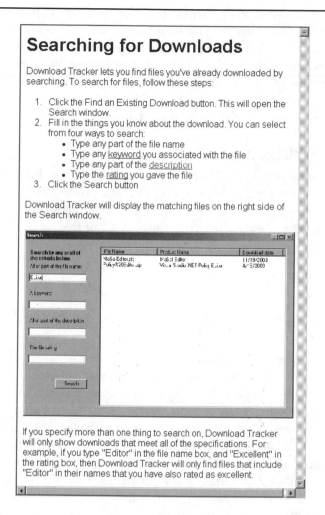

Major conceptual help topics, on the other hand, tend not to be linked directly to the user interface. Download Tracker, for instance, might offer a help topic explaining the concept of background downloads and a download queue, even though the user won't need to directly manipulate the queue. Such topics are generally not linked to the user interface. Instead, they might be available as "See Also" links, or definitions that pop up from the task-related help. You can use these background topics to supply additional information for users who need a conceptual framework to understand what they're doing.

When you're writing help topics, remember that succinctness is important. Resist the temptation to show off how smart you are and how cool your code is. Remember that users most likely aren't accessing help just because they want to poke around and learn more about your application. They're in the help because they're having a problem. They are likely to be unhappy with the program, stalled in the middle of a task, and ready for immediate answers. The task of the help system should be to deliver those answers, not to brag about your cool implementation of asynchronous events or the Observer pattern. If you simply can't restrain yourself, put an appendix in the table of contents to hold the technical details—and don't link to those topics from the user interface.

Organizing Information

Despite your best efforts at context sensitivity, it's likely that users will end up at the wrong help topic (that is, one that doesn't contain the information they need at the moment) from time to time. With all of the modern help formats (such as Windows Help or HTML help), you get some standard navigational aids "for free":

- Table of contents
- Index
- Search

These are all useful tools for the experienced help user, but you can still do more to make the user's life easier.

For starters, think about how you're organizing your help as you build the table of contents. The modern help formats support a hierarchy of files and folders to organize the table of contents; you should make use of this hierarchy. Don't just dump everything into one long list of files with no folders in sight. If users are browsing through the table of contents, you want to give them a small number of choices at each click; the traditional rule of thumb is "seven plus or minus two," but use that as a guideline rather than a rule. If a topic has only three logical subtopics, it's fine to have just three choices. On the other hand, there may be times when 15 choices are appropriate. But if you have a folder that contains nothing other than another folder, or a folder containing 100 topics, you probably need to look at organizing the information differently. Another thing to think about is that some people find scrolling a distraction. Help topics that take up more than a single screen full of information often can be profitably broken up into multiple topics.

Even while you're organizing the hierarchy, you should remember that not everyone thinks of the world as consisting of a series of hierarchies, even though that seems to be a natural way for a developer to look at things. If you're using a help format with HTML topics (which is the case with almost every help format today), you can take advantage of the richness of HTML to offer nonhierarchical alternative ways to navigate through your help file. For instance, you can provide links to closely related topics, or even to online websites that offer additional information.

You should also consider supplementing words with visual metaphors. One traditional (though limited) use of this idea entails embedding a picture of a dialog box into the help topic, with hot spots that you can click to bring up help on particular facets of the dialog box. If you're going to do that, be sure to add a caption along the lines of "Click any control for help on that control." Otherwise, users will be forced into "mystery meat" navigation, swinging the mouse pointer back and forth across the graphic in the hope that the mouse pointer will turn into the little hyperlink hand—assuming that they realize the graphic has hot spots. In addition to screen shots, you can experiment with hyperlinks from architectural diagrams, tiers of servers, and so on.

But while you're creating alternative navigation, beware of linking too richly. Everything is probably related to everything else in your mind, but each link is a way for users to leave the topic they're on and go somewhere else. If your help design contributes to the user getting as lost in the help as they are in the application, you've made no progress. In fact, you've probably provoked a phone call to your customer support organization, who won't thank you for the extra work. Every link should answer a task-oriented question that the user is likely to have in the context of the current topic: "If I'm here, how do I do this?"

NOTE   Depending on your budget, you should consider hiring a professional editor and a professional indexer to aid in preparing your help file. Very few things make a worse impression than spelling or grammatical errors in a help file, which a copy editor can prevent. An indexer will help ensure that you have a truly useful index containing terms users are likely to look up. If you can't afford such help, at least have someone else read over the help file to make sure there are no obvious mistakes.

Testing and Feedback

Don't neglect your help system when it comes to testing your application. If it's difficult to spot your own code errors, it's doubly difficult to spot problems with your own documentation. As a developer, you may find that much information that seems perfectly obvious to you turns out to be incomprehensible to your users. Having real users (or a good QA department) look over your help can identify these blind spots for you.

Encourage your testers to file bug reports any time they can't figure out how to do something on the first try. The key pieces of information are what they were looking for and where in the help they expected to find it. Then put that information in that place and go on to the next request. Of course, for this system to be a success you need to develop the help along with the product, instead of tacking it on as an afterthought.

RULE   Plan to start building help files as soon as any part of the product works well enough to require help.

Don't stop the feedback loop when you ship your product. It's to your advantage to make it as easy as possible for end users to provide feedback, not just on the help file but on any part of the application. One way to do this is to include a Send Feedback menu item on your Help menu. With the Visual Studio .NET (VS. NET) help, Microsoft went a step further: Every help topic includes a link to send feedback directly back to the writers, as you can see in Figure 12.2.

Tools for End-User Help

The starting point for building help files is Microsoft's HTML Help Workshop. A version of this tool that targets the HTML Help 1.3 format is included with VS .NET, although this isn't the latest version of the format. As you can see in Figure 12.3, HTML Help Workshop itself has a fairly dated look, and although its help files are completely functional, they might not be flashy enough to fit well with your application.

An alternative from Microsoft is HTML Help 2.0, which comes with a new version of HTML Help Workshop that integrates directly with VS .NET. You can download this version as part of the Visual Studio Help Integration Kit (VSHIK) from www.microsoft.com/downloads/ details.aspx?familyid=ce1b26dc-d6af-42a1-a9a4-88c4eb456d87&displaylang=en. HTML Help 2.0 is the help format that's used for the .NET Framework SDK and other recent help files, and it has a very modern look. Unfortunately, Microsoft has announced that it isn't planning to release the Help 2.0 runtime for redistribution; the only supported use for the VSHIK is to integrate your own help with the VS .NET help. While this is useful for component developers, it's not much help for applications that will be sold to end users. Microsoft is apparently abandoning this format to concentrate on developing new help formats for Windows "Longhorn," which is still years off as I write this.

FIGURE 12.3
HTML Help Workshop

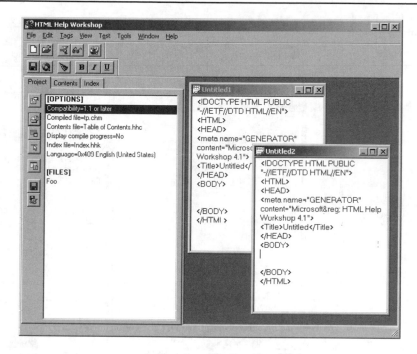

Of course, you're not stuck with Microsoft tools by any means. The Helpware Group maintains an extensive set of links to help authoring tools and information (Microsoft and otherwise) at www.helpware.net/weblinks.htm. Figure 12.4 shows eHelp's RoboHelp, one of the high-end tools in the market (now owned by Macromedia). By just looking at the interface, you can tell that RoboHelp has many capabilities beyond those of HTML Help Workshop.

Even if you don't want to invest the hundreds of dollars that a RoboHelp license costs, you can still find help-authoring tools that are much superior to HTML Help Workshop at a modest price. One tool I've used with great success on small projects is Helpware's own shareware tool, named FAR (www.helpware.net/FAR/index.html). This $49 shareware tool offers you a variety of aids for creating HTML help in both 1.0 and 2.0 formats, including ways to make the help file web friendly. Once nice feature is that it can take a folder full of HTML files and turn them into an HTML Help file; this makes it possible to use your favorite HTML tool (such as FrontPage or HomeSite) to create your help files.

FIGURE 12.4
RoboHelp 4.1

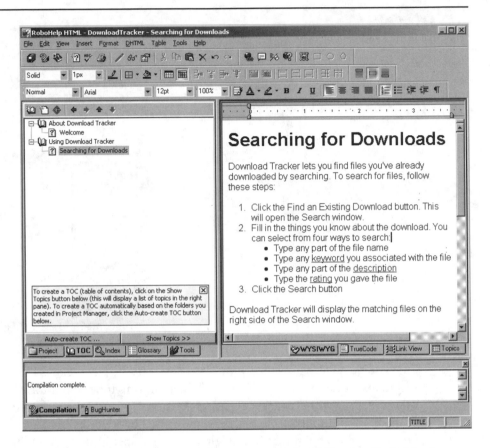

There's one more tool that every writer of documentation should be familiar with: the English language (or whatever language the file will be published in). Even if they're not great writers themselves, users will trip over spelling, grammatical, and punctuation mistakes. People read and comprehend more slowly if the text is littered with errors. Even if you're doing your own help system development, be sure to get someone who's good with the language to proofread the results.

Creating Developer Help Files

Of course, not all documentation is intended for end users of desktop applications—some is meant for other developers. I'm not thinking here of internal documentation for your own team (I'll discuss that briefly later in the chapter), but about documenting products that are aimed strictly at developers. The most obvious place this comes into play is when you're

Help in the User Interface

Although I'm concentrating on help files in this chapter, you should not neglect the application's user interface as a source of subtle but useful clues to its proper use. A well-designed application can cut down considerably on the number of times that the user has to refer to the help file at all. Consider these factors:

- People (at least those who speak one of the Western languages) tend to read left to right, top to bottom. That's why it makes sense to group the controls that indicate the end of a process (such as OK, Apply, and Cancel buttons) together in the lower-right corner of the application. Don't make users hunt around for controls.

- When entering data in a particular control is inappropriate, disable the control.

- The use of tooltips to indicate the purpose of a control can be a great help to new users. The ToolTip control makes this easy to implement on .NET Windows forms. Tooltips can also help make your application more usable for users with special needs; screen readers, for example, will pick up tooltip text. Some users find tooltips annoying, though, so you might consider providing an option to turn them off.

- For step-by-step processes, most users are accustomed to a wizard interface. It's worth using such an interface, with clear directions on each panel, for such processes.

By paying attention to the design of your user interface, you can make it possible for some users to never need the help files at all. Watching actual users interact with your application can tell you whether you're getting to this point.

delivering (and documenting) a class library. Ideally, your class library documentation should follow the format and conventions that the .NET Framework SDK established for .NET namespaces.

Fortunately, there's a free tool that makes this pretty easy to accomplish: NDoc (`http://ndoc.sourceforge.net/`). NDoc is actually the end of a process that starts with Appendix B of the C# language specification: "C# provides a mechanism for programmers to document their code using a special comment syntax that contains XML text. In source code files, comments having a certain form can be used to direct a tool to produce XML from those comments and the source code elements, which they precede." These comments are identified by being set off with three slashes instead of the two that normally introduce a C# comment.

You'll find the XML tags used by these special comments explained in the XML Documentation section of the C# Programmer's Reference. Table 12.1 lists the XML documentation tags that VS .NET can use for XML documentation. This list isn't fixed by the C# specification; different tools are free to make use of other tags.

TABLE 12.1 XML Documentation Tags for VS .NET

Tag	Meaning
`<c>`	Embedded code font in other text
`<code>`	Multiple lines of source code
`<example>`	An example of using a member
`<exception>`	Specifies an exception that can be thrown by the current member
`<include>`	Includes an external documentation file
`<list>`	The heading row of a list
`<para>`	A paragraph of text
`<param>`	A method parameter
`<paramref>`	A reference to a parameter in other text
`<permission>`	The security permission required by a member
`<remarks>`	Supplemental information
`<returns>`	Return value of a method
`<see>`	An embedded cross-reference to another member
`<seealso>`	A reference in a "See Also" list
`<summary>`	A summary of the object
`<value>`	The value of a property

NOTE   Although these XML comments are defined only for C# projects, several efforts have been made to extend the same concept to Visual Basic .NET (VB.NET). The VS .NET PowerToys download includes a VB Commenter add-in (www.gotdotnet.com/team/ide/helpfiles/VBCommenter.aspx) to give VB this capability, for example. In the "Whidbey" release of VS .NET, due in early 2005, VB.NET will have this capability natively.

As an example, here's a piece of the code for the DownloadEngine class, with embedded documentation comments:

```
/// <summary>
/// Replace a possibly null string with another string.
///
/// </summary>
/// <param name="MaybeNull" type="string">
///     <para>
///         A string that might be null or empty.
///     </para>
/// </param>
```

```
/// <param name="Replacement" type="string">
///      <para>
///          A replacement string to be used
➡ if the first string is null or empty.
///      </para>
/// </param>
/// <returns>
/// Returns the original string if it's not null or
➡ empty, otherwise returns the replacement string
/// </returns>
private string ReplaceNull(string MaybeNull,
    string Replacement)
{
    if((MaybeNull.Length == 0) ||
        (MaybeNull == null))
    {
        return Replacement;
    }
    else
    {
        return MaybeNull;
    }
}
```

Embedded in your code, these comments don't do a lot of good for your customers, but VS .NET can collect these comments into an external XML file. To enable this collection, right-click on the project in the Solution Explorer and select Properties. Then select the Build page and enter a name for the XML documentation file, as shown in Figure 12.5.

FIGURE 12.5
Activating XML documentation in VS .NET

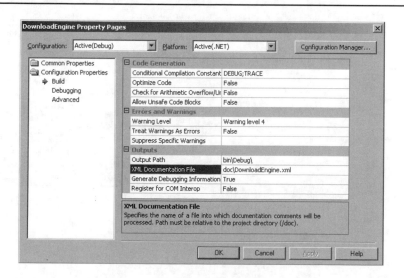

After you've built the XML comments file for your application, NDoc can do its work. Figure 12.6 shows the NDoc user interface.

You can select one or more assemblies to document and tell NDoc where to find the XML comments file for each assembly. NDoc will combine the information in the XML comments file with information determined by examining the assembly itself, and then build MSDN-style documentation for you. Figure 12.7 shows a part of the resulting help file.

For an even better developer experience, you can integrate your class library help files directly with the help for VS .NET. The Visual Studio Help Integration Kit, which I mentioned earlier in this chapter, contains the necessary tools and instructions for this process.

FIGURE 12.6
Using NDoc to build a
help file

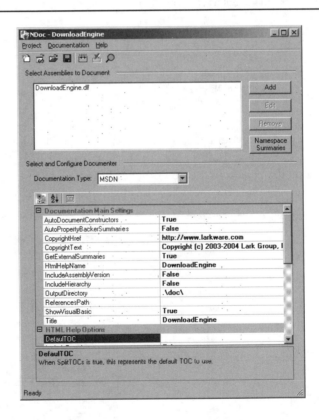

FIGURE 12.7
Developer-style help
for a class library

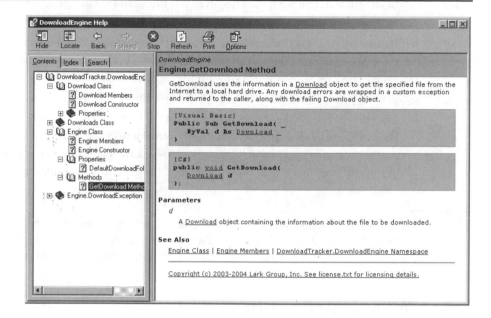

Writing Manuals

There once was a time when every software application came with complete written documentation—or at least, if there wasn't such a golden age of documentation, many aging developers remember it that way. In recent years, the rise of online help in various formats has led to a definite decrease in the quantity (and some would say quality) of documentation. Some applications still include written manuals. Others include part of their documentation in writing but refer the user to help files for details. Still others include Adobe Acrobat (PDF) files that you can print yourself—or no written documentation at all.

Whether to include a written manual with your application needs to be a business decision as well as a technical one. The plain fact is that printing manuals is expensive, and in an age of cost-driven purchasing decisions, raising your price can be fatal to your sales. But if you do decide that a manual is warranted, here are some things to think about:

- Your help file can be a good starting point for your manual, but it likely will not supply the entire content for the manual. The written manual is more often used for reference than for task-based help, and so is a good spot to expand on technical details and background information.

- Consider starting the manual with overview and tutorial material that doesn't really fit into a help file. Remember, users will have the help file for task-oriented help to use as an adjunct to any tutorial you present. This gives you the flexibility to introduce topics in the manual in a structured fashion, knowing users can go back to the help if they want to jump around.

- If your program is at all difficult to install, then detailed installation instructions belong in the printed manual (and in a readme file on the installation medium as well). Remember, users won't be able to use your help file until after they're installed the application, so installation instructions in the help file won't do much good.

- Do your best to make the manual interesting to read. If it's a hopelessly dull recitation of the application's features, with nothing to teach users or motivate them to understand the underlying concepts, it will likely be just a waste of dead trees. You should think about what you want your manual to accomplish, and then try to accomplish those aims with a light, easy style.

> **TIP**   One thing to consider when deciding whether to include a printed manual with your product: a lengthy manual can act as an unobtrusive antipiracy device. Although it's possible for pirates to scan a manual back to a file, in practice most casual pirates won't bother.

Writing Team Documentation

All of the documentation I've talked about so far has an audience outside your company; it's all intended for users of your application. But that's not the only potential audience for documentation. In particular, if you're working with a development team or as part of a continuing development organization, there's a need for internal documentation that will likely never leave the company. I've mentioned various internal documents along the way, such as the top five risks lists, project requirements, and specifications. I'd like to point out two other important documents specifically: the development log and the postmortem.

Development Log

When you're working by yourself on an application, it's usually pretty easy to remember what you've done already, what you still need to do, and what the next five steps in the process should be. However, when you add in a team of people, perhaps scattered around the globe, the problem of keeping track of development becomes much more complex. I've seen projects waste a lot of time because developers didn't coordinate their actions, in some cases overwriting each other's work time after time.

Many strategies are available to combat this problem. In some cases, a strong manager can impose such order on a team that the manager's feel for the process controls everyone's actions. In other teams, particularly long-lived ones that put out multiple versions of a product, one developer will end up being the team's institutional memory. This is the person who, in any given meeting, can recall the discussions from three years back and remind people why a particular decision was made. (If your team depends on such a person, treat that individual well; his or her contribution is irreplaceable).

But particularly if your team is community based rather than hierarchical, it can be useful to replace these ad-hoc solutions with a written development log. Such a log need not (and should not) be a detailed description of every change made to the code; your source code control system should be able to supply that when you need it. Instead, it's a place where team members can look up key facts about the project:

- What the overall architecture of the application is, and why that architecture was chosen over alternatives

- Who's responsible for each part of the application or for each function on the team

- Where key pieces of the network are located: Which server handles source code control? Which one is the build machine?

- What tricky problems came up, and how they were solved

In the ideal world, the development log contains the information you need whenever a question comes up in a meeting and people can't quite remember what happened. In the past, I've used Word documents and web pages for development logs, with all team members having the necessary permissions to edit the joint document when they have something to add. These days, I think I'd use wiki or weblog software for this purpose, since those tools have developed to allow easy joint editing of shared content. A SharePoint site would be another good alternative.

Postmortem

In contrast to the development log, the postmortem is typically written only after the application is finished and shipped. The purpose of a postmortem is to record the lessons that the team or the manager learned in the course of building the software (or the things that they wish they had known before they started). A typical postmortem might include these sections:

- Overall description of the project
- Who was involved on the team
- How the project's scope and features changed from initial design to final ship
- A list of things that were done well during the project
- A list of things that could have been done better
- A list of the tools used, along with an evaluation of their quality
- A list of tools that team members wish they had had available

- A list of important project documents with their locations

- Recommendations for the next project: How can things be done better?

  Postmortems are most useful when all team members have an opportunity to add to them, and when they're encouraged to speak freely. You should never tie performance reviews to postmortems. Instead, provide a mechanism for anonymous contributions from team members who feel threatened by the process. In a healthy software organization, postmortems are an accepted part of software development, and one with a history of helping rather than hurting careers.

TECHNOLOGY TRAP

Experience in a Locked Cabinet

Douglas Adams wrote of a particularly critical piece of documentation being stored "at the bottom of a locked filing cabinet stuck in a disused lavatory with a sign on the door saying 'Beware of the Leopard.'" This is not what you want to have happen to your team documentation. There's little point to spending time creating a postmortem if no one is ever going to read it.

If you're introducing postmortems to your organization, think about ways to make sure the lessons learned are shared by everyone who can benefit from them. Some things to consider:

- Establishing an e-mail alias to notify people when such documents exist

- Storing the documents in a specific folder on the network or on an intranet site

- Reminding managers to make reviewing past postmortems a part of planning any new project

Of course, if you're a lone developer, this sort of process issue won't apply to you. You'll just have to remember to review your own postmortems. Reminding yourself of this in a postmortem report is a futile gesture!

Documentation Checklist

Documentation, whether help files, manuals, or team reports, needs to be planned into your project from the beginning. When you're thinking about documentation, consider these factors:

- Help files and manuals are for users, not for you.

- Most help should be context sensitive and task based.

- Use "See Also" topics for additional background information.

- Most help topics should be short and focused.

- Use the table of contents, index, search, and hypertext features to organize the help in multiple ways.
- Consider supplementing words with visual aids.
- Test the help as well as the application.
- Provide a way for users to send feedback easily.
- Supply developer help in a familiar format.
- Use a printed manual for tutorials, overviews, and installation instructions.
- Create development logs and postmortem reports to aid team development.

By now I've discussed much of the development process, and I've mentioned several tools that you'll want to run on a regular basis (such as unit testing and documentation tools). In the next chapter, I'll focus on the actual process of building your software. There's more to it than just running the compiler.

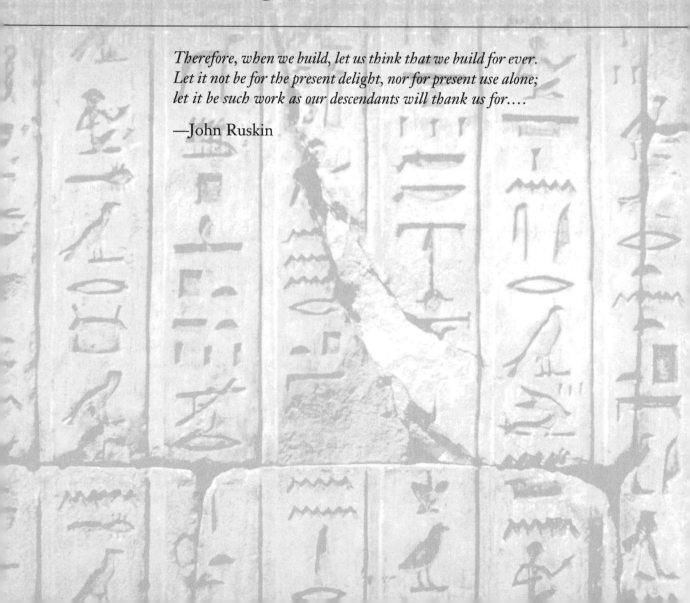

CHAPTER 13

Mastering the Build Process

Therefore, when we build, let us think that we build for ever.
Let it not be for the present delight, nor for present use alone;
let it be such work as our descendants will thank us for....

—John Ruskin

Ruskin had the advantage of being an architect (of the sort who works with buildings, not with source code). Those of us who build software are lucky if what we build lasts a year, and often we can't even manage a day before some tester comes back and tells us that the roof is caving in. But some teams are in even worse trouble: They can't build their application at all, at least not in a documented, reliable, repeatable way. In this chapter, I'll look at the importance of having a formal build process, and show you some of the many .NET tools available to make this process easier.

If you've never run across the concept of a build process, it may need some explaining. The idea is fairly simple. Putting all the pieces of your software together, from the source code to the help files to the setup program, is too important to be left to chance. A build process might be a manual checklist of everything that you need to do to produce your application from source files, but these days it's much more likely that all or most of your build process will be automated.

Developing a Build Process

There are many ways to tell whether a software project is in trouble, but here's a three-question pop quiz on the subject:

1. Can you, right now, produce a fresh copy of the application and all of the surrounding artifacts (such as documentation or data files), starting from source code?

2. Can you reproduce the application and all of the surrounding artifacts as they were on this day last week?

3. Can you go get a cup of coffee while all this is happening automatically?

If the answer to any of these questions is "no," then your build process could use some work.

The Big Picture

Just building your application is easy: Decide whether you want a debug or a release build, and then select Build Solution or Rebuild Solution from the Build menu in Visual Studio .NET (VS .NET).

TIP   The Build menu item rebuilds only the components that have changed since the last build; the Rebuild menu item cleans out all of the intermediate files and rebuilds everything from scratch. In theory, you should always be able to use Build after the first time. In practice, life tends not to be so simple. When you've made major code changes, or when strange errors start cropping up, or when VS .NET fails trying to rebuild the project, switch back to Build for your next run. I tend to do a full build the first time I build a project each day as well.

But the simple approach is not sufficient for a project of any reasonable size. That's because manually building just the code when you think about it doesn't account for all of the other tasks that are involved in turning out the final package. If you're working with other developers, for example, you need to remember to get the latest pieces from your source code control system before building. You might also have unit tests to run through, documentation to update, and so on.

The problem with attempting to put all the pieces together by hand is that people tend to forget things. When you're trying to pull together a product, forgetting things can vary from being a nuisance (forgetting to run the unit tests before you check in code that breaks someone else's work) to becoming a full-fledged disaster (shipping an old version of the help file to customers with the released product). That's why you should be using an automated build tool for any project.

I'll look at a number of build tools in this chapter, but they're all designed to bring two main benefits to developers:

Simplicity   Instead of needing to remember a dozen or more separate steps to turn out a complete copy of your software, you launch the build tool and tell it to go to work.

Reliability   Because the steps to create a build are programmed into the tool, the build process never skips steps or forgets things.

But there's more to using a build tool than just producing reliable builds easily. Once you have your build process under control, you can proceed to implement a daily build routine. Actually, it doesn't so much matter whether your daily builds are done daily, twice a day, or once every two days. What's important is that you have a regular schedule for building your software from scratch.

It seems obvious when you think about it, but in order to actually ship a product, you're going to need a perfect build, where everything works just the way it's supposed to: no errors in compilation, no failing tests, no missing files. The best way to get to the point of being able to produce such a perfect build is to produce a perfect build (or as close as you can get) every day. The ritual of building serves as a bit of clockwork for the project, a way to ensure that you're constantly moving forward. It also affords you a quick check on the quality of your work: If the daily build fails to finish, something is seriously wrong.

Teams that build high-quality software take the daily build routine seriously indeed. On major Microsoft products, for example, "breaking the build" is such a serious issue that any developer who's responsible is liable to be the one who has to stay late to fix things. While you may not want to make yourself stay late when you're a team of one, implementing daily builds will still help you keep in mind that the goal is to ship software, not just to write code.

RULE   If the daily build fails, fix it before you do anything else.

Tasks for Daily Builds

When you're ready to choose a build tool and set up a build process, the first step is to figure out just what it is that you want to automate. Different projects will have different needs, but in general, the more you can do automatically the better. Here's a selection of tasks I've done as part of daily builds on various projects:

- Get the entire source code tree from the source code control system to a clean directory. You should avoid doing an incremental get; the source code control system is your record of what you're building, so you should always make sure that what you build from is exactly what is stored.

- Create a build number, date stamp, or other unique identifier for this build. VS .NET will generate random-looking build numbers automatically, but I prefer to impose my own numbering system. I'll discuss this later in the chapter, in the "Managing Software Versions" section.

- Label the source code tree with today's date or another identifier, to make it easy to verify in the future exactly which pieces are included in this build.

- Build the source code. This may involve multiple compilation steps if your product is split up into a variety of executable and library files. Here, again, you should do full builds rather than incremental builds. You might also want to build multiple versions of each file, such as debug and release versions, with different target folders.

- Run the unit tests for the project and verify that they pass. If running all of the unit tests would take too long to be feasible, it's usual to design a set of targeted "smoke tests" to ensure that nothing too serious is wrong—the equivalent of plugging in a new appliance and watching to see whether smoke comes out of the case.

- Apply obfuscation, signing, or licensing tools to create the versions of the application that will be shipped to end users.

- Build the documentation and help files for the application.

- Build the installer for the application. I'll talk more about installers in Chapter 15, "Delivering the Application."

- Produce a report on exactly what was done and distribute it to interested parties. This might mean sending e-mail to members of your team, or automatically creating a daily XML file that can be displayed on a website with a suitable XSLT style sheet.

- Save an archived copy of all of the outputs from the daily build (including software, documentation, installer, reports, and anything else that's not in the source code control system) as a Zip file in a known location.

- Distribute the finished products via e-mail, network share, FTP, or other means to interested team members.

Not all build tools can handle all of these tasks, of course. When you're evaluating build tools, one thing to consider is how much of your process a particular tool can handle.

Tools for Daily Builds

Developers have recognized the benefits of build automation and daily builds for a long time. That's one reason there are many build tools out there to choose from. Some are XML based, others graphical, and they range in price from free up to several hundred dollars. In this section, I'll survey the build tools I've found that work with .NET applications. To give you a feel for how they work, I'll implement a very stripped-down build process for Download Tracker with each tool:

1. Get the latest source code from Vault to a clean directory.

2. Compile all of the code in the various projects (DBLayer, DownloadEngine, DownloadEngineTests, DownloadTracker, DownloadTrackerTests, DTInterfaces, and DTLogic) in both debug and release mode.

3. Execute the unit tests in both DownloadEngineTests and DownloadTrackerTests.

4. Produce a report on the build.

I'll cover the tools in alphabetical order so as not to play favorites:

- Daily Build
- FinalBuilder
- Hippo.NET
- NAnt
- Visual Build Professional

I'm not including any Microsoft solutions in this list, even though Microsoft has tried several times to produce a build utility for .NET. That's because the Microsoft offerings are not yet sufficiently flexible for most developers to use. One alternative is BuildIt, available from `http://msdn.microsoft.com/library/en-us/dnbda/html/tdlg_app.asp`. Unfortunately BuildIt can only use Microsoft Visual SourceSafe for source code control, which rules it out for many developers. There are also the .NET Solution Build & Deployment Process & Tools (`www.gotdotnet.com/Community/UserSamples/Details.aspx?SampleGuid=2cb20e79-d706-4706-9ea0-26188257ee7d`), a Microsoft community effort that still has lots of rough edges. Microsoft should become a more credible player with the release of VS .NET "Whidbey" in late 2004, which is slated to include an integrated build tool as part of VS .NET. This tool, MSBuild, is apparently patterned closely on NAnt, which I'll discuss later in the chapter. But since NAnt is an open-source tool, Microsoft refuses to even consider it as part of its officially endorsed process.

NOTE Although I'm not impressed with the public Microsoft build tools, its advice on the build process is well worth reading. "Team Development with Visual Studio .NET and Visual SourceSafe," from the Patterns & Practices group, is an excellent set of prescriptive processes for those using all-Microsoft tools, You can get it from `http://msdn.microsoft.com/library/default.asp?url=/library/en-us/dnbda/html/tdlg_rm.asp`.

The tools I'm looking at here are the ones that I think are affordable for the single developer or small team. Other build tools are available that are aimed at much more complex projects. These enterprise build tools carry a price tag to match, typically thousands of dollars. Tools in this class include OpenMake (`www.openmake.com`), which uses a distributed architecture and a knowledge base server to handle builds of both Java and .NET applications, as well as many other types of software, and Merant Build (`www.merant.com`), which handles many software environments and integrates with Merant's other software configuration management tools.

Daily Build

Daily Build, from Positive-g (`www.positive-g.com/dailybuild/index.html`) is the simplest of the graphical build tools I've seen. I'm including it in this list because it's affordable ($85) and it can manage just about any build process. But it does this by letting you identify Windows executables and supply command lines for them. Much of what you could do with Daily Build you could also do with a well-written batch file. Figure 13.1 shows the Daily Build interface.

FIGURE 13.1
Daily Build

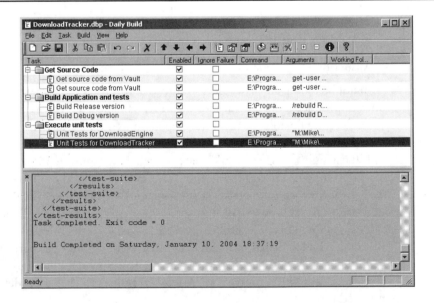

Of course, there are at least a few advances over batch files here. You can use indenting and grouping to organize your build as a tree, making it a bit easier to keep track of what's going on. Daily Build can also collect the output from the entire build into a single log file, so you get a record of what went on. And it installs a command-line e-mail tool to allow you to hook up notifications (by authoring more command-line tasks, that is).

Daily Build works out to be a pretty solid automation tool for any sort of repetitive set of tasks, not just builds. However, plenty of other tools have more direct integration with .NET.

FinalBuilder

Atozed Computer Software's FinalBuilder 2.0 (www.atozedsoftware.com/finalbuilder/) is a professional graphical build tool, with pricing starting at €299. Figure 13.2 shows the Download-Tracker build project open in FinalBuilder, displaying the results of a successful build.

To set up a build script with FinalBuilder, you drag and drop actions from the Action Types window to the Main window. An action might be as simple as copying a file, or checking something out of source code control, or calling a compiler. Each action has properties that dictate exactly what it does, which you can view with the Action Inspector. If you need further customization, FinalBuilder supports a rather complete scripting language. For example, I've used scripting to put custom messages into the build log, to calculate a version number based on information stored in an external file, or to construct the text of an e-mail to developers on my team.

FIGURE 13.2
FinalBuilder

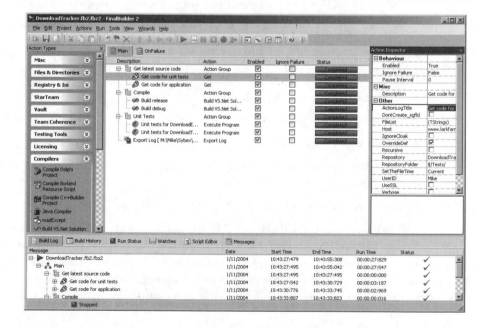

Actions can be arranged into action lists and then called from other scripts (like adding sub-routines to your build processes). You can set up variable watches to keep an eye on what's happening inside of complex scripts.

FinalBuilder derives a lot of ease of use from its extensive selection of actions. When you're using an action for something like a VS .NET build, you don't have to work out the proper command line yourself; you just specify the solution file and the configuration and Final-Builder does the rest. Version 2.0 includes 19 groups of actions:

- CD Burning actions that can directly produce a CD-ROM at the end of the build process
- Compiler actions for project types, including VS .NET, Visual Basic, Delphi, and Java
- CVS actions for working with the CVS source code control system
- File and directory actions for manipulating the file system
- Help Compiler actions for building help files
- Install Builder actions for building setup files
- Internet actions that can automate FTP, HTTP, Telnet, and other protocols
- Licensing Tools actions that use popular tools for applying licenses
- Miscellaneous actions, including user prompting, looping, and XSLT transformations
- Perforce actions for working with the Perforce source code control system
- Registry and INI actions that can read and write to Registry and INI files
- SourceSafe actions for working with the Visual SourceSafe source code control system
- SQL Server actions for automating Microsoft SQL Server
- StarTeam actions that work with the StarTeam source code control system
- Team Coherence actions that work with the Team Coherence source code control system
- Testing Tool actions that can launch a variety of tools from AutomatedQA
- Vault actions that work with the Vault source code control system
- Windows actions for executing programs, using WMI, controlling services, and other purposes
- Zip actions for working with Zip-format archives

If that's not enough, there's an API for building further actions (though you'll need to use Borland Delphi to do so) and some newsgroups that support users who are aiming for that level of customization. For example, if you use a help compiler that FinalBuilder doesn't support natively, you could create an action to call that compiler. Your custom action will integrate with the user interface and the FinalBuilder engine just like native actions do. The Windows action group contains actions for running either DOS programs or Windows executables, so you don't need a custom action if you want to call a new tool that has a command-line interface.

Overall, I've been quite impressed with FinalBuilder as a build tool. One nice touch is that it can produce XML log files, which are ideal for including as web output from your daily builds.

Hippo.NET

Hippo.NET is an open-source project (`http://hipponet.sourceforge.net/`) specifically for .NET projects. It uses a client/server model so that your entire team can share a single build machine. The developers are planning to add continuous integration features (I'll discuss continuous integration later in the chapter). Unfortunately, I wasn't able to test Hippo.NET with Download Tracker, because the tool assumes that you're using Visual SourceSafe for your source code control system. Being focused strictly on building the software, it's also less flexible than the other tools I've considered here. Still, the price is right, and the support for build machines could be useful if you're using all-Microsoft tools.

NAnt

NAnt is a well-developed open-source build tool for .NET applications. You'll find its home page at `http://nant.sourceforge.net/` and some additional content that hasn't yet made it into the main project at `http://nantcontrib.sourceforge.net/`. NAnt is based on the similar Ant build tool for Java applications, and like Ant, it has no user interface. You create a NAnt build file by writing XML using the tool of your choice, and execute it from the command line. Here's a build file for the parts of Download Tracker that I've been looking at in this chapter:

```
<project name="DownloadTracker" default="debug">
  <target name="compile">
    <vaultgetfile
      url="http://www.larkfarm.com" username="Mike" password="xxxx"
      repository="DownloadTracker" file="$\Code" />
    <vaultgetfile
      url="http://www.larkfarm.com/" username="Mike" password="xxxx"
      repository="DownloadTracker" file="$\Tests />
    <csc target="library"
      output="./DownloadEngine/bin/Debug/DownloadEngine.dll" debug="${debug}">
      <sources>
          <includes name="./DownloadEngine/*.cs" />
      </sources>
    </csc>
    <csc target="library"
      output="./DownloadEngineTests/bin/Debug/DownloadEngineTests.dll"
      debug="${debug}">
```

```
      <sources>
          <includes name="./DownloadEngineTests/*.cs" />
      </sources>
      <references>
          <includes
            name="E:/Program Files/NUnit V2.1/bin/nunit.framework.dll" />
          <includes name="./DownloadEngine/bin/Debug/DownloadEngine.dll" />
      </references>
    </csc>
    <csc target="library" output="./DTinterfaces/bin/Debug/DTInterfaces.dll"
      debug="${debug}">
      <sources>
          <includes name="./DTInterfaces/*.cs" />
      </sources>
      <references>
          <includes name="./DownloadEngine/bin/Debug/DownloadEngine.dll" />
      </references>
    </csc>
    <csc target="library" output="./DTLogic/bin/Debug/DTLogic.dll"
      debug="${debug}">
      <sources>
          <includes name="./DTLogic/*.cs" />
      </sources>
      <references>
          <includes name="./DTinterfaces/bin/Debug/DTInterfaces.dll" />
          <includes name="./DownloadEngine/bin/Debug/DownloadEngine.dll" />
      </references>
    </csc>
    <csc target="library" output="./DBLayer/bin/Debug/DBLayer.dll"
      debug="${debug}">
      <sources>
          <includes name="./DBLayer/*.cs" />
      </sources>
      <references>
          <includes name="./DTinterfaces/bin/Debug/DTInterfaces.dll" />
          <includes name="./DownloadEngine/bin/Debug/DownloadEngine.dll" />
      </references>
    </csc>
    <csc target="exe" output="./DownloadTracker/bin/Debug/DownloadTracker.exe"
      debug="${debug}">
      <sources>
          <includes name="./DownloadTracker/*.cs" />
      </sources>
      <references>
          <includes name="E:/WINDOWS/Microsoft.NET/Framework/v1.1.4322/
➥ Microsoft.VisualBasic.dll" />
          <includes name="./DTinterfaces/bin/Debug/DTInterfaces.dll" />
```

```
            <includes name="./DownloadEngine/bin/Debug/DownloadEngine.dll" />
            <includes name="./DBLayer/bin/Debug/DBLayer.dll" />
            <includes name="./DTLogic/bin/Debug/DTLogic.dll" />
        </references>
    </csc>
    <csc target="library"
      output="./DownloadTrackerTests/bin/Debug/DownloadTrackerTests.dll"
      debug="${debug}">
        <sources>
            <includes name="./DownloadTrackerTests/*.cs" />
        </sources>
        <references>
            <includes name="./DTinterfaces/bin/Debug/DTInterfaces.dll" />
            <includes name="./DownloadEngine/bin/Debug/DownloadEngine.dll" />
            <includes
              name="E:/Program Files/NUnit V2.1/bin/nunit.framework.dll" />
            <includes name="./DTLogic/bin/Debug/DTLogic.dll" />
        </references>
    </csc>
    <nunit2>
      <formatter type="Plain" />
      <test assemblyname=
        "./DownloadEngineTests/bin/Debug/DownloadEngineTests.dll" />
    </nunit2>
    <nunit2>
      <formatter type="Plain" />
      <test assemblyname=
        "./DownloadTrackerTests/bin/Debug/DownloadTrackerTests.dll" />
    </nunit2>

</target>

<target name="debug">
  <property name="debug" value="true" />
  <call target="compile" />
</target>

<target name="release">
  <property name="debug" value="false" />
  <call target="compile" />
</target>

<target name="both">
  <call target="debug" />
  <call target="release" />
</target>
</project>
```

NAnt does not support Vault out of the box, but there are Vault tasks for NAnt available from the public Vault server at `http://vaultpub.sourcegear.com`.

NAnt uses tasks as a unit of work. A single NAnt task might invoke a compiler, send a mail message, or import a type library. NAnt supports dozens of tasks and NAntContrib adds dozens more, which makes it likely that this build tool can handle even your most complex projects. Table 13.1 shows the tasks that are included in NAnt 0.84, which is the current version as I write this.

TABLE 13.1 NAnt 0.84 Tasks

Task	Summary
al	Invokes `al.exe`, the assembly linker.
asminfo	Generates an `AssemblyInfo` file using the attributes given.
attrib	Changes the file attributes of a file or set of files.
available	Checks if a resource is available at runtime.
call	Calls a NAnt target in the current project.
cl	Compiles C/C++ programs using `cl.exe`.
copy	Copies a file or set of files to a new file or directory.
csc	Compiles C# programs.
cvs-checkout	Checks out a CVS module to the required directory.
cvs-update	Updates a CVS module in a local working directory.
delay-sign	Signs delay-signed .NET Assemblies, or re-signs existing assemblies.
delete	Deletes a file, fileset, or directory.
description	A do-nothing task that lets you add comments to a build file.
echo	Writes a message to the build log.
exec	Executes a system command.
fail	Exits the current build by throwing an exception.
foreach	Loops over a set of items.
get	Gets a particular file from a URL source.
if	Allows conditional branching in a build file.
ifnot	The opposite of the if task.
include	Includes an external build file.
jsc	Compiles JScript.NET programs.

TABLE 13.1 CONTINUED NAnt 0.84 Tasks

Task	Summary
lib	Runs `lib.exe`, the Library Manager.
license	Generates a `.license` file from a `.licx` file.
link	Links files using `link.exe`.
loadtasks	Loads tasks from a given assembly or all assemblies in a given directory or fileset.
mail	Sends an SMTP message.
mc	Compiles messages using `mc.exe`, the Win32 message compiler.
midl	Runs the IDL compiler, `MIDL.exe`.
mkdir	Creates a directory or directory hierarchy.
move	Moves a file or set of files to a new file or directory.
nant	Runs NAnt on a supplied build file. This can be used to build subprojects.
nantschema	Creates an XSD file for all available tasks.
ndoc	Runs NDoc to create documentation.
nunit	Runs tests using the NUnit V1.0 framework.
nunit2	Runs tests using the NUnit V2.1 framework.
property	Sets a property in the current project.
rc	Invokes `rc.exe`, the Win32 resource compiler.
readregistry	Reads a value or set of values from the Windows Registry into one or more NAnt properties.
regex	Sets project properties based on a regular expression.
regsvcs	Installs or removes .NET Services.
resgen	Converts files from one resource format to another.
script	Executes the code contained within the task.
servicecontroller	Allows a Windows service to be controlled.
sleep	Delays the build for a specified time.
solution	Compiles VS .NET solutions (or sets of projects), automatically determining project dependencies from inter-project references.
style	Processes a document via XSLT.
sysinfo	Sets properties with system information.
tlbexp	Exports a .NET assembly to a type library that can be used from unmanaged code (wraps Microsoft's `tlbexp.exe`).

TABLE 13.1 CONTINUED NAnt 0.84 Tasks

Task	Summary
tlbimp	Imports a type library to a .NET assembly (wraps Microsoft's `tlbimp.exe`).
touch	Touches a file or set of files to update their file time.
tstamp	Sets properties with the current date and time.
unzip	Extracts files from a zip file.
vbc	Compiles Visual Basic .NET programs.
vjc	Compiles Visual J# programs using vjc, the J# compiler.
xmlpeek	Extracts text from an XML file at the location specified by an XPath expression.
xmlpoke	Replaces text in an XML file at the location specified by an XPath expression.
zip	Creates a zip file from a specified fileset.

NAnt is extremely powerful, and it's the closest thing there is to a standard build utility for open-source projects. On the downside, no good tools are available yet for writing NAnt build files. You need to be comfortable writing XML files by hand to make effective use of NAnt. Personally, I prefer using one of the graphical build tools. Then again, I like trackballs better than mice, too.

Visual Build Professional

Kinook Software's $295 Visual Build Professional 5.1 (`www.kinook.com/index.html`) offers another full IDE for managing complicated build processes, as shown in Figure 13.3.

In addition to dozens of built-in actions (including the ability to run arbitrary Windows programs as part of your build process), Visual Build Professional has a full macro language for custom programming. A nice touch is the explicit provision of failure steps, to be executed if something goes wrong in the main build. For example, you could roll back any changes you made to a data file, or undo a checkout of a file you'd planned to update, as part of the failure steps.

Visual Build Professional supports nine broad groups of actions, each with several different actions:

- Built-in actions include writing a log message, running an external program, and grouping actions together.
- Borland actions let you build Delphi or JBuilder projects.
- Files actions include copying files, transforming XML logs, writing to INI files, and managing zip files.

- Installer actions let you invoke common setup applications, such as InstallShield or Wise.

- Microsoft actions build a variety of project types, such as VB6 or VS .NET. SourceSafe integration is also included in this action group.

- Miscellaneous actions include Help & Manual compilation, writing to the Registry, or pausing for a set interval.

- Network actions can communicate with FTP, e-mail, or Telnet.

- Server actions can register COM or COM+ applications, install an assembly to the GAC, work with SQL, or interact with Windows services.

- Version Control actions interact with CVS, Perforce, Surround SCM, or Vault.

FIGURE 13.3
Visual Build
Professional

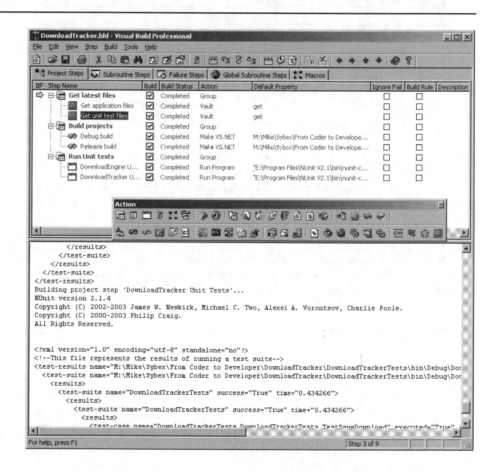

You customize individual actions by filling in dialog boxes, so you're protected from the details of the underlying software.

Unlike the other tools I've covered, Visual Build Professional offers some level of integration with VS .NET. In version 5.1 this is limited to launching Visual Build Professional from within VS .NET, which automatically creates a new action for compiling the current solution.

With its flexible programming and macro capabilities and good support for a variety of tools, Visual Build Professional is an excellent choice if you're prepared to spend the money for a graphical build tool.

TECHNOLOGY TRAP

The Dirty Build

When you're setting up your daily build process, you also need to consider where the process will take place. The temptation is to set up the builds on the same computer you use for development, because that's most convenient. Unfortunately, there's a trap lurking in that convenience.

If you use a development machine for builds, you lower the reliability and repeatability of the process somewhat. Suppose you ship out a build to beta-test customers on January 1, and then use the computer where the build was performed for other purposes, including daily web surfing and installing new software. When a bug comes in on February 1, you might find it difficult or impossible to re-create the build environment, and you won't know exactly which versions of which libraries were installed on the build machine when you tested the beta build. Most of the time this won't matter, but the times when it does matter the bugs can be subtle and hard to find.

Ideally, you'll set up a dedicated build machine, with a carefully controlled software environment, that does nothing but build the software. If you can't dedicate a physical computer to nothing but builds, set up a virtual machine with VMware or VirtualPC, and use that as your build computer.

Continuous Integration

Continuous integration is another practice that comes out of the Extreme Programming movement. If daily builds are good, XP practitioners realize, then even more frequent builds are better. After all, the sooner you spot a problem in a build, the sooner you can get to work fixing it. The logical extension of this line of reasoning is to rebuild your application every time anyone checks a change into your source code control system.

Of course, you wouldn't want to spend all of your time doing builds by hand. That's why people have invented continuous integration utilities. These applications monitor your source code control repository for check-ins. When they detect an updated file, they get the current code, build the project, and look for failures. With instant feedback via e-mail or a web page, they can help you be sure that no one has accidentally checked in untested code. I know of two continuous integration utilities for .NET, both of which are open-source projects:

- CruiseControl.NET (`http://ccnet.thoughtworks.com/`) can work with CVS, Subversion, VSS, Perforce, StarTeam, or PVCS repositories. It integrates with NAnt for builds and NUnit for testing. It can give you immediate feedback on builds through a website, e-mail, or system tray notification.

- Draco.NET (`http://draconet.sourceforge.net/`) uses CVS or VSS for source code control, and can create builds with either NAnt or VS .NET. It distributes build results via e-mail.

The main drawback that these projects have at the moment is that they don't offer wide tool support. If you're using Vault for source code control, or csunit for unit testing, or Visual Build Pro for your builds, they won't help you. But if your tools are on the supported list (or you're willing to write the code to add them), and you can spare a separate machine to be a continuous integration server, they're worth considering for any project with multiple developers.

WARNING If you're using continuous integration to kick off a test build process, make sure that the process doesn't alter anything in your source code control repository. Otherwise, you can up in a situation where the continuous integration server does new builds in an endless loop, detecting its own changes and rebuilding as a result.

Problems and Solutions

Automation is a lovely thing to have, but you may run into some problems when trying to automate your current manual build processes. Other issues will pop up when you try to share an automated solution with a team of developers. In this section, I'll look at four common problems and suggest ways to solve them:

- Tools that can't be automated
- Developers with different environments
- Losing time over broken builds
- Keeping versions up to date

Automating Intractable Tools

You may also run into situations where a particular part of your process is difficult to automate. Earlier versions of RoboHelp, for example, did not expose any command-line interface or automation API. A manual built with these versions of RoboHelp was difficult to work into a build process no matter what tool you used. When you're seriously committed to build automation, you'll probably find yourself making sure that there's some way other than a graphical user interface to drive any tool that you start using. But what can you do in the meantime?

For times when there's no other solution, you can fall back on a user-interface automation program. Various applications are available that will let you record and play back mouse clicks and keystrokes so that you can automate processes that have no API. While such applications are inherently fragile (what if a window is in a different location than it was when you recorded the macro, or you forget and move the mouse while the macro is executing?), they can be the only workaround available at times. One free automation tool that I've used in the past with good results is AutoIt, which you can find at `www.hiddensoft.com/AutoIt/`. A commercial alternative with more power and a good track record is WinBatch (`www.winbatch.com`).

Handling Developer Idiosyncrasies

Developers are funny creatures. It may seem completely obvious to you that NUnit belongs in `c:\nunit`, but the person you're collaborating with might have her copy in `f:\utilities\ bin\nunit`. This can pose a problem if the two of you are trying to share a build script: the path to NUnit is going to be wrong for one of you.

There are two possible solutions to this dilemma. The first is to move all of the builds to a dedicated build machine, and to make that machine the one that matches the build script. This works well to make the build reliable, but doesn't do much good if individual developers want to execute test builds on their own machine before checking changes in to the source code control system.

A better approach is to make use of environment variables. Just about every build tool can use environment variables in its work. For example, you might call NUnit from `%NUnitPath%\ nunit-console.exe`. Each developer can then set his or her own environment variables using the Control Panel System applet so that the script works with that individual's particular arrangement of directories.

Fixing Broken Builds

If your code base hasn't yet settled down to something of high quality, you might lose a lot of developer time to broken builds. This can happen if you execute the daily build overnight, starting after everyone has left, but don't look at the results until the next morning. This can leave you with a single developer trying to figure out the reason for a broken build while everyone else waits around with nothing to do.

If you're in this predicament, the most productive thing to do is to make use of some of those hours between when the build is finished and when the team comes in the next morning. Your build tool can most likely send e-mail when the build is done, with a success or failure notice. Rent a pager with an e-mail gateway (which is common these days) and send the notices to the pager. Hand it to one of your developers each evening. If the pager goes off, that person gets to come in and get a head start on fixing things before the rest of the team.

Because this leads to someone working at 2:00 in the morning, you'll need to be a bit creative to keep from being unfair. One alternative is to give the designated build-fixer the afternoon off. Another is to make the person who actually contributes bad code that breaks a build the designated build-fixer until someone else manages to mess things up.

Managing Software Versions

VS .NET stores assembly version information in the `AssemblyInfo.cs` or `AssemblyInfo.vb` file. For example, in a C# program you'll find this by default:

```
// You can specify all the values or you can
// default the Revision and Build Numbers
// by using the '*' as shown below:

[assembly: AssemblyVersion("1.0.*")]
```

Unfortunately, this scheme of numbering is not very flexible. The build numbers that VS .NET selects will increase with each build, but they won't follow any regular pattern. You can either put in version numbers by hand, or you can let VS .NET select them based on the time and date. Most developers would prefer to have some sort of auto-incrementing build number that goes up by a predictable amount with each build, or one that's set according to a pattern that they specify.

If your build tool of choice doesn't offer a way to force the version number, take a look at Matt Griffith's UpdateVersion utility, available from `http://code.mattgriffith.net/UpdateVersion/`. This command-line utility lets you force the build number according to a variety of schemes, from using a fixed number to using calendar dates to auto-incrementing. I've used this utility from build tools several times, and it's performed perfectly. In addition, Matt makes the source code available, so if you have a new numbering scheme in mind you can add it yourself.

Build Process Checklist

Building your software is one of those things that can seem simple on the surface but that gets complex fast when you really think about it. Here are some rules of thumb to keep in mind when designing your build process:

- Use a build automation tool to make your build process simple and repeatable.
- Build your software on a regular basis. Many developers find daily builds to be the best frequency.
- Archive copies of the outputs from the daily build.
- Evaluate a variety of build tools to find one that integrates well with the rest of your process and that fits your budget.
- Use continuous integration to make sure that the build is never broken for more than a few minutes.

With your software built, you're ready to start sending it out in the world—or are you? Before shipping copies, you should consider certain issues that revolve around protecting your intellectual property. Maybe you want to give away the fruits of your labor, but if not, move on to the next chapter to see what you can do about it.

CHAPTER 14

Protecting Your Intellectual Property

Property is Theft.

—P. J. Proudhon

Proudhon was an anarchist, which goes a long way to explain his feelings about property. If you have other ideas, though, you need to give at least a few moments of thought to the intellectual property contained in your software. When you release your newly minted code into the world, you also need to decide what rights to release along with it. If you don't, someone else will decide for you—and you might not like the results. In this chapter, I'll examine some of the property issues that developers need to think about, from contracts to licenses to making it hard for someone else to read your source code.

I've written code in a variety of situations over the past couple of decades: as a full-time employee (with and without stock options), as a partner compensated only by a share of the profits, and as a contractor to other companies. I've seen a lot of different ways to structure consulting arrangements, and I've seen a lot of different software licenses. Over this time, I've learned a fair amount about software contracting and the pitfalls that it can involve. This chapter is designed to give you the knowledge that you need to make intelligent decisions in these areas.

WARNING   Although I can lay out the major issues in this chapter, bear in mind that I'm neither a lawyer nor an accountant. Get real professional advice before making any decisions that have large amounts of money riding on them.

Writing Software Contracts

The first set of issues I want to consider are those that involve software you write for someone else under contract. Although most of us prefer to spend our time developing our own little programs for resale, the need to pay the bills often dictates taking consulting jobs of one sort or another. This means that you're going to have to actually write a contract (or, perhaps more likely, review a contract that someone else has written). I'm not going to worry about things like insurance and delivery dates here. Instead, I want to focus on one of the key areas that is often neglected: *making sure you protect your own intellectual property as you develop software for someone else*.

Staking a Claim

When you agree to write a program for a client, you probably think you're selling them the code that runs on their computers and nothing more. If the customer is running a chain of gas stations, say, you could be writing a database application that tracks hour-by-hour sales to make it easier to predict when to refill the tanks with minimum customer inconvenience. After a few months of work, you hand over a couple of CD-ROMs with the executable code and instructions for their network administrator to install the database. What could be simpler?

But in the absence of any contract, your customer's point of view is unlikely to be the same as your naive developer's ideas. Depending on how technically savvy your client is, what they think they can get away with, and how outrageous they feel your fee is, they might demand any or all of these things:

- A copy of the source code

- Exclusive ownership of the source code, so you can't sell any part of it to any other client

- A royalty for every copy of the application you sell to any other company

- The right to make copies of your application and sell it themselves

- The right to prevent you from marketing the application to their competitors for a limited time (or for an unlimited time, for that matter)

- The right to veto any attempt on your part to sell copies of the application to other companies under any circumstances

- Patents, trademarks, and copyrights on any breakthroughs you made while writing the code

- Ownership of any code you wrote during the entire contract period, whether you were writing it for them or not

Generally, it's in your interest to give the company as little of this as possible, and it's in their interest to demand as much as they can get. This is why there are contracts.

Creating the Contract

What can you put in a contract? There's a simple answer to that one: anything you like—well, anything that doesn't break the laws of the appropriate jurisdictions or contravene public policy, anyhow. But that still leaves a pretty broad range of potential contract clauses. Of course, your clients will have their own ideas about what belongs in a contract, so you'll likely need to negotiate somewhat to settle on a document that you can both sign.

Although you may find the entire thought of dealing with lawyers and negotiating contract details to be an annoying distraction from writing code, you must go through the process. Working without a contract is one of the best ways possible to set yourself up for a disaster. Without the contract negotiation, you and the customer may have vastly different ideas of what you're being paid to do. Worse, it may come down to paying expensive lawyers (which they can probably afford better than you can) to settle whose ideas were right.

RULE   Don't do contract work without a contract.

Here are some of the intellectual property issues that any well-written software consulting contract should include the following.

A description of the work product   A description of the work product is essential. It should spell out what the deliverables are, both in terms of functionality and in actual physical terms: Are you turning over object code, source code, design documentation, end-user documentation, or some combination of these? If you can't determine this at the start of the contract because details won't be clear until you've worked on the job for a while, consider a contract that explicitly allows attaching addenda with agreed-upon work products and schedules—and then remember to keep the attachments up to date.

Confidentiality   Make sure that you know what information the client considers confidential, and under what circumstances you are freed from any confidentiality provisions. For example, if they publish their customer list on the Web, are you free from the obligation to keep such information confidential? More important from the standpoint of your own property, make sure that any confidentiality provision is not written so broadly as to encompass your own work, unless you're getting compensated for this. You might even consider a contract with a two-way confidentiality provision, prohibiting the client from releasing information about your own operations.

If your work involves proprietary techniques or code that you want kept secret, you should consider having a separate *nondisclosure agreement (NDA)* that you ask clients to sign before you'll discuss their projects in depth. That way, your trade secrets are protected even if a particular sales call doesn't lead to a contract.

A description of rights purchased   A critical issue is what you're selling the customer. From the consultant's point of view, it's often best to sell the client a perpetual, nonexclusive license to use the software rather than selling them the software itself. This will leave you free to sell the same (or very similar) software to other customers. If the client balks at this, you can negotiate what you mutually consider reasonable limitations; perhaps what they really want is exclusive rights for a period of time, or within a particular industry. Also, keep in mind that there are many different software licenses; I'll discuss a few options in the next section.

Ownership of utility code   Code reuse is a fact of life in the software business, and as a working developer you probably bring a toolbox stocked with utility code to each assignment. Your contract should make it clear that you retain ownership of these common subroutines, even if the overall application is owned by the customer. It's also worth spelling out how such common subroutines will be identified (one approach is to use comments directly in the source code to assert your ownership).

Copyrights, trade secrets, and patents   Spell out ownership of copyrights, trade secrets, and patents in the contract. This is one area that you need to settle before the question arises. Once again, you might find it simplest to grant a nonexclusive use license to the customer for anything you find patentable, assuming that the customer will agree.

Limitations on client actions   There are also actions you may legitimately wish to prevent the client from taking in the future; for example:

- Disassembling or reverse-engineering the program
- Installing the program on more than the agreed-on number of computers
- Reselling the program to other companies
- Creating derivative works
- Making copies for any purpose other than backups

Means of settling disputes   Any contract should include information on how disputes will be settled. If at all possible, specify that disputes related to your contract will be settled by arbitration rather than by going to court. Arbitration is less expensive and more informal, and it's much easier to argue your side in front of an arbitrator (and get a fair hearing) than a judge if you're not an attorney.

You may feel awkward raising some of these issues with your customers. You might even worry that you'll lose the contract by seeming intransigent. But if the customer is reasonable, they're expecting you to negotiate a contract. And if they're not reasonable, wouldn't you rather find out about that *before* starting the work than when you're sitting across an arbitrator's conference table or in a courtroom?

TIP   Pay your lawyer to draw up a boilerplate contract that you're happy with, with a blank for the customer's name. Then you can present this contract to your customer as your standard terms. Sometimes you'll get lucky enough that they sign it without even negotiating. In any case, it's a good place to start the negotiations.

Licensing Your Software

Whether you're writing code for commercial sale as a shrink-wrapped application or as part of a consulting contract, you need to think about software licenses. The license is the piece of paper (or, more likely these days, the text file) that governs the users' rights to use the software. There are a wide variety of licenses that you can use, and it's worth understanding some of the basic differences.

Public Domain

By default, your code is protected by copyright. For all practical purposes, this means that you own the code and you can dictate the terms under which others can (or cannot) use it. If you wish to give up ownership completely, you can do so by placing the code in the public domain.

You can do so by including a simple statement when you distribute the source code, perhaps in a comment:

```
// The author of this code dedicates any and all copyright interest
// in this code to the public domain. I make this dedication for the
// benefit of the public at large and to the detriment of my heirs
// and successors. I intend this dedication to be an overt act of
// relinquishment in perpetuity of all present and future rights
// to this code under copyright law.
```

Placing code in the public domain is the most extreme action you can take with regard to your copyright; you're essentially nullifying the copyright completely. For less extreme actions, which allow you to retain some rights while granting others some rights, you'll need to use a software license to spell out your desires.

NOTE   Once you put code in the public domain, that's it. Anyone can take your code, alter it, use it as is, include it in another product, or profit from it, without crediting or compensating you.

Open-Source Licenses

Open-source licenses are a class of licenses designed to encourage sharing computer software. Many popular and successful computer applications these days are distributed under an open-source license, including the Linux operating system and the Apache Web server. If you're interested in making your code freely available, an open-source license may be ideal for you.

Although there is some debate over what "open source" means (and whether it's the same as "free software" or something different), the Open Source Initiative (OSI) offers a reasonably authoritative definition at www.opensource.org/docs/definition.php. The OSI offers these general characteristics of open-source licenses:

- Free redistribution of software
- Distribution with source code
- Permission for derived works under the same license
- Distributing modified code or patch files allowed
- No discrimination against persons or groups
- No discrimination against fields of endeavor
- No additional licenses required
- No forced bundling
- No attempt to restrict other software
- No special technology required by the license

A wide variety of licenses conform with these guidelines. As of this writing, the OSI has certified nearly 50 different licenses as being conformant with its concept of open source. I'll introduce a few of the better known of these licenses here: the GNU General Public License, the BSD License, and the Mozilla Public License. If you visit the OSI website, you'll find links to many other open-source licenses to choose from.

Open-source licensing has been a topic of much debate and more than a few flame wars. In particular, the Free Software Foundation (FSF), the originators of the GPL, often seem to be at odds with everyone else over philosophical differences. A visit to the FSF website (www.gnu.org) will give you all the licensing philosophy you could ever want to read. Microsoft, too, has had many critical things to say about open-source licensing. I'm going to concentrate on the practical aspects of the various licenses as I understand them, and try to avoid the philosophy.

NOTE   An interesting sidelight to open-source licenses is the Creative Commons project (http:/ /creativecommons.org), which is crafting analogous licenses for creative works. You may want to look into these licenses for manuals or other nonsoftware artifacts.

GNU General Public License (GPL)

The GPL is the best-known (perhaps *notorious* would be a better word) open-source license. You'll find the authoritative version online at www.gnu.org/copyleft/gpl.html. The GPL allows you to distribute copies of the source code and application that you receive, under certain conditions. The condition that troubles some people is section 2b of the license:

> *You must cause any work that you distribute or publish, that in whole or in part contains or is derived from the Program or any part thereof, to be licensed as a whole at no charge to all third parties under the terms of this License.*

This clause makes the GPL an *infectious* (or *viral*) license. For example, if you find a graph control that you like, and it's licensed under the GPL and you use this control in your own application, then you must likewise license your application under the GPL. This means that your own application is subject to all of the requirements of the GPL, including the requirement to make your source code available.

The GPL includes copyright as a sort of fallback provision. Section 5 of the GPL reads:

> *You are not required to accept this License, since you have not signed it. However, nothing else grants you permission to modify or distribute the Program or its derivative works. These actions are prohibited by law if you do not accept this License. Therefore, by modifying or distributing the Program (or any work based on the Program), you indicate your acceptance of this License to do so, and all its terms and conditions for copying, distributing or modifying the Program or works based on it.*

In other words, when you license code under the GPL, you're explicitly not placing the code in the public domain. Instead, you're setting out conditions under which users may redistribute your work, including explicitly the condition that they accept the GPL.

The GPL limits the people who receive your source code, not you. If you like, you can still use other licenses. For example, you could release the first version of your application under the GPL, and the second version under a proprietary license. You can even license some users of the first version under a different license. For example, you might offer a license that includes support and custom modifications but does not include the right to redistribute the custom modifications to paying customers. What you cannot do with the GPL is remove the rights of anyone who received the code under the GPL license. In the scenarios I've outlined here, people who get version 1 under the GPL can continue to redistribute it, and works based on it, as long as they like (and as long as they remain in compliance with the GPL terms themselves).

BSD License

BSD originally stood for Berkeley Source Distribution, the version of Unix that included the first version of this license (the license has since been modified somewhat). Unlike the GPL, which contains several pages of legalese, the BSD license has just two essential clauses (preceded by an assertion of copyright and followed by a disclaimer of warranty). Here's the version used by the FreeBSD variant of the operating system (`www.freebsd.org/copyright/freebsd-license.html`):

> *Redistribution and use in source and binary forms, with or without modification, are permitted provided that the following conditions are met:*
>
> *1. Redistributions of source code must retain the above copyright notice, this list of conditions and the following disclaimer.*
>
> *2. Redistributions in binary form must reproduce the above copyright notice, this list of conditions and the following disclaimer in the documentation and/or other materials provided with the distribution.*

There are continued debates over whether the BSD license is freer than the GPL. On the one hand, it allows users of the software much more latitude than the GPL. On the other, it allows them to take from the community without giving back. Microsoft, for example, is known to have incorporated BSD-licensed networking code into Windows. As long as it includes the appropriate legalese, this is perfectly legal, and it has no obligation to reveal the source code of Windows. Unlike the GPL, the BSD license is not viral.

Mozilla Public License (MPL)

The Mozilla Public License was developed by the open-source Mozilla web browser project. You'll find it (and various related documents) at www.mozilla.org/MPL/. The MPL is even more complex and loaded with legalese than the GPL, apparently because Netscape's lawyers had a hand in crafting it. To get an idea of what this means, consider part of the source code licensing terms from the MPL:

2.1. The Initial Developer Grant.

The Initial Developer hereby grants You a world-wide, royalty-free, non-exclusive license, subject to third party intellectual property claims:

(a) under intellectual property rights (other than patent or trademark) Licensable by Initial Developer to use, reproduce, modify, display, perform, sublicense and distribute the Original Code (or portions thereof) with or without Modifications, and/or as part of a Larger Work; and

(b) under Patents Claims infringed by the making, using or selling of Original Code, to make, have made, use, practice, sell, and offer for sale, and/or otherwise dispose of the Original Code (or portions thereof).

(c) the licenses granted in this Section 2.1(a) and (b) are effective on the date Initial Developer first distributes Original Code under the terms of this License.

(d) Notwithstanding Section 2.1(b) above, no patent license is granted: 1) for code that You delete from the Original Code; 2) separate from the Original Code; or 3) for infringements caused by: i) the modification of the Original Code or ii) the combination of the Original Code with other software or devices.

While the GPL is written so that the average developer can understand it, the MPL is clearly written by and for lawyers. Despite this complexity, the MPL is largely compatible with the GPL; it grants nearly the same rights under the same conditions. However, there's one major difference between the two. The GPL forbids combining GPL code with proprietary code in a larger work. The MPL expressly allows this. The MPL thus occupies a sort of middle ground between the GPL and BSD licenses.

Shared-Source Licenses

Shared source is Microsoft's answer to open source. As such, it is not currently a very popular licensing model, but it's one that you should know about as you consider the spectrum of available licenses for your code. You can learn more at www.microsoft.com/resources/sharedsource/default.mspx, where you'll also find some polemics about why the GPL is bad for the software industry.

Under various licenses that it groups into the Shared Source Initiative, Microsoft has opened up selected portions of its source code to nonemployees without giving up copyright and other protections. Instead, it has granted specific rights for different programs. For example, in some programs licensees can use the source code only for reference and debugging. In others, they have the right to modify the code and distribute the results (this is how Windows CE is licensed to embedded manufacturers, for example).

Microsoft does not generally make the text of its shared-source licenses available to non-licensees. An exception is the license for the shared-source implementation of the Common Language Infrastructure, which you can read at `http://msdn.microsoft.com/msdn-files/027/001/901/ShSourceCLIbetaLicense.htm`.

Proprietary Licenses

Most developers will probably want to ship their applications using a proprietary license. This is a license that specifies the rights of the user to use the software but that normally does not grant any source code or redistribution rights.

Unlike open-source licenses, proprietary licenses do not have any central repository. This can make it tough to find one to use with your software. I know of three general approaches you can use when crafting a license to use with your product.

Perhaps the safest alternative is to hire a lawyer to write the license for you. Assuming you find a lawyer with a working knowledge of the software industry (which may be tough, depending on where in the country you're located), this should get you a solid, usable license ideally fitted to your needs. It's also undeniably going to be the most expensive alternative, and the expense may be unmanageable depending on the size of your operation.

Another way to develop your own proprietary license is to find a software package that you admire and commandeer its license, changing the company name to your own. While inexpensive, this is a risky strategy; depending on the license, there may be some terms that don't apply to your product, or other things besides the company name (such as the state whose laws apply) that you should change.

Finally, you can split the difference and go the legal self-help-route. One good book is *Web & Software Development: A Legal Guide*, by attorney Stephen Fishman (Nolo Press, 2002). In addition to a chapter on licenses, this book includes much other information of use to the small developer, including the basics of copyright, trade secrets, and patents, employment agreements, and domain name issues. You can order a copy of either the printed book or an e-book version from Nolo's website, `www.nolo.com`.

There's no way I can give you a one-size-fits-all license agreement to use with your software. But here are some areas that are often covered in a proprietary license:

- A notice that the software is licensed rather than sold, and instructions for returning it if the user does not agree.

- A notice that you retain title in the software and all of your intellectual property rights.

- The rights the users are granted, including how many computers they may use the software with simultaneously and how many backup copies they can make.

- The term of the rights, whether perpetual or limited to a term of years.

- A list of things users *cannot* do. Typically this includes decompilation, reverse-engineering, sublicensing, renting, or leasing the software.

- A limited warranty. Normally this translates to the absolute least warranty allowed by law, with the only remedy being a new copy of the software.

- Termination provisions. Normally users are required to destroy all copies if they break the license.

- A notice of which state any legal action will be taken in. You always want this to be your home state; the expenses of pursuing legal action in another state can be substantial.

RULE   Be sure you understand which rights your license is granting to your customers.

Using Obfuscation to Protect Your Algorithms

I mentioned code obfuscation briefly in Chapter 7, "Digging Into Source Code." Now I want to dig into this topic a bit more, and show you an example of obfuscation in action.

Why Obfuscation?

Any time you're delivering software without selling the source code (or the rights to the source code), you need to worry about reverse-engineering: obtaining the original code by inspecting the compiled version that you deliver. This is a special concern when you're working in a modern language that supports reflection, which makes decompilation a trivial affair. Java and .NET both suffer from this potential weakness; you saw in Chapter 7 how easy it is to get the source code back from a .NET application.

This is where obfuscation comes in. Code obfuscators are programs that take your application's executable code and remove some of the information that the computer doesn't really need. For instance, you might have a method named `MasterLicenseCheck`. The computer doesn't care if that's renamed to `Plergb`, as long as the change is made everywhere in the application. An obfuscator will go through your compiled code, changing all of the identifiers to remove any clues that a human with a decompiler can use to make sense of your code.

The goal of an obfuscator is to make recovering the source code from the compiled version difficult or impossible. In practice, there's a continued arms race between manufacturers of obfuscators and manufacturers of decompilers, but a good obfuscator can certainly help you attain this goal.

Approaches to Obfuscation

Obfuscators can use many sneaky tricks to make it harder to understand your compiled code. This isn't an exhaustive catalog (and new methods are invented all the time), but I'll show you some of the cleverness that can go into this effort.

Identifier renaming   By changing the names of classes and members such as `Download`, `Engine`, and `GetDownload` to a, b, and c, an obfuscator can make it difficult to guess what code does by looking for keywords. In addition, this change helps optimize execution times by cutting down the length of variable names.

Method overloading   The .NET framework allows two methods to have the same name so long as they have different parameters. Obfuscators can thus rename two methods to the same nonsense identifier, even if the two methods have nothing to do with each other, as long as they take different parameters.

Metadata removal   Microsoft Intermediate Language (MSIL) files contain some metadata that isn't needed by the application at runtime. Removing this metadata can make it harder to determine what the assembly is meant to do.

String encryption   Encrypting hard-coded string constants can remove another layer of information from your compiled code.

Resource obfuscation   Some obfuscators may also scramble, mask, or otherwise hide bitmaps, animations, and other resources embedded in your executable.

Control flow obfuscation   There's more than one way to write many bits of code. For example, you probably know that a `For Each` loop can be changed to a `Do While` loop with the introduction of a variable and a logical test. Some obfuscators will perform such transformations to turn your application into spaghetti code while maintaining the logic.

Use of MSIL-only features   C#, Visual Basic .NET, and other languages are all compiled to MSIL. Some MSIL features are not used by some source languages. If an obfuscator can figure out how to use these features in the MSIL, they can prevent it from being decompiled back to source code in the affected language.

Unused code removal   You may have methods or properties in your code for future use. If an obfuscator can detect this code and remove it, you'll have an application that loads faster and that is harder to understand.

Cross-assembly obfuscation   Even public members can be renamed if you also fix up calls to them from other assemblies at the same time.

Decompiler protection   Some obfuscators inject code sequences that will crash or confuse existing decompilers.

Not all obfuscators implement all of these forms of obfuscation, nor do they all perform equally. If you're thinking of using obfuscation for your product, you should evaluate the available obfuscators to determine which one works best for you. Here are some of the .NET possibilities:

- Demeanor for .NET (www.wiseowl.com/products/Products.aspx)
- Dotfuscator (www.preemptive.com/dotfuscator/index.html)
- Salamander .NET Obfuscator (www.remotesoft.com/salamander/obfuscator.html)
- Spices .NET (www.9rays.net/cgi-bin/components.cgi?act=1&cid=86)

Obfuscation in Action

To give you a feel for the obfuscation process, I'll run through obfuscating Download Tracker using the Professional Edition of Dotfuscator. To start, take a look at the information that you can get out using Ildasm on the unobfuscated assembly. Figure 14.1 shows a bit of the Ildasm interface; you can see all of the control and method names here, among other things.

Ildasm can go further than just showing you the classes and members in your code. Here's a small piece of the IL code from DownloadTracker.exe:

```
    IL_008c:  callvirt    instance void
➥ [DownloadEngine]DownloadTracker.DownloadEngine.Download::
➥ set_ProductName(string)
    IL_0091:  ldloc.2
    IL_0092:  ldstr       "Enter the Description:"
    IL_0097:  ldstr       "Download Info"
    IL_009c:  ldloc.2
    IL_009d:  callvirt    instance string
➥ [DownloadEngine]DownloadTracker.DownloadEngine.Download::
➥ get_Description()
```

```
IL_00a2:  ldc.i4.0
IL_00a3:  ldc.i4.0
IL_00a4:  call        string
➡ [Microsoft.VisualBasic]Microsoft.VisualBasic.Interaction::
➡ InputBox(string, string, string, int32, int32)
IL_00a9:  callvirt    instance void
➡ [DownloadEngine]DownloadTracker.DownloadEngine.Download::
➡ set_Description(string)
IL_00ae:  ldsfld      class [System]System.Diagnostics.TraceSwitch
➡ DownloadTracker.Form1::ts
IL_00b3:  callvirt    instance bool
➡ [System]System.Diagnostics.TraceSwitch::get_TraceError()
IL_00b8:  brfalse.s  IL_00d4
IL_00ba:  ldstr       "Downloading "
IL_00bf:  ldloc.2
IL_00c0:  callvirt    instance string
➡ [DownloadEngine]DownloadTracker.DownloadEngine.Download::
➡ get_ProductName()
IL_00c5:  call        string [mscorlib]System.String::Concat(string,
                                                             string)
IL_00ca:  ldstr       "DTAction"
IL_00cf:  call        void
➡ [System]System.Diagnostics.Trace::WriteLine(string, string)
IL_00d4:  ldloc.1
IL_00d5:  ldloc.2
IL_00d6:  callvirt    instance bool
➡ [DTLogic]DownloadTracker.DTLogic::UpdateDownload(
➡ class [DownloadEngine]DownloadTracker.DownloadEngine.Download)
IL_00db:  pop
IL_00dc:  ret
} // end of method Form1::btnGo_Click
```

It's not the easiest thing in the world to read without practice, but the MSIL does contain all of the logic and identifiers from the original source code.

The first step in obfuscating this code was to add a new Dotfuscator project to my Visual Studio .NET solution (one reason I like Dotfuscator is that it's integrated with the Visual Studio .NET IDE). Figure 14.2 shows the solution open in the IDE. The various nodes of the project specify the assemblies that should be obfuscated and the options that I've chosen for obfuscation. The Output node brings up a report on the obfuscator's actions.

Obfuscating the assembly is then just a matter of building the solution. When all of the other projects have been built, Dotfuscator builds its own project, turning out obfuscated versions of the libraries and executables in its own folder. Figure 14.3 shows the obfuscated assembly loaded into Ildasm.

FIGURE 14.1
Looking at an unobfus-
cated assembly

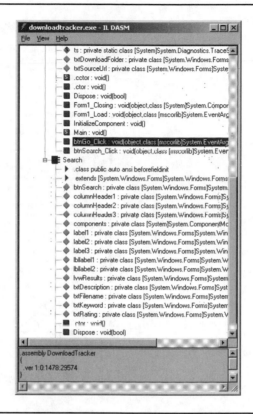

FIGURE 14.2
The Dotfuscator
project in the Visual
Studio .NET IDE

FIGURE 14.3

Looking at an obfuscated assembly

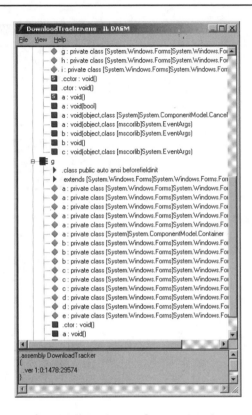

As you can see, the real names of all of the classes and members have vanished, replaced by single letters. And these single letters are overloaded, referring to two, three, or more different members. For comparison, here's the same section of code that I disassembled earlier, after obfuscation:

```
IL_00d7:  callvirt   instance void [DownloadEngine]f::a(string)
IL_00dc:  ldloc.2
IL_00dd:  ldstr      bytearray (62 28 47 2A 5F 2C 48 2E 5D
➡ 30 11 32 47 34 5D 36   // b(G*_,H.]0.2G4]6
                          52 38 19 3A 7F 3C 58 3E 4C
➡ 40 22 42 31 44 2C 46   // R8.:.<X>L@"B1D,F
                          37 48 3D 4A 22 4C 22 4E 21
➡ 50 6B 52 )             // 7H=J"L"N!PkR
IL_00e2:  ldloc      V_3
IL_00e6:  call       string a$PST06000001(string,
                                          int32)
IL_00eb:  ldstr      bytearray (63 28 46 2A 5C 2C 43 2E 43
➡ 30 5E 32 52 34 51 36   // c(F*\,C.C0^2R4Q6
```

```
                              17 38 70 3A 55 3C 5B 3E 50
➥ 40 )                    // .8p:U<[>P@
  IL_00f0:  ldloc       V_3
  IL_00f4:  call        string a$PST06000001(string,
                                          int32)
  IL_00f9:  ldloc.2
  IL_00fa:  callvirt    instance string [DownloadEngine]f::e()
  IL_00ff:  ldc.i4.0
  IL_0100:  ldc.i4.0
  IL_0101:  call        string
➥ [Microsoft.VisualBasic]Microsoft.VisualBasic.Interaction::
➥ InputBox(string, string, string, int32, int32)
  IL_0106:  callvirt    instance void [DownloadEngine]f::b(string)
  IL_010b:  ldsfld      class [System]System.Diagnostics.TraceSwitch
➥ a::a
  IL_0110:  callvirt    instance bool
➥ [System]System.Diagnostics.TraceSwitch::get_TraceError()
  IL_0115:  brfalse.s  IL_0142
  IL_0117:  br         IL_001a
  IL_011c:  ldstr      bytearray (72 28 5A 2A 4E 2C 5F 2E 0F
➥   30 52 32 5F 34 5C 36   // r(Z*N,_..0R2_4\6
                              54 38 52 3A 5E 3C 59 3E 1F
➥ 40 35 42 2B 44 20 46   // T8R:^<Y>.@5B+D F
                              67 48 0E 4A 24 4C 6D 4E 2D
➥ 50 24 52 27 54 21 56   // gH.J$LmN-P$R'T!V
                              38 58 37 5A )
➥                          // 8X7Z
  IL_0121:  ldloc       V_3
  IL_0125:  call        string a$PST06000001(string, int32)
  IL_012a:  ldstr      bytearray (63 28 7D 2A 62 2C 43 2E 49
➥ 30 5E 32 41 34 58 36   // c(}*b,C.I0^2A4X6
                              56 38 4D 3A 52 3C 52 3E 51
➥ 40 )                    // V8M:R<R>Q@
  IL_012f:  ldloc       V_3
  IL_0133:  call        string a$PST06000001(string,
                                          int32)
  IL_0138:  call        void [System]System.Diagnostics.Trace::
➥ WriteLine(string, string)
  IL_013d:  br         IL_004b
  IL_0142:  ldloc.1
  IL_0143:  ldloc.2
  IL_0144:  callvirt    instance bool [DTLogic]e::
➥ a(class [DownloadEngine]f)
  IL_0149:  pop
  IL_014a:  ret
} // end of method a::c
```

TECHNOLOGY TRAP

If It's on Their Machine, They Own It

Obfuscation is not a panacea. It will not prevent reverse-engineering MSIL into a higher-level language, though that language might not make a lot of sense. You can't prevent people from decompiling Java or .NET code, but you can go a long way to ensure that what they get as a result is a stew of confusing jumps and meaningless names. The bottom line, though, is that code that runs on someone's computer can be analyzed, and potentially understood, by that person. For example, instead of trying to understand the code only from static disassembly, a determined attacker who can run the application can hook up a debugger and monitor the process memory, learning what variables are stored and how they change during execution. From this and other information, and lots of patience, even obfuscated code can yield original algorithms.

Sometimes this state of affairs is not satisfactory. If you're dealing with encryption algorithms, or other extremely sensitive code, you may want to implement an even higher level of protection than obfuscation can offer. How can you do this? The answer is to never run the sensitive code on the user's machine. Instead of implementing your sensitive algorithms in a library that resides on the user's computer, implement them in a library that runs only on your own server. Then provide a remote interface, through web services or some other API, to allow users to invoke the library and get back results. Obviously there are drawbacks to this scenario (you need to worry about the server's reliability and ability to handle the load, and remote method calls over the Internet are likely to be slow), but you can be sure that no one is reverse-engineering your actual code.

While you can still extract some meaning from this (for example, it's still clear that the code calls the Visual Basic InputBox function), the actual logic flow of the application is a good deal more obscure than it was in the original.

Property Protection Checklist

Some people are content to just give their code away to the world, and that's fine for them. Most of the rest of us need to worry about protecting our property for one reason or another. Here are some intellectual property issues to consider when you're writing code:

- Make sure you have a contract before doing contract programming.
- Consider the various alternative licenses for your software (public domain, open source, shared source, proprietary) and choose one that makes sense for your desires and circumstances.
- If you need to write a proprietary license from scratch, get professional help.

- Use obfuscation to make it harder for users to reverse-engineer your code.
- For truly sensitive code, consider running on a protected server with a web services interface.

Now you've finally got all the pieces put together, the manual written, and the license chosen. There's only one step left: preparing an installation program. That's the subject of my final chapter.

CHAPTER 15

Delivering the Application

Installing new software is like drilling teeth;
It's painful above, and it's painful beneath.

Not nearly so simple as seen on the telly—
My knees, as I watched, like two bowls full of jelly.

If it crashes, I thought, I will just blame Bill Gates,
And then sign myself into Norm's Hotel Bates.

—from *The Night Before Y2—K, eh,* by Ted Warnell

It's amazing that the simple act of installing software is so often painful and terrifying. Some of that is due to the underlying architecture of Windows, and there's not much that you can do about it. But some comes simply from shipping poorly designed installers (or no installer at all). Think about this: Your setup program is the first piece of your software that your users will run. Doesn't it make sense to have it leave a good first impression? In this chapter, I'll look at some of the choices you can make when it comes to delivering your application.

Writing Robust Installers

When you're ready to start delivering your application to customers, you probably feel as if you're at the end of a long journey. The journey's not quite over yet, though. In some cases, you may be able to get away with just handing out the compiled executable to customers with some instructions. For example, if your product is a simple library of functions designed to be called from other applications, you probably don't need to do much more than zip it together with the help file and hand it out. As soon as the installation becomes more complex (say, because the help files need to be integrated with the default .NET Framework help), you'll find that an installer is helpful. As a rough rule of thumb, whenever setup becomes so complex that it requires step-by-step instructions, you should automate the process.

In most cases, you'll need a formal setup program (an *installer*) for your application. A typical installer these days performs dozens of tasks, from copying software to the hard drive, to setting up websites, to providing product registration, to building desktop icons, and more. Creating this extra piece of software is often not a trivial job, but it's worth the effort.

Surveying Installation Creators

When you're ready to build your installation, the first choice you need to make is how to create it. You can find a variety of programs out there designed to help you create software installations for Windows. Choosing between them is, as with other categories of software, a matter of features and budget, but I recommend you choose one of these existing installation creators.

RULE   Don't roll your own setup.

Setup applications are pretty complex beasts. They need to run perfectly on many different versions of Windows, whether or not the user has administrative privileges. They must integrate with the Add/Remove Programs Control Panel applet. They need to support a user interface that's already familiar to users. With all these requirements (and more), you're much better off buying an existing product, or using one of the free alternatives.

Table 15.1 lists some of the major installation creators that I've seen used for .NET applications. Let's review them briefly.

TABLE 15.1 Some Representative Installation Creator Software

Package	URL
Inno Setup	`www.jrsoftware.org/isinfo.php`
InstallAnywhere.NET	`www.zerog.com/products_ianet.html`
InstallShield DevStudio	`www.installshield.com/`
InstallShield Express	`www.installshield.com/`
NSIS	`http://nsis.sourceforge.net/site/index.php`
Visual Studio .NET	`http://msdn.microsoft.com/library/en-us/vsintro7/html/vboriDeploymentInVisualStudio.asp`
Wise for Visual Studio .NET	`www.wise.com`
Wise for Windows Installer	`www.wise.com`

Inno Setup   Inno Setup is a free tool (and it's free whether you're using it to install free applications or commercial ones). It performs the basic setup tasks: installing files, creating shortcuts, modifying INI files, and making Registry entries. It also handles the corresponding uninstall tasks. Inno Setup can be extended by writing code in a Pascal-like scripting language. It uses its own setup engine rather than the Windows Installer service. Inno Setup depends on plain-text scripts (which resemble INI files) to control its actions, but there's an optional user interface called ISTool available that provides a nicer way to edit these scripts. You can't customize the user interface of installers created with Inno Setup, other than by omitting certain steps to the wizard (for example, you can decide whether to collect user information).

InstallAnywhere.NET   InstallAnywhere.NET was originally named ActiveInstall, before its purchase by Zero G Software. As of this writing, it's unavailable pending the first release under the new branding, but I had the opportunity to test-drive ActiveInstall and presumably the new version will have the same general capabilities. ActiveInstall provides a full IDE for creating and editing Windows Installer–based setup programs, modeled on the Visual Studio .NET (VS .NET) IDE. The IDE contains sections for tasks such as modifying the Registry or working with Internet Information Services (IIS). The IDE is scriptable with Visual Basic for Applications (VBA) and includes source code control integration. ActiveInstall handles quite a number of high-end tasks, including SQL scripting, COM+ application deployment, and IIS virtual directory creation. It features a .NET project wizard, as well as a log analyzer and a runtime debugger, and is a promising entrant in the high end of the market. (Active-Install 2.0 had a $899.95 price tag).

InstallShield DevStudio and InstallShield Express   InstallShield DevStudio, at $1199, is one of the top competitors in this market. It can create scriptable setups that use either the Windows Installer service or InstallShield's own engine, and runs in either stand-alone mode or integrated into VS .NET. In addition to regular installers, it can build merge modules and patches, installers for web projects and Smart Device projects, and more. It can create a setup directly from your VB .NET or C# project. The Project Assistant provides you with step-by-step help on every aspect of building an installer, and you can also edit everything at the most detailed level possible. DevStudio can customize every aspect of the installation, and it handles high-end tasks like COM+ setup or Microsoft Data Access Components (MDAC) installation. Some projects might find the complexity of DevStudio to be overkill, but the InstallShield people have tried to cover every setup contingency in this product. The $349 InstallShield Express is a stripped-down version of the same product, missing some features (such as dialog editing and merge module creation), but it will work for many setups.

NSIS   NSIS is the Nullsoft Scriptable Install System, a free and open-source alternative from the creators of the popular WinAmp music player. Like Inno Setup, it relies on your writing a special plain-text scripting file to drive the installer (and there are a couple of free editors available to make this easier). NSIS has very low overhead and is designed to compress the files you're installing as well, to achieve the minimum possible download size. You can write custom dialog boxes and web setups, as well as patch installers, with NSIS. The whole system is extensible through a plug-in interface, and NSIS includes many contributed plug-ins. This means that NSIS can do just about anything that you can write C++ code to implement. NSIS uses its own setup engine.

Visual Studio .NET   If you own VS .NET, you can build Windows Installer–based setup programs directly in the IDE. You do this by inserting a new Setup and Deployment project into your solution. VS .NET has a wizard to build a basic setup, or you can start with an empty project and customize it from scratch. The various editors built into setup projects let you specify the files, file types, Registry keys, user interface, and launch conditions associated with your setup program. You can also build custom actions, which are pieces of .NET code that will be executed during the setup project. However, there are a couple of drawbacks to the built-in setup projects. First, there's no direct editor to get into the Windows Installer tables, so some of the power (and complexity) of the Windows Installer service is hidden from these projects. Second, you must arrange to deliver the .NET Framework before these setups will work at all.

Wise for Visual Studio .NET and Wise for Windows Installer   Wise Solutions is another major vendor of software that creates setup programs. Wise's .NET-aware products include Wise for Windows Installer (starting at $549) and Wise for Visual Studio .NET (starting at $1199). As you can probably guess from the name, the latter version integrates directly with VS .NET. Wise offers an Installation Expert user interface that lets you fill in dialog boxes to dictate your setup's options, as well as other editors that will let you see the exact script and table entries that the Expert generates. Wise can start from existing VB .NET or C# projects, and handles high-end tasks like configuring IIS virtual directories and .NET Framework security, installing COM+ components, and executing SQL Server scripts. Wise also supports mobile devices as well as core Windows Installer features (like merge modules and setup validation).

In addition to these products, there are two other useful resources you should know about when you turn your attention to building a setup. First, the Microsoft Windows Installer SDK contains all of the information you need to understand what's going on inside the Windows Installer, though it's not always easy to read. The SDK also contains some essential tools and a bare-bones setup editor. You can download it from `www.microsoft.com/msdownload/platformsdk/sdkupdate/`. Second, InstallSite (`www.installsite.org/`) offers a wide variety of resources related to the Windows Installer, including links to products, reviews, troubleshooting information, and more.

To give you some hint as to what the high-end setup solutions look like, Figure 15.1 shows an InstallShield DevStudio project open within VS .NET. I won't actually be using this setup, because I don't need the high-end capabilities that DevStudio provides for this simple application.

FIGURE 15.1
InstallShield
DevStudio in Action

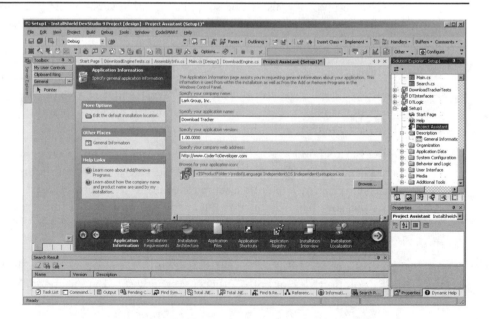

Choosing an Installation Creator

Given all these choices, how do you decide which installation creator to use? Here are some factors to consider:

Cost   With a few tools, the spread in cost is as wide as it is in setup programs, from free applications to high-end versions of professional tools that can run over a thousand dollars. While the more expensive products are also more capable, many applications can get by with the less expensive alternatives.

Functionality   With a high-end package, you'll find some advanced operations to be as easy as basic ones. For instance, creating a virtual directory for an IIS server (important when you're deploying an ASP.NET application) can be a matter of filling out a dialog box. You can still perform these actions with basic packages, but you'll invest more of your time in writing and testing custom scripts to do so.

Customization   The level of customization you can apply to the setup process varies from package to package. In some cases, you might only be able to put your application's name into otherwise standard dialog boxes. In others, you can redesign and extend the user interface that users see when they're setting up your application.

Windows Installer support   The Windows Installer service is Microsoft's built-in set of APIs for setup programs. It's present in all modern versions of Windows. The Windows Installer service provides such things as setup logging, uninstall cleanup, and *install-on-demand* (where a feature isn't actually installed until the first time that a user attempts to use it). Some setup programs use the Windows Installer service, while others implement their own custom setup engine instead. The custom engines are often simpler and smaller than the Windows Installer service. But the Windows Installer service provides a consistent user experience, and its use is a requirement to obtain the "designed for Windows" logo from Microsoft, which may be important to your marketing efforts.

Delivery mechanisms   Any installation creator can build a setup program that's designed to run from a CD-ROM or a downloaded file. But some have additional flexibility. For example, you may be able to build a setup that runs from a website and that only downloads necessary files, or a patch or update to an existing application to bring it to a new version. If these delivery mechanisms are important to you, you'll want to make sure that they're supported by your program of choice.

Integration   Some of the installation creators integrate with VS .NET, or can read VS .NET solution files, or both. Others are strictly stand-alone affairs. You'll find it easier to build a setup for a .NET application using an integrated product.

Given all these factors, I think that many .NET developers will find that the VS.NET setup and deployment projects hit the sweet spot. When and if you outgrow this solution, you can look at some of the more full-featured commercial applications.

General Installation Tips

When you're creating the setup program for your application, there are some factors that you should keep in mind. Here are some suggestions on building good setup programs:

Build your setup with your application.   As with your help files and documentation, you should be building your setup program concurrently with your application. That's because, like everything else, the setup program will need to be tested. Although your development team and internal testers could probably do their work without the formal setup program, that doesn't do anything to ensure that the setup program will work for end users. As soon as you've got any files to install, you should be crafting the means to install them.

Install everything.   The setup program should offer to do as much work as possible when installing your application so that users can carry out a single process and have a working program. If your application requires a database, you should set up the database. If it runs in conjunction with a website, build the IIS virtual directory. If it installs a service, you should register the service so that it runs when the operating system is restarted. There are few things more annoying than clicking Finish, waiting for the setup program to finish, and then discovering a readme file with a dozen more steps.

Leave the user in control.   Some changes are so sweeping, though, that you shouldn't make them without user consent. Take setting up a SQL Server database, for example. While you could just search for a database server and use the first one that you find, that wouldn't be very friendly. It's far better to prompt users for a server name and login information, and to then use the server that they selected. Your setup program should be capable of doing everything, but for things like creating websites or installing databases, make sure users know what they're getting into. If your application is very complex, you may even want to offer to install only parts of the application. You've probably seen the dialog box shown in Figure 15.2, which is the one that Microsoft Office 2003 uses for this purpose. Most installation creators offer some support for a similar dialog box.

Don't do the unexpected.   Some setup authors seem to think they can do whatever they want to a user's computer. It's certainly possible to write a setup that deletes or disables a competitor's product, hijacks a file extension, or insists on creating a desktop icon. In general, you shouldn't make changes to the system that will surprise the end user. Things can get even worse if your setup disables features that the user depends on. For instance, imposing your own system color scheme can make it impossible for a sight-impaired user to even read the screen.

FIGURE 15.2
Choosing the pieces of
Office 2003 to install

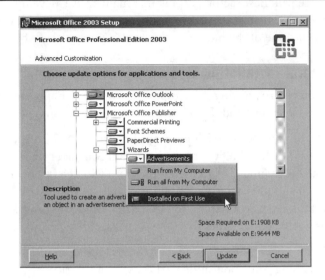

Clean up on uninstall.   If the user should decide to remove your application, your setup program (or, if it's a separate application, your uninstaller) should do the best that it can to clean up and reverse any changes that the setup made to the system in the first place. This includes removing files and Registry keys, deleting Start menu entries, and so on. There's one exception to this general rule: You may not want to delete databases and data files that were created or altered by the user without asking first. That way, if users decide that removing your application was a mistake, their previous work will still be waiting when they reinstall the application.

Test your setups.   Like your application, your setup program should be tested in the environments where you expect it to work. Try installing your application to make sure that it works properly, and then try removing it to make sure that the setup program cleans up properly. You'll need to carry out these same tests on a variety of operating systems to make sure that everything works. As with other testing problems, virtual machines can be very helpful here.

RULE   In general, your setup program shouldn't do anything that you wouldn't like some other application's setup program to do to your computer.

Building a Setup for Download Tracker

Download Tracker doesn't have any especially demanding setup requirements, so I'm going to use VS .NET to build a setup program for it. In this section, I'll work through the process to give you an idea of what's involved.

Handling Licensing

Developers take a wide range of attitudes toward licensing code within their software products. Some depend on the honor system to make sure that people don't install illegal copies. Others require you to enter a serial number, while others might require online product activation before you can use the application.

For some reason, licensing support isn't built into most installation creators. Instead, you'll need to build your own licensing piece, or buy a solution. Given the complexity of building a strong license (one that's hard for hackers to get around), I recommend buying a solution if you need licensing support in your products. Here are some of the available solutions for .NET products:

- Aspose.License (`www.aspose.com/Products/Aspose.License/`; free)

- Desaware Licensing system (`www.desaware.com/DlsL2.htm`; starting at $1495)

- XHEO|Licensing (`www.xheo.com/products/licensing/default.aspx`; starting at $259.99)

The first step in the process is to add a new Setup and Deployment project to the overall solution file. I chose to use the Setup Wizard, and called the new project **DownloadTrackerSetup**. After an introductory screen, the Setup Wizard offers four choices, as shown in Figure 15.3:

- Windows application setup

- Web application setup (this is appropriate for ASP.NET applications)

- Merge Module (this is appropriate for libraries that will be included in other products)

- Downloadable CAB file (this is appropriate for controls downloaded to a web browser)

For this project, I chose to create a Windows application setup and clicked Next. The wizard next presents a list of components that it can incorporate into the setup automatically. This includes the outputs, resources, documentation files, debug symbols, content files, and source files from every project in the solution. For Download Tracker, I want to install the primary outputs (that is, the DLL and EXE files) for each of the nontest projects.

The fourth step of the Setup Wizard lets you add additional files to the setup. This is where you'd put in help files, license files, and anything else that you want to install with your product. For Download Tracker, this includes the Microsoft Access database. The last screen of the wizard just confirms the choices you made earlier; clicking Finish at this point creates the project and opens it in VS .NET.

FIGURE 15.3
Choosing a project
type

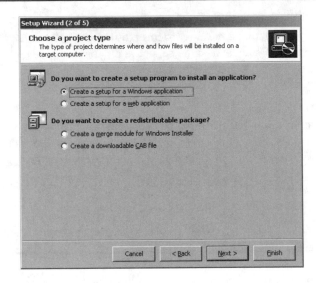

The new project opens displaying the File System Editor. This is one of the six dedicated editors that allow you to modify a setup project. Toolbar buttons at the top of the Solution Explorer window let you switch between them:

File System Editor   Allows you to add files and folders to the installation, and specify where they should be installed on the user's system. You can also install shortcuts by right-clicking on a file and selecting Create Shortcut. The File System Editor knows how to deal with many special folders on the target system; right-click on the root node and select Add Special Folder to see the list.

Registry Editor   Allows you to add Registry keys to the installation.

File Types Editor   Allows you to add file associations (for example, Microsoft Word is generally associated with the .doc file extension) and specify the actions that can be performed on those files.

User Interface Editor   Allows you to adjust the dialog boxes that will be displayed by the setup program. Figure 15.4 shows the list of dialog boxes that you can add. VS .NET provides you with the ability to add limited customization to these dialog boxes by setting properties, but there's no general dialog-box editor available.

Custom Actions Editor   Allows you to add arbitrary pieces of .NET code to your setup, to be executed on install or uninstall.

Launch Conditions Editor   Allows you to specify conditions that must be satisfied before your application can be installed. For example, you can specify that the .NET Framework must already be installed, or that a particular file or Registry key must be present.

In addition to working in the specific editors, you'll need to customize the properties of the setup project itself. Figure 15.5 shows the Properties window for the DownloadTrackerSetup project.

FIGURE 15.4
Dialog boxes for setup
projects

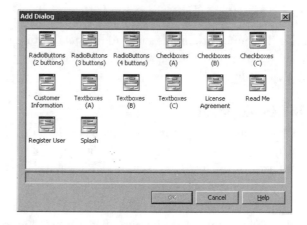

FIGURE 15.5
Properties for a setup
project

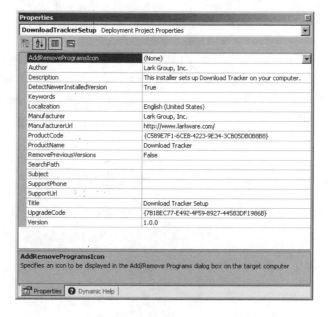

When you're done making choices in the setup editors, you can create the setup program simply by compiling the solution. After building the installer, you can test it by right-clicking on the setup project in Solution Explorer and selecting Install. By default, the installer will contain three panels: a welcome panel, a second panel that lets you select the location where the product will be installed, and a confirmation panel. Figure 15.6 shows the start of the Download Tracker setup program.

Alternatives to Traditional Installers

The .NET Framework brings some additional flexibility to the setup story, compared with earlier software platforms. In particular, you should know about XCOPY deployment and no-touch deployment.

XCOPY Deployment

XCOPY is a command-prompt utility that's built into Windows. Its job is simple: It takes a source directory structure and creates an exact duplicate of that structure elsewhere. XCOPY deployment need not actually use the XCOPY command. Rather, it refers to installing an application by making a copy of all the relevant files and folders on the target system, without doing anything else.

Previous generations of Microsoft applications were typically not good candidates for XCOPY deployment. That's because they depended on registering components in the Windows Registry, which XCOPY cannot do. But with .NET, the picture is somewhat changed. The .NET Framework's components contain their own metadata and thus do not depend on the Registry. That makes it possible to deploy some .NET applications by simply copying all of the files from a CD to your hard drive, or by unpacking a zip file.

FIGURE 15.6
The completed
installer

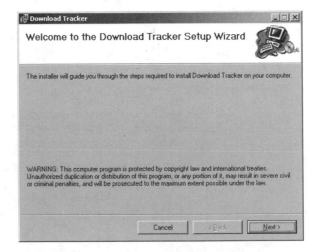

For simple applications, this is the easiest deployment that you could possibly ask for. However, for more complex applications, it falls down. Here are some of the things that you can't do in a purely XCOPY deployment:

- Create shortcuts

- Allow installing only part of an application

- Require assenting to a license

- Add assemblies to the Global Assembly Cache (GAC)

- Create or configure databases

- Add custom event logs

- Check whether .NET is installed

- Present a custom user interface for the setup

- Uninstall via the Add/Remove Programs applet

For simple utilities or internal-use applications, you may find XCOPY deployment to be an attractive choice. Most real-world projects will run into at least one snag that makes a pure XCOPY deployment difficult to implement.

No-Touch Deployment

The .NET Framework also supports a new means of deployment called *no-touch deployment*. With no-touch deployment, instead of building a setup program you drop your application and its supporting libraries (EXE and DLL files) on a web server. Then you provide your users with a URL to the main application file.

Assuming that users have Internet Explorer 5.01 or later and the .NET Framework on their computer, when they go to the specified URL, the code will be downloaded to their computer. Whenever they need code in a different library, that too will be downloaded. These downloaded files are stored in a special cache. When users launch the application a second time, their computer will check the original URL for an updated version; if there are no updates, the cached copy will be used instead.

No-touch deployment is attractive for some scenarios. In particular, if you're constantly updating your application, it's easier to update a single copy on the web server than it is to have every user run a new setup. Yet there are some drawbacks to no-touch deployment as well. For starters, unless you build a special loader stub application for the client, the application will run in the Internet security zone, which prohibits many common actions (such as saving files). You also can't deliver nonexecutable files this way, install services or local databases, register COM+ components, or satisfy other advanced scenarios.

NOTE   For more information on no-touch deployment and other deployment issues, you can download a copy of "Deploying .NET Framework-Based Applications," a product of the Microsoft Patterns & Practices group, from www.microsoft.com/downloads/details.aspx?FamilyId=5B7C6E2D-D03F-4B19-9025-6B87E6AE0DA6&displaylang=en.

TECHNOLOGY TRAP

Is That All There Is?

You've been with me for almost 300 pages now, and you've learned about dozens of things, large and small, that separate coders from developers. Now you know it all, right?

In a word, *no*.

I've been developing software for upward of a quarter-century now, and I've learned (I hope) a thing or two in that time. But I certainly haven't learned everything about developing software. Although I've tried to be comprehensive in this book, I've inevitably missed some important topic. Perhaps you'll be the one to ship a new category-defining product next year, creating the need for a chapter that I haven't even envisioned yet.

If there's one thing that distinguishes good developers from the rest of the pack, it's an attitude toward learning. Good developers just don't stop learning. There's always some new part of the software universe to explore, some new language to learn, or some new tool to test-drive. As you hone your own development skills, I urge you to make use of the resources of the Internet to continue learning and exploring.

Delivery Checklist

You've come to the end of your project! Before you go out for that celebratory dinner, spend a moment to review this checklist:

- Create a setup program that leaves a good first impression.
- Don't roll your own setup; use an existing installation creator instead.
- Build and test your setup program as you're going along.
- Provide a comprehensive but flexible setup program.
- Consider whether nontraditional alternatives, such as XCOPY deployment or no-touch deployment, can work for your application.

Best of luck as your career as a developer continues!

Index

Note to the Reader: Throughout this index, **boldfaced** page numbers indicate primary discussions of a topic. *Italicized* page numbers indicate illustrations.